# Excel

Get the Results You Want!

# SmartStudy 9

# English

Catherine Minett

Reprinted 2019, 2021, 2024, 2025

ISBN 978 1 74125 604 8

Pascal Press
PO Box 250 Glebe NSW 2037
www.pascalpress.com.au

Publisher: Vivienne Joannou
Project editors: Mark Dixon and Rosemary Peers
Edited by Michael Wyatt
Answers checked by Justine Hodgson
Proofread by Barbara Bessant
Cover and typesetting by Kim Webber
Printed by Vivar Printing/Green Giant Press



**Students**
All care has been taken in compiling this book, but please check with your teacher about the exact requirements of the course as these can change from year to year.

# TABLE OF CONTENTS

# TABLE OF CONTENTS

# STUDY STEPS TO SUCCESS!

## Step 1 Reading Work

- In each chapter, read the main text.
- Read the annotations on the text. These notes identify key features of the text and will be useful as you complete the questions and activities in each section.
- The main texts have been categorised as either informative, narrative or persuasive. However, some texts have features of more than one category and so the categorisation in this book depends upon the specific elements of style they contain. These, in turn, depend on each particular writer's purpose for creating that text. For example, someone writing a biographical text may have been more interested in telling a good story than merely providing factual information about the subject's life. They may have given the text all the hallmarks of a narrative.

## Step 2 Comprehension Work

- Read and answer the questions, using the hints to help you.
- Check each multiple-choice answer to ensure that it is the best response to the question.
- Re-read your longer answers to ensure that they make sense.

## Step 3 Spelling Work

- Read all of the information, rules and hints provided about spelling.
- For most questions, use the List Words provided to complete your answers.
- For open or creative questions, avoid writing basic or obvious responses.

## Step 4 Vocabulary Work

- Read all of the information and hints provided about improving your vocabulary.
- Check that you have the skills and knowledge you need to successfully complete the topic.
- Complete the questions and activities to test your knowledge and skills.

## Step 5 Grammar Work

- Read all of the information, rules and hints provided about grammar.
- Check that you have the skills and knowledge you need to successfully complete the topic.
- Complete the questions and activities to test your knowledge and skills.

## Step 6 Punctuation Work

- Read all of the information, rules and hints provided about punctuation.
- Check that you have the skills and knowledge you need to successfully complete the topic.
- Complete the questions and activities to test your knowledge and skills.

## Step 7 Writing Work

- Read the information about language forms and structures.
- Refer back to the main text to understand these forms and structures in context.
- Answer the questions to test your knowledge and understanding.

## Step 8 Writing Sample

- Study the writing sample carefully, reading all of the explanatory notes.
- Compare this text with the main text studied throughout the chapter so far, to reinforce your learning.

## Step 9 Writing Your Own Sample

- Check that you understand the terms and techniques relevant to this task.
- Using the sample text and the explanatory notes as a guide, compose a similar text inside the scaffold. You may wish to do this on separate paper or electronically, in order to give yourself more room.

## Step 10 Check Your Answers

- Check all of your answers at the back of the book.
- Whether or not you got the answers right, read through the whole answer section. Sample answers are provided along with explanations of why multiple-choice options are right or wrong.
- If you cannot understand a particular answer, revise the chapter notes and text annotations or ask your teacher for help.
- You should always attempt a question, even if you aren't confident in your answer, because in English you may still get some marks for a good attempt. Reading sample answers will help you write better answers next time.

## Step 11 Tips for the Sample Tests

- These useful tips appear on page 122. Read them before you attempt one of the Sample Tests.

## Step 12 Sample Tests

- Two Sample Tests are provided at the end of the book.
- Before attempting the Sample Tests, make sure that you have completed all of the work in the book and have worked through the answers to all questions that you answered incorrectly.
- Set aside the time allowed for the paper and complete it under test conditions—no sneaking a look at your notes!
- Work through the answers (at the end of the book) to any questions that you were unsure about. Write down your total marks for each section in the Your Score boxes at the end of each part of the paper, then add them up to get a total percentage for the test.

# HOW TO USE THIS BOOK TO STUDY FOR A CLASS TEST, HALF-YEARLY OR END-OF-YEAR EXAM

Depending on your teacher or school, you will be given a variety of tests and exams each year. There may be a single-topic test, a test that covers a number of topics, a semester test or exam, or even a half-yearly or yearly exam.

**Step 1**

## **Find out** which topics will be covered in the class test.

- To do this, look at your class workbook/textbook, laptop/tablet or online study program, and ask your teacher.
- For example, your class test may be on grammar.

**Step 2**

## **Match** the topics that your test is on to the topics in this book.

- For example, each unit has questions on grammar.

**Step 3**

## **Use** this book to study the topics being tested.

- Pages 6, 16, 26, 36, 46, 56, 66, 76, 86, 96, 106 and 116 all cover grammar. You can do the questions on these pages to study for your class test on grammar.

**Note:**

- When you are using this book to study for a **half-yearly** test, follow the same steps as above—the only difference being that you will have more topics to revise, of course.
- When you are using this book to study for an **end-of-year** test, you will more than likely need to study the whole book.

# READING
## *Types of Questions*

### Literal questions—the answer is right in front of you

This is the simplest type of reading task question that asks you to find a 'literal' answer.

**To answer these questions** you just have to locate specific facts and details to find the meaning.

For some literal questions you might have to:

- find facts, details and other forms of information from the text
- consider certain features of the text, including spelling, punctuation or common language techniques
- recount (or retell) details, sometimes in your own words
- consider the order in which facts are presented in a text
- recognise synonyms that are used for particular details and search for slightly different words from those in the question
- use your vocabulary
- use your comprehension
- identify who, what, where, when and how.

### Interpretive questions—the answer requires a synthesis of textual details

This type of question asks you to interpret the meaning of words, phrases and sentences.

**To answer these questions** you will have to combine facts and details to synthesise the meaning.

For some interpretive questions you might have to:

- synthesise meaning by putting various facts together to reach a conclusion—we synthesise meaning from texts all the time without even realising it
- consider multiple aspects of the text at once
- use logic to find additional meaning beyond the words
- interpret the meaning of facts and details as the meaning of some parts of the text may not be obvious from just a straightforward reading
- do simple calculations to find an answer
- look at language-related matters, such as meanings conveyed by certain words, phrases or symbols
- think about the connotations of words—meanings that extend beyond the words on the page
- describe, recount, explain, compare, summarise or give reasons
- make small but important distinctions between ideas. The words *bad*, *evil*, *naughty* and *diabolical* all mean a similar thing—but they have quite distinct shades of meaning. We might call a disobedient puppy naughty but not evil. Likewise, we wouldn't call a murderer naughty.

# READING
## *Types of Questions*

### Applied questions—the answer is conceptual and is not present in the text

These questions require you to understand a text's implications—the logical extension of facts and connotations. A writer can imply meaning, rather than simply state it. This allows us to extract meanings that go beyond the literal denotation (straightforward meaning) of the words a writer uses.

**To answer these questions** you have to apply multiple skills to infer the meaning.

Students sometimes confuse the terms 'imply' and 'infer'. Put simply, the writer implies meaning in a text and the responder infers meaning from the text.

For some applied questions you might have to:

- explain, prove, judge, evaluate, predict, solve, discuss or critique aspects of the text
- make an informed judgement or evaluation based on evidence from the text
- apply 'assumed knowledge'—information or understanding that the writer assumes you possess already
- interpret facts using additional knowledge from outside the text, such as allusions
- consider facts or details in specific combinations to arrive at a logical conclusion
- consider what you already know about textual features and their effects on meaning
- consider the usual rules of genre, form or type of text
- 'read between the lines' to infer meaning from the text
- 'read beyond the lines' to understand implications
- engage your senses
- apply thinking skills to develop insights and personal opinions
- consider what information may be missing from the text.

# INFORMATIVE TEXT

## News article

READING WORK

# Black Saturday

Wednesday, 11 February 2009

Firefighters were practically powerless against the inferno.

Last Saturday, 7 February, fire crews in country Victoria were on alert for a potentially busy day. 'Busy' would turn out to be a cruel understatement. During the worst heatwave Victoria has ever seen, coming on the back of an unprecedented rainless two months, when temperatures skyrocketed well above 40 degrees and conditions were at their most searing, a fire broke out in bushland at Murrindindi. At this stage, investigators suspect that the fire may have been deliberately lit but they are at pains to tell the public that arson has not yet been confirmed.

From this initial blaze, and others like it in the surrounding areas, came the world's worst bushfire in recorded history. With the power of 1500 atomic bombs—enough energy to last Victoria for a year—this hurricane of flames was simply unimaginable and undefeatable. One of the worst accomplices of the killer fire was the wind, the speed of which often exceeded 100 kilometres per hour. The gusts drove fire fronts together to create an impossibly powerful and fast-moving inferno. The wind was also particularly lethal because it was exceptionally dry and hot, having passed across the vast desert centre of Australia.

Casey Mills, a volunteer firefighter with the CFA (Country Fire Authority), describes what confronted her when she arrived in Marysville, a rural township that was completely levelled:

'The fire was travelling unbelievably fast. There were these massive fireballs crashing through the treetops and just leaping over the roads—some of them hundreds of metres in the air—it was just surreal. I could not believe my eyes. And the heat was just indescribable. It literally sucked all the oxygen out of the air so you couldn't breathe. The randomness of the fire's path was really weird. I saw whole streets where everything was burnt completely beyond recognition, then occasionally, a single house and a bit of lawn that had escaped untouched.

'At one point, I had to get out of the truck to move a fallen limb off the road. I couldn't see any flames or burning material nearby. I cleared the road pretty quickly, and by the time I got back in the truck, the bush on both sides of the road ahead was alight. The flames on either side were leaping so high that they joined up in mid-air. I turned the vehicle around and put the pedal to the metal. I had to get back to the oval—it's a clearing where I'd seen a lot of cars gathering. I made it back and took shelter under a fire blanket on the back floor of the truck. The fire was moving so quickly that it just sped right over the area in a big rush and kept going. So all the people on the oval survived. If I'd delayed turning around by even a minute or two, I know I wouldn't have made it out alive.'

Saturday's fires have seen the highest number of deaths by bushfire in Australia's history. A hundred and seventy-three people have lost their lives; around 120 people in one firestorm alone. More than 2030 houses and 3500 other structures have been destroyed, thousands more buildings damaged and a string of picturesque towns, including Kinglake, Marysville, Narbethong, Strathewen and Flowerdale, entirely decimated. Around 7000 people are now homeless. The combined destruction has claimed half a million square kilometres of land, an area roughly the size of Spain.

Even more tragic than the victims' deaths is the fact that many of them could have been spared, had they not chosen to stay and defend their homes. Like a host of others, Casey Mills believes that people should be required by law to leave their properties in the event of a fire emergency or even a serious threat. It is anticipated that a number of investigations will follow this disaster—possibly even a Royal Commission. In any case, it is becoming increasingly clear that lives could have been saved if better warning systems and compulsory evacuation plans had been put into practice in those nightmarish hours that will forever be known as Black Saturday.

- The **headline** of this news story is simple, yet dramatic and eye-catching. It is in much larger font than the rest of the text, and in bold, to draw the eye of the reader.
- The **image** of firefighters against a wall of flames is dramatic and suits the mood of the story. It also provides factual visual information that matches the story's content.
- The **first paragraph** of the article provides readers with the 'who, what, when and where' of the story. The writer will go on to explore more of the 'what', along with the 'how and why' of the events in question. This reporting approach is called an inverted pyramid structure and is the traditional format for news stories of this kind.
- The language in the interview section is **colloquial** (informal), in contrast with the formal language of the rest of the piece. This is because these words were said spontaneously by the witness, recorded by the journalist, then transcribed verbatim (written down word-for-word).
- **Details and statistics** are provided to show the scale of the destruction and perhaps to impress upon readers the need to help people left homeless by the fires.
- The writer builds on the main story by **drawing conclusions** and **making suggestions**, incorporating the opinion of the expert witness.
- This is an **analogy** that aids our understanding of the fire's power. It is not exactly a literal analogy, which compares two things that are practically the same, but it is also not a figurative analogy (like a simile or metaphor) because the things being compared are literally similar in many ways.
- The fire and the wind are **personified** (the fire is called a 'killer' and the wind is called its 'accomplice'). This technique adds drama and danger to the subject, suggesting how terrifying and serious the events of that day were.
- In the final line, the writer reinforces the suggestion of a need for better warning systems, reminds the reader that this was a 'nightmarish' event and **repeats** the headline. Not only does this repetition emphasise the article's most important ideas; it also creates a neat structure.
- An **expert witness**—a person who fought the fires—is interviewed to give extra detail and credibility to the article. Someone who saw and survived the fires is telling readers what it was like in a first-hand account.

# INFORMATIVE TEXT

## News article

**COMPREHENSION WORK**

### Literal questions

*Hint: Read the text carefully to locate specific facts and details.*

**1** What does the word 'conditions' mean in the context of the first paragraph?

**a** moisturises **b** weather **c** climate

**2** What analogy adds to the description of the 'hurricane of flames' in lines 28–31 (1st column)?

_______________

**3** What is the highest number of deaths caused by bushfire in Australia's recorded history?

*Hint: Look for a number in the text.* _______________

### Interpretive questions

*Hint: These questions require you to combine facts and details to synthesise the meaning.*

**4** 'Firefighters were practically powerless against the inferno.' What is the purpose of this line in the article?

*Hint: There may be more than one purpose.*

_______________

**5** Why is Casey Mills an expert witness? *Hint: Read the third paragraph and the notes beside the text.*

_______________

**6** Finish the sentence below based on the information presented in the second paragraph.

The wind was particularly lethal because it was

**a** fast-moving, dry and hot. **b** vast, drier and eternal. **c** passed, fast-moving and across.

**7** What natural occurrence led to the worst bushfire in recorded history?

**a** an act of arson **b** a severe heatwave **c** a black Saturday

**8** Re-read the second paragraph. What was simply 'unimaginable and undefeatable'?

**a** the 100-kilometre winds **b** the atomic bombs **c** the power of the flames

**9** What does the expression 'a string of picturesque towns' tell us about the towns named in lines 14–15 (3rd column)?

**a** They are strung out. **b** They are neighbouring towns. **c** People take pictures of them.

**10** Give one word or phrase to describe the tone of this article. _______________

### Applied questions

*Hint: These questions require you to understand a text's implications to infer meaning from the text.*

**11** 'At this stage, investigators suspect that the fire may have been deliberately lit but they are at pains to tell the public that arson has not yet been confirmed.' Why? *Hint: Arson is the crime of deliberately starting a fire.*

**a** The public might become obsessed with blaming someone for the fires.

**b** The public might get ideas from the investigators and start other fires.

**c** The public might not know what 'arson' means.

**12** Give evidence that the writer's main message is that more lives could have been saved on Black Saturday.

_______________

# INFORMATIVE TEXT

## SPELLING WORK

### List Words

All of the words in the box below appear in the text 'Black Saturday'.

| | | | | |
|---|---|---|---|---|
| potentially | initial | inferno | deliberately | cruel |
| skyrocketed | arson | kilometres | volunteer | authority |
| weird | picturesque | tragic | commission | compulsory |

**1** One list word in each of these sentences is spelt incorrectly. Find the word and rewrite it correctly.
*Hint: Some sentences contain more than one list word. Only one is spelt incorrectly.*

**a** The cruel inferna may have been started deliberately. ____________________

**b** I voluntere for the Country Fire Authority. ____________________

**c** The picturesqe village was razed by the bushfire. ____________________

**d** Some say that abandoning properties in a bushfire should be compolsory. ____________________

**2** Shuffle the letters to form words from the list.

**a** wired ____________________ **b** ilitain ____________________

**c** crumpyloso ____________________ **d** innofer ____________________

**3** Separate the list words in these letter chains using slashes ( / ). Spare letters appear at the ends of each chain to trick you. Cross these out then find the three list words hidden inside each chain.

**a** SYKSKYROCKETEDINITIALARSONICO **b** MWINDWEIRDINFERNOPOTENTIALLYALOT

**c** UNTRAGICCOMMISSIONAUTHORITYN **d** EDELIBERATELYKILOMETRESPICTURESQUEUE

The following two questions involve finding vowels that have been removed from list words.

**4** These letters are list words with some vowels removed. Which three vowels are missing?

| rsn | werd | uthrty | ntl | nfern |
|---|---|---|---|---|

Answer: ____ ____ ____

**5** These letter groups are list words with different vowels removed each time. Write the vowels on the lines.
*Hint: One or two vowels may be missing from a word.*

**a** trgc ____________ **b** athrity ____________ **c** vluntr ____________

A **prefix** is a letter or group of letters that can be placed ('fixed') before ('pre-') a word to change its meaning, often to the opposite of the root word. For example, in the word *indirect* the prefix *in* means 'not'. Many words begin with *in* but it is not necessarily a prefix. Check by removing *in*: is a whole word left?

**6** **a** The letters *in* begin seven words in the text, once as a prefix. Write the words on the line, separated by commas.

________________________________________

**b** A prefix meaning 'with' or 'together' is used twice in the list. Which words have this prefix?

____________________ ____________________

# INFORMATIVE TEXT

## News article

**VOCABULARY WORK**

In our writing, particularly in non-fiction texts like news articles, we should always aim for clear meaning. This means that we should always choose the most **precise** word, not necessarily the most impressive-sounding one.

**1** Complete each sentence by inserting the most appropriate list word. A synonym of each word is provided.

a Angry Mr Fosset was ______________________________ to even the best-behaved students. (mean)

b 'Did you ______________________________ destroy your homework?' asked Ms Evans. (intentionally)

c A natural disaster is always a ______________________________ event. (terrible)

d I find it ______________________________ that people drink hot tea in summer. (strange)

e The price of petrol ______________________________ over the long weekend. (surged)

f 'This is such a ______________________________ meadow,' enthused the artist. (scenic)

**2** Are these word meanings true or false? Write the answer beside each definition.

| Word | Meaning | True or False? |
|---|---|---|
| a picturesque | a photograph | ______________ |
| b volunteer | an unpaid worker | ______________ |
| c commission | an official group or panel | ______________ |
| d arson | criminal | ______________ |

**3** **Antonyms** are words with the opposite meaning to a given word. Circle each word's antonym.

| | | | |
|---|---|---|---|
| a cruel | uncruel | kindest | kind |
| b volunteer | pay | unpaid | employee |
| c weird | ordinary | odd | wired |

**4** Write words on the lines to complete definitions of list words or slightly altered versions of them.

| | |
|---|---|
| a kilometre | a unit of measurement consisting of one ____________________ metres |
| b compulsory | something that is ____________________ optional |
| c deliberate | done ____________________ purpose |
| d inferno | an exceptionally ____________________ ____________________ |

### Idioms

An **idiom** is an expression used by people from a certain area, era or group. Here are some idioms and their meanings based on their use in the context of the news article.

- surreal: bizarre; unbelievable; like a dream
- could not believe my eyes: found the situation difficult to accept or understand
- put the pedal to the metal: accelerate hard; drive fast
- a host: many; possibly too many to count

**5** Use the above idioms to complete new sentences. *Hint: Check the article for their meanings in context.*

a I ______________________________ when I saw my Lotto numbers appear on the screen.

b We ______________________________ when we saw how late we were.

c 'If you don't like these tiles, we have ______________________________ of other styles,' urged the salesman.

d Bumping into my favourite actor at a café was ______________________________ .

## Compound words

There are two common types of **compound words** that are easy to spot because of the presence or absence of a hyphen. Technically, however, there are three compound word types: **hyphenated** (such as *over-excited*), **closed** (such as *baseball*) and **open** (such as *full moon*). The last type can be easy to miss, because the two words that make the compound are separated.

Compound words:

- offer writers a chance to add detail to texts without using too many words
- can change over time, particularly from hyphenated to closed (for example, *mail-box* to *mailbox*)
- that are created by adding a prefix are usually not hyphenated (for example, *antibacterial*)
- often have plurals with the *s* somewhere apart from the end (for example, *sons-in-law*).

Answer these questions about compound words based on the information above and your own knowledge.

**1** What are the three main types of compound words?

______________ ______________ ______________

**2** Which three words in this sentence are compound words? *Hint: They can be any type of compound word.*

My grandmother was devoted to ice-cream and used to make her own triple-chocolate variety at home.

______________ ______________ ______________

**3** Complete these eight compound words from the text 'Black Saturday'. Some letters have been provided as clues.

**a** tow ______________ p **b** tre ______________ ps **c** und ______________ ent

**d** sk ______________ ted **e** fire ______________ lls **f** f ______________ rm

**g** bu ______________ nd **h** he ______________ ve

**Adverbs** modify verbs, adjectives or other adverbs. They provide the how, where, duration or extent of an action or description. Adverbs can be easy to spot because they often end in *ly*.

**4** Which word in each sentence is an adverb? Circle it. *Hint: One does not end in* ly.

**a** It was truly the most terrifying experience I've ever had.

**b** Sometimes, during power cuts, we cook on the old pot-belly stove.

**5** Sort these adverbs and adjectives by writing them in the correct columns.

late tasty green nearly daily frightening

| Adverbs | Adjectives |
|---|---|
| | |
| | |
| | |

**6** Pair up these fragments to form adverbs from the news article. Write the eight full adverbs on the line provided.

| Beginnings: | im | except | comp | for | rou | partic | lite | quic |
|---|---|---|---|---|---|---|---|---|
| Endings: | kly | ghly | ionally | rally | letely | ever | ularly | possibly |

______________________________________________

# INFORMATIVE TEXT

News article

## PUNCTUATION WORK

### Apostrophes in contractions

The **apostrophe** has only two functions: to **show ownership** or to **indicate one or more missing letters**. The second function is used in words called contractions (pairs or groups of words combined to form one word, such as *would've* for *would have*). Apostrophes are never used to make plural words. They are also unnecessary in plural numbers (such as *the 1970s* and *10s and 20s*), but they are more forgivable in these situations than in words. In recent times the use of apostrophes in plural numbers began to be phased out. Eventually they will be gone altogether.

**1** In the following contractions the apostrophe shows that something is missing. Write the missing letter or letters on the lines. *Hint: The required number of spaces are provided as a guide.*

**a** haven't ____ **b** it's ____ or ____ ____ **c** that's ____ or ____ ____

**d** should've ____ ____ **e** I'll ____ ____ **f** we'd ____ ____ or ____ ____ ____ ____

**2** Add an apostrophe to each highlighted word to complete it as a contraction.

**a** I **cant** believe he said that.

**b** **Its** normal to see our cat buried in its blanket.

**c** **Wed** all love to come to the party, thanks!

**d** The receptionist said '**Youre** welcome.'

Now challenge yourself to find contractions without help. Add the apostrophes to complete each contraction.

**e** Youve got to know when youve over-stayed your welcome.

**f** The concert wouldve been great if wed been seated closer to the front.

**g** I couldnt tell you whether its Wednesday or Thursday.

**3** There are two punctuation errors in each sentence below. Circle the mistakes. *Hint: Remember that apostrophes are not used to make plurals.*

**a** Thered be far fewer crime's on trains if cameras were operational in each carriage.

**b** 'welcome to our class on punctuating contractions,' said the Teacher.

**c** I have'nt been to the ARIAs but I'd love to go.

**d** This cruise is costing—us a fortune?

**e** Tomorrow, well all go to the well and see why all is not well

**4** Proofread these sentences about bushfires then add any missing punctuation marks. *Hint: Re-read the sentences a couple of times to ensure you get the right answers.*

If you live anywhere near bushland even in a built-up area bushfires pose a very real threat to your home and your family Be aware of your bushfire risk wherever you live. Also before you can properly protect your property youll need to prepare a survival plan

**5** There are three full stops, three capital letters, a hyphen and an apostrophe missing from this passage. Insert them in the correct spaces. *Hint: Reading the passage aloud will help you work out the answers.*

the information presented in so called factual news stories is often sensationalised its unfortunate that news is tainted by exaggeration and unnecessary drama many journalists should be more careful with their words

# INFORMATIVE TEXT

## News article

**WRITING WORK 1**

### News articles

**News articles** are informative texts that provide factual details about a topic. They exist in a variety of forms, and are published in newspapers, magazines and digital media settings. Graphics, including photographs, illustrations, charts and diagrams, help make news articles more effective and more believable.

**1** A photo of firefighters is used in the text 'Black Saturday'. What is a different image that could replace it?

______________________________________________________________

### Inverted pyramid structure

The information in news articles is presented in an **inverted pyramid structure**, with the most important details first, the body of the report in the middle and extra information or commentary at the end.

**Lead**: who, what, when, where

**Body**: how, why, more detail, background, evidence, statistics, interviews, quotes

**Tail**: extra detail, commentary, evaluation

**2** Complete the blanks in the passage below to show your understanding of the inverted pyramid news structure.

In the text 'Black Saturday', most of the __________ section is an interview that provides ev__________ from a w__________s who was there. This part of the report adds d__________ to the main facts of the lead section, and the st__________s (numbers) provided act as a transition into the __________ section.

**3** Which statement best describes the writer's main purpose in composing the text 'Black Saturday'?
*Hint: The purpose is made clear in the final paragraph (tail) of the article.*

- ☐ The writer wants to inform readers about the bravery of volunteer fire fighters on Black Saturday.
- ☐ The writer wants to urge the community to work towards improving bushfire safety.
- ☐ The writer wants to frighten Victorians into moving away from bushfire zones.

### Features of a news article

To write a news article successfully, a writer must:

- decide whether a topic or event is newsworthy (worth reporting as a news story)
- conduct research and interviews to use in writing the piece
- find and provide key details, facts, statistics, names and/or quotations
- compile the main 'who, what, when and where' details in the first paragraph
- present the story using language (often formal) that is clear, engaging and economical
- create a headline that sums up the story and grabs attention
- locate and caption at least one appropriate image.

Ideally the information in a factual newspaper article should be reported without bias. Of course, because humans with their own thoughts and opinions report the news, this does not always happen in reality.

**4** What do you think the word 'bias' means? ______________________________

**5** In the text 'Black Saturday' Casey Mills gives her opinion but this is not a case of biased reporting. Why?

______________________________________________________________

# INFORMATIVE TEXT

## News article

**WRITING WORK 2**

The text 'Black Saturday' is an example of a well-written **news article** because the writer has packed it with facts and details, used language economically and crafted an impactful piece without relying on exaggeration, emotion or sensationalism. The article also has a message but remains informative.

**6** Complete the table about the 'Black Saturday' journalist's style by writing in the blank cells. *Hint: Use the annotations on the original text to help you. Some of the answers are explicitly contained there*.

| | Language feature | Example from the text | Effect in the text |
|---|---|---|---|
| Elements of news writing | formal language | | **a** |
| | **b** strong ad__________s | cruel, worst, unimaginable, fast-moving, lethal, vast | **c** |
| | strong adverbs | **d** | **e** |
| Elements of authoritative writing | numbers and statistics | **f** | These help readers understand the scale of the crisis and add authority and reliability to the article. |
| | **g** | I saw whole streets where everything was burnt completely beyond recognition. | Adds credible detail from a witness and gives a personal, human face to the tragedy. |
| Other techniques | **h** __________y | … the power of 1500 atomic bombs—enough energy to last Victoria for a year … | Aids the understanding of the reader by making a direct and vivid comparison. |
| | **i** | One of the worst accomplices of the killer fire was the wind … | Adds drama and danger to the subject, suggesting how terrifying and serious the events of that day were. |
| | strong synonyms | inferno | **j** |
| | **k** m__________ | hurricane of flames | This direct figurative comparison adds necessary drama and shows that conditions were extreme. |

# INFORMATIVE TEXT

## News article

**WRITING SAMPLE**

Here is a sample text showing you how to structure and write a news article.

## Danes prove clean energy is no fairytale

✱ **Write a headline that captures attention by naming an important current issue.** This headline alludes to fairytales, for which Denmark is known.

The Danish rural region of Thy—particularly its capital, Thisted—produces clean energy from entirely renewable natural sources, and it's not a new venture. They've been quietly doing this for the past thirty years. The region has implemented a proven model for communities across the globe who are seeking local, workable solutions to their energy problems.

✱ **Write a paragraph to open the lead section that contains the main details of the news article.** This article names the region at the centre of the story. Two contractions ('it's' and 'they've') make this paragraph fairly informal, drawing the reader in.

*Wind farm*

✱ **Find and label an appropriate image that reinforces the topic.** The chosen image features a wind farm, which readers immediately associate with clean energy. It also features a rainbow, which is a symbol that can mean hope, promise and a fresh start.

Thy hit two milestones in 2007, achieving selection for Denmark's first official National Park and winning the European Solar Prize for its renewable energy accomplishments. The region is a worthy winner: the capital Thisted produces 100 per cent of its electricity by clean, renewable means and meets more than 80 per cent of its heating needs with renewables also. Because of its position on the windy North Sea, wind power helps serve the needs of the region instead of coal and oil. But wind power is not the only resource that has enabled Denmark's best and brightest to switch from fossil fuels to clean energy.

✱ **Begin writing the body of the article, giving specific details, including statistics, to flesh out the story.** The body of this article continues to the end of the fifth paragraph (the second-last paragraph). Background information about Thisted's location is provided. A hook (interest-grabber) closes this paragraph.

Thisted's biogas plants use two common waste products that everyone wants to get rid of: straw (leftover stalks and stubble from grain crops) and household garbage. This rubbish is collected from farms and residential areas and used to fire power plants. Massive reductions in electricity bills are delivered, with most customers' energy costs slashed by two thirds.

✱ **Answer the question raised by the hook in this paragraph.** Readers are told about power sources other than wind. Background information is provided about generating clean energy and what this means for regular people and their way of life.

Even more climate-conscious cleverness is on the way for the region. With a recent proposal designed to reduce carbon dioxide emissions from school buses, Thy goes to the top of the class. A bold plan is being developed to stagger school opening times so that the same bus can be used to transport all students in fewer loads. Not content to rest on its climate-saving laurels, Thy is continuing to look for new sustainable resources, with operations under way in solar power, wind energy, garbage recycling, agricultural and forestry waste, tidal energy and geothermal (underground) heat.

✱ **Look to the future.** Here the writer looks to the future of clean energy in the region being celebrated. In this section, which includes a list of specific details (from 'solar power' to 'geothermal (underground) heat'), a message is implied: if a community already achieving 100 per cent clean energy can do even better, all communities can achieve at least some progress.

Most admirably of all, Thy's governors are keeping energy solutions local. On accepting the European Solar Prize, Mayor Erik Hove Olesen said: 'I am very proud and grateful that we today receive this award. Not we as authorities claim the honour. Our 46 000 citizens [and] … 1700 local companies made the change … They have together made Thy self-sufficient with energy.' This region is living out an object lesson, proving that entirely clean energy is a real and achievable goal for all communities.

✱ **Expand the story.** This story is expanded to demonstrate how leaders can inspire and help citizens work towards clean energy goals. A quote from an expert (Thy's Mayor) backs up the point made in this paragraph's first line. The body's final line acts as a bridge to the tail.

Thanks to Hans Christian Andersen, Denmark has long been famous for its fairytales. Thanks to a Tasmanian named Mary, it is also loved by Australians for its royal family. Now, the nation has re-established itself on the map for even more important and impactful reasons. The great Danes are showing the world how working together and using good old common sense can bring clean, green power to the people.

✱ **In the article's tail, make a comment or evaluation.** The writer gives a brief commentary on who and what Denmark is famous for and makes a pun ('great Danes') for impact. The writer concludes by identifying the article's issue of clean energy as 'important and impactful'.

# INFORMATIVE TEXT

## News article

**WRITING YOUR OWN SAMPLE**

Plan your sample on the lines provided.

- **Write a headline that captures attention by naming an important current issue.** Try to use a technique such as an allusion.
- **Write a paragraph to open the lead section that contains the main details of the news article.** Use a contraction to make this paragraph fairly informal and draw the reader in.
- **Find and label an appropriate image that reinforces the topic.**
- **Begin writing the body of the article, giving specific details, including statistics, to flesh out the story.** Provide background information about the places and people at the centre of the story. Close the paragraph with a hook that will encourage the reader to continue.
- **Answer the question raised by the hook in this paragraph.** Provide background information about the topic, and any implications for regular people and their way of life.
- **Look to the future.** In this section include a list of specific details, and suggest or state a message.
- **Expand the story.** Give a quote from an expert to back up the point made in this paragraph. Write the body's final line as a bridge to the tail.
- **In the article's tail, make a comment or evaluation.** Try to include a technique (like a pun) for impact. Conclude by repeating the article's issue in a new and interesting way.

# INFORMATIVE TEXT

## Interview

**READING WORK**

### Embracing the world with Rotaract

*Courtney is a Bachelor of Management graduate from Sydney, Australia, but thanks to her involvement in* ***Rotaract****, a community organisation for young adults, she is also a citizen of the world.*

**Tell us, Courtney: what is Rotaract and what do they do? Also tell us a bit about Rotary International.**

Rotaract is a non-profit organisation for 18–30-year-olds interested in bettering the community—both locally and internationally. Anyone can join a Rotaract club. Different clubs have different areas of focus and projects, depending on location, local needs, member interests and resources. Rotaract is a branch of Rotary International, a global organisation with six main focus areas: peace and conflict prevention/resolution, disease prevention and treatment, water and sanitation, maternal and child care, basic education and literacy, and economic and community development. There are other branches of Rotary International, too: Interact, for 12–18-year-olds, Inner Wheel, for women only, and Probus, for retired or semiretired people wanting social interaction.

**Rotary sounds like a whole world in itself! How did you first hear about Rotaract and what led you into student exchange?**

I first heard about Rotaract and Rotary at my high school. We had a school Interact club, and each year we hosted a Rotary Youth Exchange (RYE) student from a different country. I'd joined Interact at the end of year 10 and met the Finnish boy who was currently at the school. Then, while studying HSC Beginners French, I was approached by the school to host a French exchange student. After spending four months with her, I thought it would be amazing to do what she did and go to a different country (knowing no-one!), live with locals and go to high school. So after the HSC, I applied and was accepted for RYE in France in 2012.

**Tell us about your year of international exchange.**

We RYE kids have a saying: 'Exchange isn't a year in your life, it's a life in a year'. On exchange, you go through the full range of emotions: you love it one day, you hate it the next, you meet incredible people from all around the world, you make friends with locals. Exchange did a few things: it exposed me to so many different cultures, giving me the opportunity to learn from them and realise that, while we may not speak the same language or even drink coffee the same (French people drink it from bowls in the morning), we are essentially all the same—I just happened to be born in Australia. It showed me that, as much as I love Australia, I want to live and work overseas and learn a third language. It gave me a travel bug that drains my savings every year like crazy! But it proved to me that I could move out of my comfort zone and everything would be okay.

**What about later Rotaract experiences?**

I helped create a Rotaract Club at UTS [The University of Technology, Sydney] and was Club President for a year. Starting a club from scratch was hard work, but incredibly fulfilling. I joined a Rotaract trip in Serbia, continuing to Montenegro and then solo to Croatia, where I met with local Rotaract clubs. On returning, I attended the Australian Rotaract Conference in Hobart, then I ran an Australian East Coast trip for Rotaractors from Canada, Algeria, Mexico and Great Britain, participated in the Australian Rotaract Games and took on a leadership role with RYLA [the Rotary Youth Leadership Awards] program. You get out of Rotaract what you put in. So far I have gone to ten different countries because of Rotaract, and learned that being outside my comfort zone is where the magic happens.

**Head-spinningly busy! So what is one way in which you and other Rotaractors make a difference globally?**

Currently, Australian Rotaractors are working on a project called RAM: Rotaractors against Malaria. In the '80s, polio was the disease to beat, but now, through the collective work of Rotary International and its partners, it's nearly eradicated. Malaria is the next disease we're trying to combat—it kills one person every thirty seconds somewhere in the world. We're doing this through various fundraisers to provide mosquito nets, education and awareness to those who need it.

**That is awesome. Lastly, what can you say to encourage young people reading this to get involved in Rotaract?**

You'll never meet a Rotaractor who isn't friendly, warm and genuinely interested in you, your life and your goals. Rotaract is a group of people who want to impact the world in ways we can be proud of. We also like to have a good time doing good things! You can go anywhere in the world and instantly make friends. I just visited the Rotaract Club of New York at the United Nations, and met some amazing people I know I'll stay in touch with. Joining the Rotary International family has, without a doubt, changed my life. From going to France, making lifelong friends, helping people locally and internationally, building skills that help me empower people to follow their dreams … also gaining the confidence to follow my own … Rotary has allowed me to live an incredible life—so far!

To find out more about Rotaract in Australia go to: www.rotaract.org.au
To find out more about RAM go to: www.malaria.rotaract.org.au

- The **metaphorical phrase** 'embracing the world' has many connotations relating to travel, adventure and care for others. All of these are themes that emerge in the interview.
- The interviewee (Courtney) and the subject (Rotaract and student exchange) are **introduced** before the first question.
- The first question begins with the **interviewee's name** and creates a friendly, informal tone.
- An important explanation is given about the **different groups** that are named in the interview. This is done early in the text to avoid confusion for the reader.
- The interviewer responds with emotion and opinion, adding to the **informal style** of the piece. This response is followed by the next question.
- The interviewee speaks freely and in a **highly colloquial** (informal) style, appealing to the reader and making the text easy to read.
- A **catchphrase** neatly sums up the subject of the article and suggests what an exchange year is like in a concise way.
- Small, **interesting details** (such as a method of drinking coffee) bring the interview to life and keep readers engaged.
- A key **lesson learned by the interviewee** is placed in the centre of the conversation to draw attention to it.
- A **detailed list of experiences** is provided by the interviewee to show that she is a credible representative of Rotaract. This is also done to inspire young readers to do similar things.
- The interview **changes direction** a little to bring attention to an important global issue: eradicating malaria.
- The **interviewee is invited to speak directly** to readers about getting involved if they're interested. She concisely sums up what Rotaract is all about, referring to different aspects of the group, including adventure, friendships and charity.
- Relevant **web addresses** are provided at the end of the interview. Here readers can get more details about the information discussed in the interview and consider getting involved in youth exchange themselves.

# INFORMATIVE TEXT
## Interview

COMPREHENSION WORK

### Literal questions

*Hint: Read the text carefully to locate specific facts and details.*

**1** Which disease has been nearly entirely eradicated?

a polio  b malaria  c the '80s

**2** In what non-literal place does Courtney say 'the magic happens' in the fourth paragraph?

______________________________

**3** How many countries has Courtney visited because of Rotaract? ____________

### Interpretive questions

*Hint: These questions require you to combine facts and details to synthesise the meaning.*

**4** What are at least four events that kept Courtney 'head-spinningly busy'?
*Hint: Look for the key phrase 'head-spinningly busy', then find the particular events to which it refers.*

______________________________

**5** What is the relationship between Rotaract and Rotary International?

a one is the opposite of the other  b one is a branch of the other

c one is for women only

**6** Is the following statement true or false? Read the introduction to the interview then circle your answer below.

Being born in Australia and also being a 'citizen of the world' means Courtney has dual citizenship.

True  False

**7** What factors led Courtney to join the RYE (Rotary Youth Exchange) Program?

a joining Interact and studying French  b meeting a Finnish boy and a French girl

c both a and b

**8** The discussion of what Rotaract project leads to the response 'That is awesome' from the interviewer?

a Rotaractors  b RAM  c malaria

**9** Since joining Interact what is one thing Courtney has learned about many French people?

a they speak French  b they travel frequently  c they drink coffee from bowls

**10** What does the made-up word 'Rotoractors' suggest about the young people it describes? Give two ideas.

______________________________

______________________________

### Applied questions

*Hint: These questions require you to understand a text's implications to infer meaning from the text.*

**11** Based on the content of the interview, what might be one aim shared by the interviewer and Courtney?

a to recruit RAM workers  b to eradicate Polio  c to celebrate Rotaract

**12** The article says that Rotaractors are 'embracing the world'. In what two ways do you think they do this?

______________________________

______________________________

# INFORMATIVE TEXT

## SPELLING WORK

**List Words** All of the words in the box below appear in the text 'Embracing the world with Rotaract'.

| | | | | |
|---|---|---|---|---|
| essentially | fulfilling | disease | exchange | combat |
| lifelong | eradicated | mosquito | organisation | language |
| global | sanitation | non-profit | genuinely | fundraisers |

**1** The following passage contains many list words. Eight of them have been spelt incorrectly. Correct them on the line below.

Rotary International is a gloabal organnisation that is committed to genuenly helping people suffering from problems including disese and poor sannitation. The non-profit group has already achieved a lot, such as fighting Polio, an illness now essentially erradicated around the world. Along with fullfilling commitments to raising funds for charity, Rotary has a highly successful exchange program for students that creates livelong memories.

**2** The following names of countries from the interview are spelt incorrectly. Correct each word on the line.

**a** Montainegro ____________ **b** Sebria ____________

**c** Alegria ____________ **d** Grate Britan ____________

**3** Unscramble these letter groups to form list words.

**a** hangecex ____________ **b** blloga ____________

**c** gualaneg ____________ **d** tombac ____________

**4** Turn these list words into new words by following the instructions.

**a** Change a six-letter word into an adverb by adding *ly*. ____________

**b** Change a word in the third column into a past tense verb. ____________

**c** Remove half of a compound word to make a word that means 'existence'. ____________

**d** Add a three-letter suffix to a word to create a noun meaning 'fighter'. ____________

**5** Rewrite the following list words as plurals. *Hint: Some plurals are made simply by adding* s. *Others also need an* e.

**a** language ____________ **b** organisation ____________

**c** mosquito ____________ **d** disease ____________

A **synonym** is a word with the same or a very similar meaning to another word.

**6** The words below are synonyms for list words, but they are spelt incorrectly. Correct the synonyms on the lines provided.

| List Word | Synonym | Correct spelling of synonym |
|---|---|---|
| **a** combat | battel | |
| **b** global | worlwide | |
| **c** eradicated | erazed | |
| **d** exchange | swop | |
| **e** sanitation | hygene | |

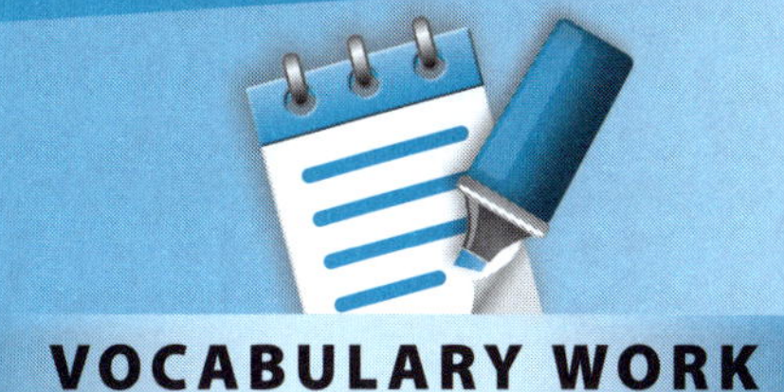

# INFORMATIVE TEXT

## Interview

## VOCABULARY WORK

### Colloquial language

In a non-fiction interview text like 'Embracing the world with Rotaract', much of the language is **colloquial** (like everyday speech) because the interviewee is relating his or her personal experiences and opinions. Even if the answers are prepared and not given spontaneously, the language is likely to be colloquial. Two common features of colloquial language—idioms and contractions—are explored below. Another feature—present participle verbs—will be explored in the Grammar Work section on page 15.

### Metaphorical idioms

You already know that an idiom is an expression used by people from a certain area, era or group. But did you know that many **idioms are also metaphors**—that is, figurative expressions that compare two things by saying one IS another? For example, the idiom *itchy feet* refers to a person who enjoys travelling or moving from place to place. The expression suggests that, because the person's feet are itchy, he or she can't stay still.

**1** Supply definitions for these three travel-related metaphorical idioms from the text 'Embracing the world with Rotaract'. *Hint: Read the idioms in context.*

a travel bug ____________________

b comfort zone ____________________

c drains my savings ____________________

**2** From this list of phrases from the text 'Embracing the world with Rotaract', circle another five idioms. *Hint: Read the phrases in context.*

| from scratch | where the magic happens | stay in touch | those who need it | tell us about |
|---|---|---|---|---|
| I love Australia | follow their dreams | essentially all the same | like crazy | retired or semiretired |

The **contraction** is one of the most common features of colloquial speech. It is created by contracting two words together, dropping one or more letters and replacing them with an apostrophe. For example, *can't, that's, I've.*

**3** Match these contractions from the interview with their full forms by drawing connecting lines.

| | |
|---|---|
| a I'd | you will |
| b isn't | we are |
| c it's | it is |
| d you'll | is not |
| e I'll | I had |
| f we're | I will |

**4** Complete these sentences by choosing the correct list word from the options given. *Hint: When spelling is not an issue, a word is usually correct or incorrect in a sentence based on context.*

a This movie is essentially / genuinely about growing up.

b The party hosted by the non-profit / fundraisers group raised a lot of money.

c One of Rotary's goals is to bring organisation / sanitation to places where disease is common.

**5** Can you find the countries in the list of words below? Circle them. *Hint: Some cities and country-based adjectives have been included to distract you.*

| ALLEGORY | MEXICAN | ALGERIA | MONTENEGRO | NEW YORK | CROATIA |
|---|---|---|---|---|---|
| CREATURE | FINNISH | FINISH | DENMARK | HOBART | FINLAND |

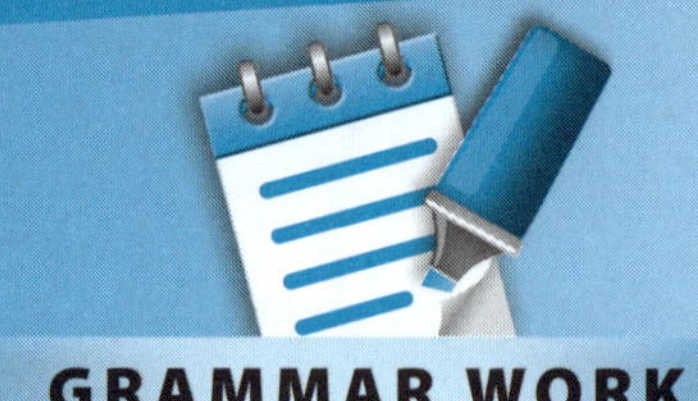

# INFORMATIVE TEXT

## Interview

## GRAMMAR WORK

A verb is a word denoting an action, state or happening. A **present participle** is a verb form that ends with *ing*, like *wondering, leaving.* Like contractions and idioms, these verb forms are often used in texts featuring colloquial language. Not all verb forms ending in *ing* are participles.

**1** Write a present participle beside each word meaning or synonym provided. *Hints: All of the answers are in the text 'Embracing the world with Rotaract'. Some first letters are given. Look in the text for words ending in* ing.

| | | | | | |
|---|---|---|---|---|---|
| **a** | b__________ing | improving | **b** | g__________ing | offering |
| **c** | __________ing | beginning | **d** | __________ing | assisting |
| **e** | w__________ing | desiring | **f** | __________ing | being productive |
| **g** | g__________ing | getting or acquiring | **h** | c__________ing | going on or forward |
| **i** | __________ing | coming back | **j** | __________ing | making an attempt |
| **k** | d__________ing | performing an action | **l** | __________ing | using money |

A **proper noun** is the capitalised name of someone or something (such as a person, place, product or time period). In a text like 'Embracing the world with Rotaract', which is about different countries, many proper nouns are used. Most of the proper nouns in the text are names of countries.

**2** What else do proper nouns name? Circle or underline each proper noun used below. *Hint: Apart from the first letter of each sentence or question, all capital letters have been removed.*

**a** The german shepherd breed of dog is also called an alsatian.

**b** Can we please go to movie world today, dad?

**c** As a charity group, rotary international brings aid to developing countries in the so-called third world.

**Proper adjectives** are derived from proper nouns. One of their uses is to describe people's nationality. For example, *Vietnamese* is the proper adjective form of *Vietnam* and *Irish* is the proper adjective form of *Ireland.*

**3** **a** In the text, three proper adjectives describe people from different countries. Write them on the lines below. The first letter of each word is provided.

F____________ F____________ A____________ (also a proper noun)

**b** Pair up these word fragments to form four more country-based proper adjectives. Write them on the lines.

IRA ISH LEBAN LIAN BRIT QI ITA ESE

____________ ____________ ____________ ____________

**Abbreviations** can save space in texts. Some of the abbreviations used in the text stand for programs run by Rotaract and/or Rotary. These programs have long titles so abbreviating them makes sense.

**4** The following abbreviations are used in the interview. Find them in the text and write what they stand for.

**a** RYE ________________________

**b** RYLA ________________________

**c** HSC ________________________

**d** RAM ________________________

In this, the age of the emoticon and the emoji, the **exclamation mark** tends to be overused because it conveys emotion. Double, triple and many more multiples of the exclamation mark, along with interrobangs (?!) litter social networking pages, text messages, chat or comment forums and blogs. While the exclamation mark can be a word-saving way to express yourself, it is a lazy practice to frequently use it in place of words and phrases.

**1** These sentences have been adapted from the text 'Embracing the world with Rotaract'.

- **a** We are providing mosquito nets and health care!
- **b** Rotaract is one of many branches of Rotary?!
- **c** We like to have a good time doing good things!
- **d** We RYE kids have a saying!
- **e** Travelling drains my savings like crazy!
- **f** It sounds like you were head-spinningly busy!

Only three of those sentences actually need exclamation marks, based on what is being said. Which ones?

____ ____ ____

**2** What other punctuation marks can be used to end a sentence? Circle or underline them in the list below. *Hint: Some of these items are not punctuation marks at all.*

period    ellipsis    grammar    pause    capital letter    semicolon    quotation mark

**3** The passage below is partly punctuated. Finish punctuating it by adding one capital letter, one full stop, one quotation mark, one exclamation mark, one question mark, one apostrophe and five commas.

in the past decade its become common for students finishing school to opt for a 'gap year overseas young people enjoy the exposure to the world the independence the new friendships the chance to earn money and, of course, just the adventure of it all There are benefits of an overseas working holiday but are they outweighed by the risks

**4** Change the following word pairs from the text 'Embracing the world with Rotaract' in these ways: turn three pairs into hyphenated compound words, turn four into closed compounds by removing the space between them, and add a slash to one pair to show that the words are interchangeable in the context. *Hint: All of the answers are contained in the text.*

| | | | |
|---|---|---|---|
| **a** non profit | **b** semi retired | **c** life long | **d** no one |
| **e** over seas | **f** prevention resolution | **g** head spinningly | **h** fund raiser |

### Its or it's?

These two words are so commonly misused that it is unusual to see them used correctly! Here is the difference:

- **Its** without an apostrophe is a possessive pronoun or determiner, like *my, their* and *our*.
- **It's** is a contraction, short for *it is*.

The two words are entirely different but because possessive nouns often contain an apostrophe (such as *the man's bike*) people often automatically use an apostrophe in the possessive pronoun *its*. Remember that 'its' is a possessive pronoun by thinking of the pronoun *itself,* which does not contain an apostrophe either.

**5** Select the correct word—*its, it's* or *itself*—in each of these phrases adapted from the interview.

- **a** Rotary International and its / it's / itself partners
- **b** this is a whole world in its / it's / itself
- **c** its / it's / itself really like a life in a year
- **d** as for polio, its / it's / itself nearly eradicated

# INFORMATIVE TEXT

## Interview

**WRITING WORK 1**

### Interviews

**Informative interviews** are non-fiction texts that explore an interesting subject, person, place, event or activity. There may be more than one interviewer (person asking questions) and more than one interviewee (person answering questions). Some of the basic features of this text form are listed below.

- An interview is usually structured as a series of questions and answers.
- The questions (from the interviewer) are carefully worded and kept fairly short, allowing the answers (from the interviewee) to include plenty of detail.
- Questions are open-ended, meaning that they require more than a 'yes or no' answer, avoid addressing well-known facts and encourage the interviewee to give detailed answers.
- The interviewer's questions and comments usually build towards the most important, interesting or relevant part of the text. In the text 'Embracing the world with Rotaract', for example, the RAM (Rotaractors Against Malaria) project is mentioned in the second-last paragraph and young people are encouraged to join Rotaract in the final paragraph.
- In most cases, images are not required in an interview text but they can add interest.

**1** Based on the definition of an open-ended question above, what do you think a closed question is?

______________________________

**2** Which of the following are features of most informative interviews? Circle or underline them.

| | | | |
|---|---|---|---|
| short questions | long answers | large images | |
| an interesting subject | no subject | factual information | |
| persuasive language | fictional information | 'yes or no' answers | structure |

**3** Think of the different types of written interviews you've read before. Show your understanding of some of the purposes of informative interviews by completing these sentences with specific ideas of your choice.

**a** An interview may introduce readers to ______________________________.

**b** An interview may educate people about ______________________________.

**c** An interview may help raise awareness about ______________________________.

**d** An interview may be a celebration of ______________________________.

**4** Look at the text 'Embracing the world with Rotaract' and answer these questions.

**a** List three emotive words or phrases used in the text.

__________ __________ __________

**b** If readers of the text 'Embracing the world with Rotaract' are interested in joining the fight against malaria, what can they do? *Hint: Go to the end of the interview.*

______________________________

**c** In what kind of larger publication might this interview be included?

______________________________

# INFORMATIVE TEXT

## *Interview*

**WRITING WORK 2**

### Language features of an informative interview

There are two categories of **language features** in this type of text because parts of it are planned (questions) and parts are more likely to be spontaneous (answers). For this reason these categories are separated below.

The questions in an interview text often contain these language structures and features:

- simple and concise wording
- keywords that offer ideas to the interviewee and invite detailed responses
- responses and transitions that lead to a related issue and/or a new question
- an organised structure that builds to the most interesting or relevant content
- concrete language rather than figurative expressions
- polite and, where necessary, sensitive wording and tone.

The answers in an interview text often contain these language features:

- colloquial language, including contractions, idioms, and emotive words and phrases
- repetition of key terms and ideas
- details such as dates, places, names and statistics.

**5** The following tasks are all completed by the person or people composing an interview. They are currently in a random order. Place them in their correct order using the numbers 1 (for the first task) to 8 (for the final task).

___ Transcribe (copy out) the interviewee's answers.

___ Edit the answers by cutting them down if necessary.

___ Edit the whole piece and submit it for publishing.

___ Do some research on the person or group before asking them for an interview.

___ Decide on an important or interesting person (or group) to interview.

___ Think of the target reader and the kinds of questions they would ask in the interview.

___ Interview the chosen person/group.

___ Write a series of open-ended questions.

Informative texts often include very **precise terms, names and expressions**. These words may be classed as jargon or they may simply be proper nouns associated with the subject.

**6** Find examples of precise vocabulary in the text 'Embracing the world with Rotaract' and write them below. A description or definition of each is given to help you. One letter has been provided for each word to help you.

| | | | | | |
|---|---|---|---|---|---|
| **a** | ________r | a member of Rotaract | **b** | e________ | a year-long trip for a student |
| **c** | m________ | something Rotaract is fighting | **d** | c________ | a group or organisation |
| **e** | ________t | the leader of a group or nation | **f** | o________ | in another part of the world |

The overall mood or atmosphere of the text 'Embracing the world with Rotaract' is friendly and relaxed. The **tone**, or **'voice'**, that comes across in the interview helps create this mood. The tone changes a little depending on who is speaking (interviewer or interviewee) and what is being said.

**7** What is one word or phrase that describes the tone of each of the extracts below? There are no set answers.

**a** Rotaract is a non-profit organisation ________________

**b** a travel bug that drains my savings every year like crazy! ________________

**c** you love it one day, you hate it the next ________________

# INFORMATIVE TEXT
## *Interview*

WRITING SAMPLE

Here is a sample text showing you how to structure and write an informative interview.

## An Australian alien

*Tham Vương, known as Tamma, was born in Vietnam and migrated to Australia with her family just before starting high school in a regional town. Despite her intelligence, outgoing personality and fast language acquisition, Tamma struggled to find her place in a foreign school.*

**Tamma, what was it like starting high school in a foreign country?**
To be honest, I've never enjoyed going to school, even back in my home country, and I don't think anyone *really* does, apart from aspiring scientists and mathematicians maybe. For me, not only the stress of study but also language and social problems were barriers to fun, especially in my first year of high school. It was awful enough when I found out that school started at 7:30 in the morning, and from my house to school was a one-hour drive, so I had to wake up at 5:45 am to get ready. All of this was ages ago but memories of that difficult year always flash to the front of my mind. I can't shut them out.

**So tell us about an unpleasant high-school experience you had.**
I'll never forget when one of the teachers, Mr Carter, asked me to stand up and introduce myself in front of the class of thirty people, who already knew each other from previous years. I knew no-one. Not a single person. My heart was skipping as I stood up, my stomach was crazy with butterflies, I was shaking, my mind was a blackout and I just stood there, smiling like an idiot. At that time, I knew almost nothing in English, so what could I say? All eyes were on me. Then Mr Carter broke the silence, asking 'What's your name?' I answered nervously, 'Me name Tham Vương.' After my answer I could see that people were whispering to their friends and grinning. I knew what that meant—it's the same in any language! My face started turning the colour of a dragon fruit (that's bright pink) and I imagined smoke might come out of my burning ears.

**What did your teacher do?**
Obviously he wasn't understanding that I was being humiliated, or maybe he was joining in the joke—I hope not … anyway, he asked me another question! Again, I didn't have the English words to answer. But I still tried. I said, 'I am fin, than yo.' This time, the laughter in the class exploded. At this moment I knew that either I had answered wrong or my Vietnamese accent sounded like an alien had come to town. Or both. I've never felt so embarrassed like this before. I sat down with a huge chip on my shoulder and I was very angry with my parents for sending me here.

**That's a terrible thing to go through! Did life at school improve?**
Yes, eventually—as I learned more of the language and put myself forward with confidence … sometimes pretending! As I did that, people reached out to me—I guess because now I could reach back. Now I have wonderful friends for life and I have built up my knowledge and skills more than I ever dreamed I would. High school has given me so much.

**What is one lesson that you learned outside the classroom at school?**
That high school can be hard for many people for many different reasons. I used to feel so sorry for myself, like nobody had it as bad as me. But that's not true! If everybody could understand that everybody struggles sometimes, maybe not as many people would have to. I recently did some research on experiences of high school and found lots of people saying negative things, how scary and unfriendly it was for them. But there was one comment that caught my eye: 'High school is big, it's drama-filled, and it's a place where you try and find yourself.' Those last words were very true for me. I did find myself, and I feel that there is nowhere now in the world that I could go where I could feel lost again.

---

**Give the interview an eye-catching title.** This title relies on the language techniques of alliteration ('A', 'A', 'A') and near-rhyme (*-alian/Alien*), and also sounds intriguing.

**Write an introduction to the interviewee before the first question.** This provides the reader with some basic background information and provides a link to the title.

**Ask the first question, beginning with the interviewee's name.** This creates a friendly tone. The question refers directly to the subject and purpose. The interviewee gives a long answer and additional details about her experience of and opinions about school. The interviewee is encouraged to speak informally, using colloquial language features like contractions (such as 'I've', 'don't') and hyperbole (such as 'ages ago').

**Use a transitional word to link the last line of the previous paragraph with the next question.** The word used by this interviewer is 'So'. The question is simple, allowing Tamma to speak freely and share her memories. This answer contains direct speech that adds to the interest and detail of Tamma's memories, for example, 'What's your name?' Tamma includes comparative language, such as 'My face started turning the colour of a dragon fruit' and other figurative language to express her emotions.

**Ask a direct, very brief question.** This allows Tamma to continue her story without any interruption. The interviewer also asks this because it is the question that the reader is probably asking at this point. Tamma shares her feelings of pain, anger and frustration, helping the reader empathise with her situation. A simile ('sounded like an alien') is used to enhance the emotion. It also explains the text's title.

**Begin the next question by responding to the previous answer.** This response is emotive ('terrible') and ends with an exclamation mark to show the interviewer's honest reaction and to voice the expected reaction of the reader. Tamma's story becomes more positive in this section.

**Use a language technique such as a pun in the final question of the interview.** Tamma is asked about a 'lesson' learned at school, but 'outside the classroom'. This is an appropriate way to conclude the conversation. Tamma talks about what her experiences have taught her, both about high school and about life in general. The final sentence has emotional impact and has been placed in this position by the interviewer to provide a positive and memorable ending.

# INFORMATIVE TEXT

## WRITING YOUR OWN SAMPLE

Plan your sample on the lines provided.

- **Give the interview an eye-catching title.**
- **Write an introduction to the interviewee before the first question.** If you can, link it to the title.
- **Ask the first question, beginning with the interviewee's name.** Ensure that the question refers directly to the subject and purpose of the interview. Allow for a long answer that includes details about the interviewee's experience and opinions. Encourage the interviewee to speak informally, using colloquial language features like contractions and hyperbole.
- **Use a transitional word to link the last line of the previous paragraph with the next question.** Ask a question that is simple, allowing the interviewee to speak freely and share memories. Try to get an answer containing direct speech that will add to the interest and detail of the person's memories. Encourage the interviewee to use comparative and figurative language to express emotion.
- **Ask a direct, very brief question.** Consider what question the reader is probably asking at this point, and ask that. The interviewee should share his or her feelings, which will help the reader empathise. Literary techniques such as similes can also enhance emotion. Here or elsewhere, explain or refer to the text's title.
- **Begin the next question by responding to the previous answer.** Your response can be emotive and end with an exclamation mark to show your honest reaction and to voice the expected reaction of the reader. Begin to include more positive details and experiences in this section and build the positivity until the end.
- **Use a language technique such as a pun in the final question of the interview.** This is an appropriate way to conclude the conversation. Ask the interviewee to talk about what these experiences have taught him or her, both about the situation at the time and about life in general. Write a final sentence that has emotional impact and provides a positive and memorable ending.

# INFORMATIVE TEXT

## *Autobiography*

**READING WORK**

## Excerpt from *Bleeding Blue: A Life in the Navy*

*This is an excerpt from the autobiography of a former Commander in the RAN (Royal Australian Navy). The writer has divided information and recollections about ANZAC Class frigates (warships) into Facts and Feelings. The factual first section is expressed simply, while the second section is a recount of an exciting experience.*

### The ANZAC Class Frigate: Facts

During my career, I had the honour of serving and living on two of these 'Greyhounds', as our crew affectionately called them. The warships are used as long-range escorts, and form the front line of Australia's naval defence fleet. These vessels have various roles in both military and peacekeeping scenarios, including general surface combat capabilities, anti-submarine warfare, air defence, surveillance and reconnaissance. Here are some stats:

Vessel type: Frigate    Displacement: 3600 tons    Length: 118m
Beam: 14.8m    Draught: 4m    Speed: 27 knots (or 50 km/h)
Propulsion system: one General Electric engine (including a gas turbine) and two diesel engines
Range: 6000 nautical miles (11 000 kilometres) at 18 knots (33 km/h)

Currently, Australia has eight ships in active service. ANZAC frigates are fitted with various sensors and processing systems for self-protection, including radar and sonar arrays, counter-measures, decoys, machine guns and small arms. The ships are also capable of launching deadly Sea Sparrow missiles and torpedoes and each carries a Sea Hawk helicopter. Excitingly, they are also in the process of being upgraded with what is arguably the world's best naval defence system for small warships: CEAFAR. This largely Australian-invented radar and response system decisively proved itself in a recent test off the coast of Hawaii, when the HMAS *Perth* used CEAFAR to obliterate a US Coyote sea-skimming missile moving at nearly three times the speed of sound. Understandably, I'm a little miffed that now I've retired my beloved Greyhounds are being upgraded to super-ships!

### The ANZAC Class Frigate: Feelings

Fire from the belly of the stricken enemy destroyer boiled up through its main funnel like lava. But I could see the crippled ship readying itself for a second attack. If they were going down, they clearly didn't want to go alone.

I glanced at the clock on the wall of the bridge. 1705. Would this be the last time we called in? *No*, I decided. But only seconds later, I watched, horrified, as a vertically launched warhead went streaking white across the clear sky. I knew I had to act fast.

I launched the close-in weapons defence system, flicking the four switches in rapid succession. Immediately, an enormous cloud of metallic dust sprang into the air above us. My reflexes took over: I snatched the engine-room coms and called for a sudden swing about. 'Full to starboard on my mark!' Sweat was deluging my face. 'And .... mark!' I exhaled hard as the frigate's diesel turbines screamed in response to the hasty change of course. The sea boiled as her propellers churned, steering us to a position only metres clear of the warhead's target area. The missile closed in, still appearing to have us locked in its sights. But then it swung to a minutely different course, slowed for a moment, then acquired a new target—the metallic dust cloud—because it was larger than our ship. The explosion rocked the frigate like a toy boat in a washing machine. But she held steady.

'Too bad those missiles can't think for themselves!' I said, a little too smugly, and grinned as I watched the bow of the swamped destroyer finally slip below the surface.

A series of five sharp, reassuring beeps welcomed me back to reality and confirmed a five-star mission. No casualties, no serious mistakes. At long last, I'd defeated my nemesis: The Machine. The combat simulator door unlocked with a clunk and a sigh, as though it knew I'd won and wasn't too happy.

I stepped out into the fluorescent whiteness of Training Lab 4 and tried to stiffen my jelly legs in the intimidating presence of my commanding officer. I gave the obligatory salute, murmured 'Ma'am', then asked, caj as a cucumber, 'What's for lunch?' I saw a flicker of a smile in one corner of her mouth: high praise from one of the Navy's toughest nuts.

---

- The writer takes an interesting **structural approach** to this autobiographical recount by dividing his knowledge and recollections into two distinct categories: 'Facts' and 'Feelings'.
- A greyhound is a sleek breed of hunting and racing dog known for both its speed and its affectionate and loyal nature. The name comes from the earliest dogs of the breed, which were mostly grey in colour. 'Greyhound' is an **appropriate nickname** for the sleek, grey warship being described here.
- The writer breaks down technical details about the ANZAC-class frigate in a clear, readable way. The colloquial abbreviation 'stats' fits the casual, **personal style** of the text.
- Very **casual expressions**, such as 'I'm a little miffed', remind the reader that this is a highly personal text. They also provide relief from the large amount of jargon (technical terms) and facts about warships.
- It is immediately clear that **the second section will contrast starkly with the first.** An enemy warship is personified (it has a 'belly' like a person) and a simile ('like lava') is used to describe the onboard fire that is causing it to sink.
- **Truncated sentences** (such as 'I knew I had to act fast.') help convey the action and excitement of the scene.
- As we see in the first section, there is **naval jargon** used here. This time, however, it can be fairly easily understood in the context of the action and dialogue.
- Traditionally, ships like this war frigate are **colloquially personified** using female pronouns (*she, her*, etc.).
- **Similes** like this one ('like a toy boat in a washing machine') create vivid imagery in the story that brings the action to life and aids our understanding.
- The action ends with a **twist**: the writer has not been in a real battle but was in fact completing a difficult training exercise in a simulator. Depending on the structure of a story, a twist can be included not just in fiction but also in nonfiction writing,
- The writer combines a **slang term** ('caj', short for 'casual') and an **idiom** ('cool as a cucumber') to describe his demeanour in his own unique voice.
- The writer ends the recount with a statement of victory and satisfaction, but he does it using **understatement**. This technique actually magnifies the achievement.

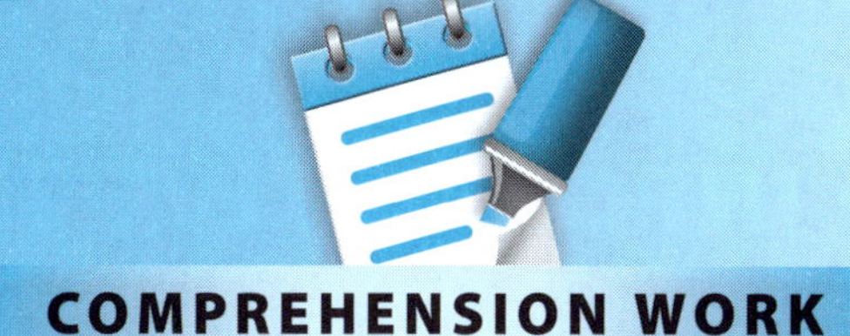

### Literal questions

*Hint: Read the text carefully to locate specific facts and details.*

1 What does the writer say the ANZAC frigates' crews often call them? ______________________

2 How many kilometres can an ANZAC frigate travel at the speed of 18 knots? ______________________

3 In what types of combat and warfare can these ships have roles?

a surface and submarine
b air and surveillance
c submarine and defence
d reconnaissance and surveillance

4 What weapons can an ANZAC frigate launch?

a missiles and torpedoes
b missiles and Sea Sparrows
c Sea Sparrows and helicopters
d helicopters and torpedoes

### Interpretive questions

*Hint: These questions require you to combine facts and details to synthesise the meaning.*

5 Which two fuels are used to power an ANZAC frigate's propulsion system?

a gas and electricity
b gas and diesel
c water and diesel
d water and electricity

6 Explain why the writer says in line 25 that the ANZAC frigates' upgrades will make them 'super-ships'.

______________________

______________________

7 What actions result in the release of 'an enormous cloud of metallic dust' in line 34?

a four rapidly successful flicks
b four rapidly flicked switches
c four rapid reflexes
d four rapid close-in weapons

8 Which two adjectives are used in the text to describe the enemy destroyer that is close to sinking?

a close-in and going down
b belly and readying
c fast and boiled
d crippled and stricken

9 In the phrase 'swung to a minutely different course' in line 40, what does the word 'minutely' mean?

a every sixty seconds
b slightly
c timely
d widely

10 How does the writer know he has achieved a five-star mission? ______________________

### Applied questions

*Hint: These questions require you to understand a text's implications to infer meaning from the text.*

11 Describe the relationship between the writer and his commanding officer.

______________________

______________________

12 What are three communication modes used by the writer and his commanding officer in the final paragraph?

______________________

______________________

**SPELLING WORK**

**List Words** All of the words in the box below appear in the text 'Excerpt from *Bleeding Blue: A Life in the Navy*'.

| | | | | |
|---|---|---|---|---|
| military | surveillance | propulsion | arguably | stricken |
| torpedoes | sensors | succession | metallic | propellers |
| starboard | frigate | nemesis | toughest | simulator |

**1** Identify list words using the clues provided below.

- **a** noun with a double letter at 7 and 8 ________
- **b** begins with a word root meaning 'pretend' ________
- **c** a celestial term begins this directional term ________
- **d** this 'p' word happens when another 'p' word moves ________

**2** Without looking back at the list, circle the correct spelling of each word.

- **a** My father had a long career in the millitary / military / mitary.
- **b** The police have us under surveillance / surveiance /surveilance.
- **c** When the propellers / proppers /propelors spin, the ship moves.
- **d** The autobiography writer calls the frilgate / frigate / friglate a Greyhound.
- **e** A metallic / mettac / metalic thud indicated that the anchor had hit an object.
- **f** CEAFAR is arguabally / argueably / arguably the best naval defence system ever.

**3** In these words, the consonants are in the right spots but the vowels have swapped places. Fix them.

- **a** fregita ________ **b** sonsers ________
- **c** somilutar ________ **d** teughost ________
- **e** matillec ________ **f** terpodeos ________

The simplest way to show the **past tense** is to add the letters *ed* to a verb. For example, *sail* becomes *sailed.*

**4** Change each of these list words to a past tense verb. None of them are in the right original form to do this, so you will need to drop and/or change some letters first, then add *ed* to create a past tense verb.

- **a** propellers ________ **b** sensors ________
- **c** torpedoes ________ **d** succession ________
- **e** arguably ________ **f** simulator ________

# INFORMATIVE TEXT
## *Autobiography*

**VOCABULARY WORK**

**1** Complete each sentence by adding the correct list word. Some letters are provided to help you.

**a** Navy, Airforce and Army are all branches of the m________________.

**b** During a war, it is common to put enemy facilities under s________________.

**c** The bad-tempered Captain was considered by many new recruits to be their ________________s.

**d** 'That session in the combat s________________ was by far the t________________ yet,' sighed the Navy cadet.

**2** Change each of these list words into a noun. *Hint: Two words are already nouns and need to become new nouns.*

**a** simulator ________________ **b** stricken ________________

**c** arguably ________________ **d** toughest ________________

**e** metallic ________________ **f** sensors ________________

**3** Which one-word ending is correct? Circle it.

**a** Someone under surveillance is being … veiled watched served surveyed

**b** If something or someone is stricken, it is … doomed domed striking strict

Like idioms, **jargon terms** are words and phrases that are often only understandable to people in a certain profession, group or field. In the text 'Excerpt from *Bleeding Blue: A Life in the Navy*', the writer uses naval jargon (that is, terms used in the Navy).

**4** Some of the naval jargon used in the text can also be used in other settings, with the same meaning. Write the meaning of each term below. *Hint: Re-reading the terms in context will help.*

**a** stats ________________

**b** on my mark ________________

**c** 1705 ________________

**5** Locate the hidden words in this naval find-a-word puzzle. The list includes jargon, nicknames, technical proper nouns and abbreviations, all from the text 'Excerpt from *Bleeding Blue: A Life in the Navy*'. Some words run backwards or diagonally and many words share letters in the grid. The unused letters spell out a catchphrase related to submarines.

**Hidden words**

| | |
|---|---|
| Warship | Bow |
| Swing about | Coms |
| Slowed | Decoy |
| Starboard | Navy |
| Knots | Mark |
| Long-range | Coyote |
| Greyhound | Sparrow |
| CEAFAR | ANZAC |
| HMAS | RAN |

| | | | | | | | | | | |
|---|---|---|---|---|---|---|---|---|---|---|
| W | A | R | S | H | I | P | H | M | A | S |
| O | R | U | W | C | K | R | A | M | N | T |
| R | S | A | I | K | E | C | O | M | S | A |
| R | L | O | N | G | R | A | N | G | E | R |
| A | I | O | G | Z | L | Y | F | E | N | B |
| P | T | T | A | A | A | N | V | A | D | O |
| S | R | B | B | U | N | C | D | A | R | A |
| D | N | U | O | H | Y | E | R | G | N | R |
| R | A | N | U | W | S | L | O | W | E | D |
| E | E | E | T | O | Y | O | C | E | D | P |

**Phrase:** Write out the unused letters in order: ______ ______ ______ ______ ______

# INFORMATIVE TEXT

## Autobiography

GRAMMAR WORK

### Past tense

Most texts in the life writing genre are written in the **past tense** because they tell the reader about events from the past.

The writer may choose, however, to write some sections of an autobiography or biography in the present tense. This creates relevance and brings events in the subject's life into the present. A recollection of the past is particularly suited to the present tense when that event or activity is still happening in the life of the writer. This is the case in the sample text featured in the Writing Sample section on page 29.

Have you noticed how the tone and style of a text can change a lot when the tense changes?

Have you struggled to maintain a particular tense in your own writing? If you have, you are not alone: it is one of the most common difficulties of English students when they write creatively.

**1** Change the tense of these sentences from the text 'Excerpt from *Bleeding Blue: A Life in the Navy*' as instructed.

**a** Rewrite in the past tense: My beloved Greyhounds are being upgraded to super-ships!

______________________________

**b** Rewrite in the present tense: I watched, horrified, as a vertically launched warhead went streaking …

______________________________

______________________________

**c** Rewrite in the future tense: I knew I had to act fast.

______________________________

**Connectives** connect parts of sentences or form bridges between sections of a text. They can be a **conjunction**, such as *and*, or a larger **transitional phrase**, such as *In contrast to this* … Connectives can help create a timeline and explain the relationship between events in a life writing text.

**2 a** Cross out the connectives in this passage from the text 'Excerpt from *Bleeding Blue: A Life in the Navy*'.

The missile closed in, still appearing to have us locked in its sights. But then it swung to a minutely different course, slowed for a moment, then acquired a new target—the metallic dust cloud—because it was larger than our ship. The explosion rocked the frigate like a toy boat in a washing machine. But she held steady.

**b** Go back through the passage: underline the nouns and circle the adjectives.

**3** Give one other connective (not one from Question 2) used in the text. ______________________________

**4** Each verb below has been taken from the text. On the lines, write antonyms (opposites) for these words. *Hint: There are different possible answers; just be careful that all of the antonyms are verbs in the matching tense.*

**a** went ____________________ **b** decided ____________________

**c** exhaled ____________________ **d** grinned ____________________

**e** glanced ____________________ **f** held ____________________

**g** moving ____________________ **h** stiffen ____________________

# INFORMATIVE TEXT
## *Autobiography*

**PUNCTUATION WORK**

**1** This passage comes directly from the text 'Excerpt from *Bleeding Blue: A Life in the Navy*'. Identify all of the punctuation errors. *Hint: There are at least ten.*

Excitingly! They are also in the process of being Upgraded with what is arguably the worlds' best naval de-fence system for small warships: CEA/FAR. This largely Australian invented radar and response system decisively proved itself in a recent test off the coast of Hawaii when the hmas Perth used CEA/FAR to obliterate a us Coyote sea-skimming missile moving at nearly three times the speed of sound. Understandably I'm a little miffed that, now I've retired, my beloved greyhounds are being upgraded to superships

**2** Rewrite the following passage with correct punctuation. *Hint: The words are based on the text but not taken from it.*

the royal australian navy boasts eight Active warships in the anzac class these ships are called frigates the writer of the autobiography bleeding blue a Life in the navy say's that many navy personnel call these ships grey-hounds

____________________________________________

____________________________________________

____________________________________________

Writers use particular punctuation marks and strategies, along with syntax (sentence structure and style), when composing sections of text that are **filled with action**. A few carefully placed exclamation marks, ellipses or colons can make all the difference between a dull piece of description and an action-packed passage. In the text 'Excerpt from *Bleeding Blue: A Life in the Navy*', the writer has shown his understanding of the power of punctuation to pack a punch.

**3** The following punctuation marks and strategies have been used in the text to create action and excitement. Complete the partial terms, add examples and suggest effects in the twin tables below.

| Punctuation mark or strategy | Example from the text | Effect on the action |
|---|---|---|
| **a** e__________n mark | **b** | conveys emotion, surprise |
| **e** contraction (two joined words with an a__________) | **f** | speeds it up by saving words |
| **i** c________n (:) | **j** | **k** |

| Punctuation mark or strategy | Example from the text | Effect on the action |
|---|---|---|
| **c** i__________ __________s | '*No*' | **d** replaces d__________ speech neatly |
| truncated (cut-off or short) sentence | **g** | **h** |
| dashes | a new target—the metallic dust cloud— | **l** |

**4** **a** Which three-part punctuation mark has been used in the text to create suspense? ________________

**b** Which single punctuation mark has also been used to create suspense? Quote the whole line in your answer. *Hint: The punctuation mark you need also appears in this question.*

____________________________________________

**5** Which punctuation mark could you use more often in your own writing to add excitement?

________________

# INFORMATIVE TEXT

## Autobiography

WRITING WORK 1

### Life writing

**Biographical and autobiographical texts** fall into the literary category of **life writing**, because they tell stories about real lives. Below are some basic details you need to know about this genre.

- The person about whom these texts are written is called the subject.
- Life writing texts usually retell events in chronological (time-based) order.
- Images such as photos, illustrations and relevant documents can be used as supporting material.
- The main language features of all autobiographical texts are similar, because an autobiography is written in the first person.
- The main language features of all biographical texts are similar because a biography is written in the third person.
- Some biographical accounts can be contained inside an autobiography or memoir. For example, an autobiography written by a famous opera singer's wife will contain a lot of biographical material about the opera singer himself.
- Forms of life writing text share main language features but can differ greatly in style. For example, subheadings or dates can be used as structural dividers. The writer of *Bleeding Blue: A Life in the Navy* has used an interesting structure in a recount, dividing it by the subheadings 'Facts' and 'Feelings'.

1 Write the names of some famous people you have read about in biographies or autobiographies. You may have read short texts like articles or biography web pages, or larger printed texts.

________________________________________

________________________________________

### Language features of biography

The writing style, chapter structure and tone of life writing (**biography**) texts can vary widely, because these **features** are based on personal choices made by the writer.

- The piece is written in third person, past tense storytelling mode.
- Contextual references are made to relevant events and people in the subject's world.
- Densely detailed, factual passages are included that include dates, names and terminology.
- A combination of direct quotes and indirect (paraphrased) speech is used.

### Language features of autobiography

The text 'Excerpt from *Bleeding Blue: A Life in the Navy*' contains a number of specific **language features** that are common to the **autobiography** text form. These include:

- first person narration, usually in the past tense
- the use of active voice
- highly detailed, descriptive and often emotive language
- limited use of dialogue
- jargon, idiom and vernacular appropriate to and used by the writer/subject.

2 What are the three types of details included in a dense, factual passage of a biography?

________________________________________

3 Why does an autobiography contain less dialogue than other forms of recount and narrative?

________________________________________

**4** Why do we find particular jargon, idioms and vernacular in an autobiography?

______________________________________________

**5** Show your understanding of first and third person modes by rewriting these lines based on the text 'Excerpt from *Bleeding Blue: A Life in the Navy*' by changing the first person to third person and the third person to first. *Hint: The writer of the autobiography is a man.*

**a** He celebrated his victory by doing something highly unusual for a Navy cadet: he took a day off.

______________________________________________

**b** Despite turning the ship sharply I still thought she was a sitting duck, but the missile missed us by a hair.

______________________________________________

**c** The enemy vessel had our ANZAC frigate in its sights and I knew that the lives of my crew were all in my hands.

______________________________________________

**6** Some of these quotes from the text contain naval jargon. Tick the boxes to show which ones.

**a** The ships are also capable of launching deadly Sea Sparrow missiles. ☐

**b** A series of five sharp, reassuring beeps welcomed me back to reality. ☐

**c** These vessels have various roles. ☐

**d** I launched the close-in weapons defence system. ☐

**e** A vertically-launched warhead went streaking white across the clear sky. ☐

**7** Complete these statements about language techniques used in the text.

**a** The writer uses understatement to show that a f______________ of a smile can actually be high ____________.

**b** An example of h__________________e in the text is 'sweat was deluging my face'.

**c** Technical proper nouns in the text include the missile names S________ S______________ and C______________.

**8** All of these language features and techniques have been used in the text—give examples of each one. Different numbers of each example are required; the numbers are shown in parentheses ( ).

**a** nickname (x2) ______________________________

**b** metaphor (x2) ______________________________

**c** simile (x2) ______________________________

**d** personification (x4) ______________________________

______________________________

**e** slang (x1) ______________________________

**f** abbreviation (x3) ______________________________

**g** idiom (x3) ______________________________

# INFORMATIVE TEXT

## Autobiography

WRITING SAMPLE

Here is a sample text showing you how to structure and write an autobiography.

### About time: an ordinary person's autobiography

✸ **Provide an interesting title to attract the reader.** This title is unusual because it declares that the person in question is 'ordinary', not famous.

The rituals practised in my family seem pretty ordinary at first glance but with a closer look I guess they're a bit odd. Take Christmas, for example. For us it's the biggie. I read somewhere that Christmas is the only time of the year when it's acceptable to sit around with other people and eat snacks out of your socks. Yep, strange. What's stranger is that every year our Christmas celebrations are virtually identical, despite the fact that we don't enjoy some of them at all! Certain things simply must occur, and in a certain order, or, I don't know … the world might end.

✸ **Begin with an orientation: one or two paragraphs that offer some context and reveal the subject of the next few paragraphs.** Here the subject is Christmas. The orientation is very similar to an introduction in other informative texts. Despite describing events that have happened, the writer uses first person present tense, because they are still happening. In other parts of the autobiography, the past tense would be used.

First there's the frenzied and stressful Christmas shopping period, when my parents consistently deny that they intend to buy presents. It's an old gag, but don't they just love it. We all try to spend less each year and find gifts that may actually be of some use but somehow we manage to send ourselves broke on a pile of pointless paraphernalia each time.

✸ **Structure the information neatly with words like *First* and *Next* as dividers and transitions.** The writer gives supporting details to expand on the subject. We read about a fairly familiar scenario in Australia: Christmas shopping, but from a personal angle.

Next is the Great Turkey Debate, where my mother asks the family to consider eating 'something different this year', to which our response is always the same: absolute outrage. We refuse to change the tradition of chowing down on a dried-up, tasteless piece of poultry, charred veggies and cloudy gravy, and promptly order the fattest behemoth parrot we can find.

✸ **Continue giving personal recollections, building humour and personal quirkiness in the descriptions and expressions each time.** For example, the ideal Christmas turkey is described here as 'the fattest behemoth parrot we can find'. This description includes metaphor and hyperbole.

On Christmas Eve we endure a televised Carols by Candlelight hosted by some TV personality that we love to hate and watch absently while we do some serious snacking to prime our bodies for the following day's overeating. Most of the carol performances are drowned out by our loud criticism of song arrangements, vocal ability, camera work, celebrities' outfits, length of Santa's beard, etc., etc., but we insist on sitting there and whining our way through this apparently unwatchable production until midnight, when we stagger off to bed.

✸ **Organise the narrative chronologically to help the reader move through the text with a clear idea of how this series of events unfolds.** Because of what we have read so far, we expect more ironic humour (like 'serious snacking to prime our bodies') and cynicism (such as 'we insist on … whining our way through this apparently unwatchable production') from the writer as we go on.

Christmas Day always starts early and, barring a quick cup of tea, presents simply must be opened first. It's also a compulsory ritual between me and my sister to give each other a pair of very loud, preferably very ugly socks and to helpfully label the wrapped package with 'Here are your socks'. A late breakfast is next and it must involve croissants. Then everyone plays with their new toys (yes, we all get them).

✸ **Write a climax or key event that will be familiar to the reader.** The most familiar part of the ritual being described—Christmas morning—is told in an anticlimactic way to surprise the reader and match the cynical tone. The writing style in this paragraph is similar to a set of instructions, as though this is a short manual on 'how to do Christmas'.

Later that day, once we've sufficiently stuffed ourselves on our substandard hot turkey dinner in the blazing heat of summer there's a brief opportunity to have 'outsiders' over, make polite conversation and palm off any presents that can be sneakily regifted. The departure of these visitors is always followed by a celebratory nap before we consume a bizarre casserole of leftovers, drink tepid, flat fruit punch and crack open any surviving choccies. This latter portion of the day is also an ideal time for a good old family argument. That's usually a thing.

✸ **In your second-last paragraph, conclude your recollections about the event or activity you have been describing.** The writer concludes their recollections about a typical Christmas and continues in the 'how-to' instructional style. Understatement is used to close this paragraph ('That's usually a thing.'). This abrupt, emotionless statement suggests that the writer is actually upset about the 'good old family argument' that often happens at Christmas.

Maybe one day we'll come up with some new Christmas rituals that make more sense, are more enjoyable and promote better health but until Santa personally shows up and tells us to do so, I guess we'll stick with the ones we've got.

✸ **The final paragraph is not a recollection.** Instead a comment is presented on the recollections that have been made earlier. This is an interesting way to conclude the passage and it echoes what the reader may be thinking.

# INFORMATIVE TEXT

## WRITING YOUR OWN SAMPLE

Plan your sample on the lines provided.

* **Provide an interesting title to attract the reader.**

* **Begin with an orientation: one or two paragraphs that offer some context and reveal the subject of the next few paragraphs.** Use the first person present tense to describe events that are a part of your life. In other sections, the past tense would be used. You don't have to write those!

* **Structure the information neatly with words like *First* and *Next* as dividers and transitions.** Give supporting details to expand on the subject.

* **Continue giving personal recollections, building humour and personal quirkiness in the descriptions and expressions each time.**

* **Organise the narrative chronologically to help the reader move through the text with a clear idea of how this series of events unfolds.** Write some recollections that include ironic humour. If you find this difficult, just focus on keeping your expression and style as personal, colloquial and honest as possible.

* **Write a climax or key event that will be familiar to the reader.** Tell this part of the anecdote in an anticlimactic way to surprise the reader. Try making your writing style in this paragraph similar to a set of instructions, as though this is a short manual on 'how to do' the event or activity you are describing.

* **In your second-last paragraph, conclude your recollections about the event or activity you have been describing.** Continue to write in a 'how-to' instructional style. Use understatement to close this paragraph. An abrupt, emotionless statement can suggest that you actually feel a different or more serious emotion than you are letting on.

* **In the final paragraph, avoid recollections.** Instead make a comment on the recollections that you have made and also try to echo what the reader may be thinking.

# INFORMATIVE TEXT

## *Informative article*

READING WORK

### Chocolate history, short and sweet

*This informative text about the history and qualities of chocolate could be found online, as part of a blog, e-zine or research database, or in printed materials such as reference books, magazines, brochures or library posters.*

Chocolate has been around for more than three thousand years. It has been passed down from the Mesoamerican Aztec and Mayan cultures. Chocolate is made from cocoa beans—the seed of the cacao plant. Cocoa beans contain sweet pulp that is dried, fermented and ground to make cocoa powder.

The beans were so prized in Aztec and Mayan society that they were often used as currency.

Chocolate began as a very bitter-tasting drink. The beans were crushed and made into a paste then combined with chilli and put in water. This made a spicy mixture called *xocoatl*. The concoction was used as a recreational drink and a medicine to fight fatigue, treat stomach ailments and ease other minor illnesses.

After the Spanish conquest of South America, chocolate was introduced into Europe, where it quickly became a royal family favourite. The Europeans added vanilla, sugar and milk to soften the natural bitterness, and by the 1600s chocolate was widely used in Europe. France's Marie Antoinette and Napoleon Bonaparte were two famous chocolate fans. Napoleon loved it so much that he insisted on having it available during his battles.

In 1689 a milk chocolate drink was developed in Jamaica, where plantations of cacao were grown. This recipe was sold to the Cadbury brothers. The 1700s saw the invention of mills where cocoa butter was extracted from the beans, which led to the creation of the hard chocolate that we eat today.

Nearly 70 per cent of all the world's cacao plants are grown in Africa and much of the labour there is done by exploited farm workers and children. For this reason 'Fairtrade' certified cocoa (cocoa bought from farmers for a fair price) is becoming more popular as consumers follow their conscience.

Some delectable *Did you knows* …

- Consuming chocolate results in a greater mental high and more pounding of the heart than kissing.
- Just inhaling chocolate's aroma increases our theta brainwaves, leading us to feel relaxed.
- Ruth Wakefield, the inventor of the chocolate chip cookie, made a deal with confectionery giant Nestlé in the 1930s to swap her groundbreaking recipe for a lifetime's supply of chocolate.
- Every single second, Americans scoff a combined total of 100 pounds (45 kilograms) of chocolate.
- The melting point of chocolate is 30 to 32° Celsius, just below our regular body temperature. That's why it can dissolve so quickly in our hand or mouth.
- Chocolate snobs insist that white chocolate is not chocolate and technically they're correct. But it does contain cocoa *butter*, just not the dark cocoa solids. This means that it has an even lower melting point than milk and dark chocolates. Good white chocolate is not white in colour at all, but a creamy off-white.

Now that you are better acquainted with chocolate, allow us to do you a favour and tell you that the antioxidant and flavonoid properties of dark chocolate make it good for you. Not just forgivable but actually beneficial. So beneficial, in fact, that nibbling a small amount every day can improve your brain function, protect your skin from UV rays and reduce your risk of heart disease by a third! The same can't be said for milk and white chocolate. You'll need to come up with a different excuse to eat those.

- The title of the article includes a **pun** on chocolate (sweet). The pun is based on the cliché *short and sweet*, which means 'agreeably brief'. This describes the brief, interesting article.
- The first few words make it clear that this is an **informal article**. The informal phrase 'been around' is used instead of a formal expression such as *existed*.
- Historical information about chocolate is expressed in a **simple manner** and the writer tends to use short sentences. These elements make the article easy to read and suit its form and purpose: an informative text.
- **Connectives** such as 'after' are used by the writer to show the unfolding events in the historical timeline of chocolate.
- Two famous lovers of chocolate are mentioned. **Specific details** like this add authenticity to the article.
- **Dates** give the article authority and show that the writer has researched the history of chocolate thoroughly.
- One of the **key purposes** of the article, which is to draw attention to the exploitation of cacao growers, becomes clear at the end—or 'now' stage—of the timeline. The labour issue is a **statistic**.
- **Scientific facts** add interest and authority to the article. Here, for example, we read about 'theta brainwaves'.
- The **colloquialism** 'scoff' lightens the tone of the article and softens the criticism of Americans' snacking habits a little.
- Another **colloquialism**—'chocolate snobs'—is used to reach out to the reader in a friendly manner. Other colloquial language features support this, such as the contraction 'they're' in the same sentence.
- In the **final paragraph**, readers are addressed directly by the writer in the second person. This is the first use of the second person in the article, which has become increasingly informal as it goes along.

# INFORMATIVE TEXT

COMPREHENSION WORK

## Literal questions

*Hint: Read the text carefully to locate specific facts and details.*

**1** What is the name of the spicy drink made from cocoa and chilli?

**a** xocoatl **b** axolotl **c** cacao

**2** Which part of the cacao plant is used to make chocolate? ____________________

**3** What proper noun is used to group the Aztec and Mayan cultures? ____________________

## Interpretive questions

*Hint: These questions require you to combine facts and details to synthesise meaning.*

**4** Based on line 18, who do you think the Spanish conquistadors were?

**a** concreters **b** conductors **c** conquerors

**5** Towards the end of which century was milk chocolate developed?

____________________

**6** Re-read the bullet points. What are two ways in which chocolate can affect our brain?

____________________

**7** What is meant by the phrase 'consumers follow their conscience' in line 30?

____________________

**8** What is the connection between the melting point of chocolate and body temperature?

**a** It melts at 30 to 32 degrees, just below our regular body temperature.

**b** The temperature of our hand or mouth is just below our body temperature.

**c** Chocolate's melting point is just below 32 degrees.

**9** Read the information given about 'Fairtrade' chocolate. What does 'trade' mean in that compound word?

**a** to exchange one product for another product

**b** to exchange a product for money

**c** to exchange chocolate fairly

**10** What is the main category of information covered in this text?

**a** the history of chocolate **b** the health benefits of chocolate **c** the ingredients in chocolate

## Applied questions

*Hint: These questions require you to make an informed judgement based on the evidence.*

**11** If this article were to be included in a reference book such as an encyclopedia, the last paragraph would need to be reworded because

**a** it is too formal. **b** it is too informal. **c** it is too uncertain.

**12** What is the purpose of the bullet-point section? Why is this information not presented in regular paragraphs?

____________________

# INFORMATIVE TEXT

## Informative article

**SPELLING WORK**

### List Words

All of the words in the box below appear in the text 'Chocolate history, short and sweet'.

| | | | | |
|---|---|---|---|---|
| chocolate | cocoa | ailments | concoction | recreational |
| delectable | exploited | minor | consumers | conscience |
| confectionery | acquainted | beneficial | antioxidant | temperature |

**1** Which three words in each sentence are incorrectly spelt? *Hint: Only some words come from the list.*

**a** Beccause chocolate is so dellectable, I just can't stop eading it.

**b** Choclate is clasted as a confectionery because it is full of shugar.

**c** Consummers offen don't relise that many people who make chocolate are exploited.

**d** The benofficial antixodiant properties of some foods are becoming more widely nown.

**e** Forlow your consense and by Fairtrade chocolate at the store.

**2** The lazy or fast pronunciation of some words results in their sounding as though they have one fewer syllable. Circle the list words below that fit this description. *Hint: You will need to pronounce all of the words aloud to check.*

chocolate concoction minor confectionery temperature

**3** Use the list words to check whether each group of letters below begins or ends a word, then sort them into the appropriate box.

rec temp ant tion ments ex able cial con

| Beginnings | Endings |
|---|---|
| | |
| | |
| | |
| | |
| | |

**4** Which four list words begin with the same group of three letters?

________ ________ ________ ________

**5** Add beginnings and endings to make list words. The number of letters needed in spaces will vary.

**a** _____ sc _____ **b** _____ per _____ **c** _____ ol_____

**6** The words in each group below contain a common group of letters, which have been highlighted. In some of the words the sound created by the letter group is different from the sound in the list word. Next to each word write a rhyming word to show that you know how the letter group is pronounced. The first group has been completed for you as an example.

| | | | | | | |
|---|---|---|---|---|---|---|
| **a** minor: | tenor | henna | orb | daub | story | gory |
| **b** ailment: | said | | mail | | air | |
| **c** temperature: | pure | | lure | | sure | |
| **d** cocoa: | goal | | oar | | cloak | |

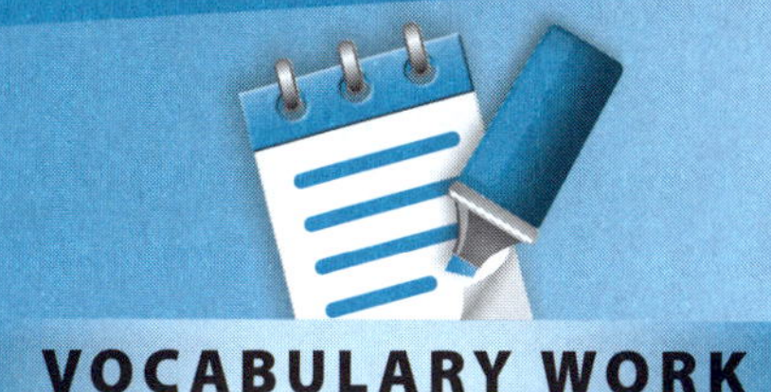

# INFORMATIVE TEXT

## Informative article

## VOCABULARY WORK

Informative articles contain many facts and details so it is vital to present them using clear expression. One enemy of clear expression in our writing is **redundancy**. When words are redundant—that is, not useful—in a sentence, remove them. Eliminating redundant words also saves space in short texts like articles.

**1** In these sentences at least two words or phrases can be eliminated without altering the meaning. In fact, their removal should make the sentence easier to understand. Cross out these redundant words. The first one has been done for you as an example.

**a** In my ~~personal~~ opinion, ~~I think~~ chocolate is the ideal snack.

**b** By the time the 1600s came, chocolate was popular all over and right across Europe.

**c** Dark chocolate is so good and healthy for you that it noticeably improves aspects of your body's health.

**d** Just eating up some chocolate brings about a stronger, more potent high than even kissing does.

**2** Reshuffle the letters in these strings of nonsense words into pairs of words from the list words.

**a** micocoanor ______________ and ______________

**b** conconsufecmerstionery ______________ and ______________

**c** aildelmentsectable ______________ and ______________

**d** bacquenefaintedicial ______________ and ______________

**e** expantiloitoxidedant ______________ and ______________

**3** Use the words in the box to answer the questions about the text 'Chocolate history, short and sweet'.

| inhaling | inventor | relaxed | high | aroma | mental | feel |
|---|---|---|---|---|---|---|

**a** Which two words in the article are associated with smell? ______________ and ______________

**b** Which five words are linked to ideas and emotions? ______________, ______________

______________, ______________ and ______________

Depending on the context we use different terms or phrases to describe the same action or state. These can be **idioms** (known to a particular group of people), **formal expressions** or **jargon** (technical words).

**4** Using the clues and letters provided, find other words for the action of eating in the article about chocolate.

**a** c______________g (formal verb) **b** ______________f (idiom or slang) **c** n______________g (verb)

**5** Change the form of a list word to complete each sentence correctly.

**a** When we ______________ chocolate, we tend to feel relaxed.

**b** It is vital that big food companies stop ______________ farm owners and workers.

**c** I once had an ______________ who was a cousin of the Cadbury brothers.

**d** A ______________ worker is someone who works hard and deserves their pay.

With its suffix *ery*, 'confectionery' can be confused for a **homophone** (word with the same sound) ending in *ary*: a confection**ary** (sweet shop or factory) is a place that sells confection**ery** (sweets).

**6** Stationery/stationary is a related pair of words ending in *ery* and *ary* that also have their suffixes easily confused. One is a noun, the other an adjective. Complete this sentence to show that you know the difference.

Stationery is a word for ______________, while stationary means ______________.

# INFORMATIVE TEXT

## GRAMMAR WORK

### Prepositions

A **preposition** is a word that shows the relationship between elements of a sentence.

- It is an essential part of a sentence that helps it make sense.
- It tells the reader when, where or why, or completes a description of something or someone.
- It is often contained within a prepositional phrase.
- It is often placed directly before a noun.

**1** Choose prepositions from the box below to complete the following sentences. Not every word in the box will be used. *Hint: The size of each space does not indicate the length of each word.*

| | | | | | |
|---|---|---|---|---|---|
| under | around | into | through | to | toward |
| with | from | in | up | on | |

**a** When you eat chocolate, electrical activity changes ____________ your brain.

**b** In many countries ____________ the world, cocoa farmers are exploited.

**c** Chocolate is flavoured ____________ sugar and vanilla to remove the bitterness.

**d** White chocolate technically does not fall ____________ the chocolate category.

**e** The cocoa bean goes ____________ a very long process to become the creamy sweet we love.

**f** Buying 'Fairtrade' chocolate helps prevent farm workers ____________ losing their income.

**2** These words from the text 'Chocolate history, short and sweet' all appear in lower case, but many of them should begin with a capital letter. Which ones? Rewrite the proper nouns but leave the common nouns as they are.

| | | | | | |
|---|---|---|---|---|---|
| aztec | ____________ | mayan | ____________ | chilli | ____________ |
| currency | ____________ | europe | ____________ | conquest | ____________ |
| cadbury | ____________ | nestlé | ____________ | celsius | ____________ |
| brain | ____________ | flavonoid | ____________ | wakefield | ____________ |

**3** These compound words all appear in the text. Circle the ones that are closed compound words. *Hint: A closed compound word is a pair of words sandwiched together; it does not contain a hyphen.*

| | | | | | |
|---|---|---|---|---|---|
| reduce | brainwaves | certified | Fairtrade | groundbreaking | plantations |
| offwhite | lifetime's | bittertasting | meltingpoint | Mesoamerican | chocolate |

**4** Adapt the list words in the table to form other parts of speech. *Hint: Some words may work as a different part of speech without changing their form.*

| Noun | Verb | Adjective |
|---|---|---|
| concoction | **a** | **b** |
| **c** | exploited | **d** |
| **e** | **f** | recreational |
| ailments | **g** | **h** |

# INFORMATIVE TEXT

## PUNCTUATION WORK

### Different kinds of emphasis

When composing a text like an informative article, a writer can use various strategies to add **emphasis** to certain parts of the text. Examples, some of which will also be explored in the Writing Work section on page 37, are:

- repetition and selective use of redundant words
- keeping sentences short (truncating them)
- italicising particular words, phrases and subheadings
- showing some words in bold
- reinforcing information in selected images.

**1** Identify the emphasis strategy that has been used in each of these extracts from the text 'Chocolate history, short and sweet' by ticking the appropriate box.

| | | | | | |
|---|---|---|---|---|---|
| **a** | Some delectable *Did you knows* … | Italics | ☐ | Short sentence | ☐ |
| **b** | Not just forgivable, but actually beneficial. So beneficial, in fact … | Image | ☐ | Repetition | ☐ |
| **c** | You'll need to come up with a different excuse to eat those. | Repetition | ☐ | Short sentence | ☐ |
| **d** | Chocolate shown in various forms | Bold | ☐ | Image | ☐ |
| **e** | But it does contain cocoa *butter*, | Italics | ☐ | Short sentence | ☐ |

**2** Correct the punctuation errors in these sentences from the article. Rewrite each sentence in full.
*Hint: You'll need to add a colon, the bullet points and the full stops.*

**a** frances marie antoinette and napoleon-bonaparte we're two famous Chocolate Fans

______________________________________________

______________________________________________

**b** Every-single second. American's scoff a combined total of '100 pounds' 4.5 kilograms of chocolate …

______________________________________________

______________________________________________

**c** thats' why It can, dissolve, so quickly in our hand, or mouth!

______________________________________________

**3** Locate examples of these punctuation features in the text and write a phrase or short sentence in which each has been used.

**a** dash ______________________________

**b** exclamation mark ______________________________

**c** capitalised proper noun ______________________________

**d** inverted commas ______________________________

**e** ellipsis ______________________________

**4** All of these punctuation marks appear in the text. Split the letter chain using slashes to show what they are.

dashcommainvertedcommaperiodexclamationmarkapostrophe

# INFORMATIVE TEXT

## Informative article

WRITING WORK 1

### Informative articles

**Informative articles** are factual texts that include lots of details. They can be found in many online and printed settings, from websites and blogs to encyclopedias and magazines. For this reason, it is helpful for both the reader and the writer if the material is well organised and expressed economically (without using too many words). When composing informative texts the use of structural devices, such as bullet points, can reduce the amount of written text and keep the content clear. Selecting appropriate images to accompany the text also helps with clarity, adds interest and helps readers remember what they have read.

### Structural features of an informative article

These types of text usually contain the following **features**:

- a title that identifies the topic
- at least one subheading
- short passages of information, including small paragraphs and bullet points
- simple sentences, sometimes truncated
- a logical sequence of information (in the text 'Chocolate history, short and sweet', the sequence is mostly chronological)
- relevant images including photographs, diagrams and tables.

1 What are two structural features of an informative article that help make it readable?

______________________________

2 What are three types of visual features that may be found in an informative article?

__________ __________ __________

3 Think about the types of informative articles you have seen, both printed or online. Show your understanding of some of the purposes of informative articles by completing these sentences using topics of your choice.

a An informative article may educate people about ______________________.

b An informative article may be useful for students ______________________.

c An informative article may help raise awareness about ______________________.

d An informative article may be included in ______________________.

4 Look at the text 'Chocolate history, short and sweet' again, then answer these questions.

a List two specific structural features that have been used in the text.

______________________________

______________________________

b What image would complement (suit and enhance) the information given in the final paragraph? Explain. *Hint: Look at the final bullet point above for ideas.*

______________________________

______________________________

# INFORMATIVE TEXT

## WRITING WORK 2

### Language features of an informative article

In order to keep informative articles succinct, clear, interesting and accurate, writers of these texts usually employ the following **language features**:

- factual descriptions and concise details that are highly relevant
- economical use of language, including short phrases and precise diction (word choice)
- jargon and specialised vocabulary
- statistics and dates that provide supporting evidence and add authority to the article
- adjectives that describe or elaborate on aspects of the topic
- concrete language and an absence of figurative expressions.

**5** Look at the text 'Chocolate history, short and sweet' and match the features listed with the examples taken from the text. Write the correct letters in the spaces to show the matches. *Hint: Using a process of elimination will help you with this task.*

| | | |
|---|---|---|
| **a** title | ______ | creamy off-white |
| **b** bullet point information | ______ | story about Ruth Wakefield |
| **c** specialised vocabulary related to the topic | ______ | 'Chocolate history, short and sweet' |
| **d** adjectives that describe a substance | ______ | cocoa beans and powder |
| **e** photograph or illustration | ______ | *xocoatl* |
| **f** statistics | ______ | reduce your risk of heart disease by a third |

As mentioned in the notes above, **precise diction** is used in informative articles. This is done to give authority to the text, to make it readable and to keep it brief.

**6** Find examples of precise diction used by the writer of the text 'Chocolate history, short and sweet' and insert the words below, using the clues provided.

**a** specific names of people groups ______________ and ______________ cultures

**b** specific names of people M______________ ______________te, R______________ ______________ld and N______________ ______________e

**c** precise nouns p______________s of c______________ were grown

**d** precise verb cocoa butter was ______________ from the beans

**7** Complete the following statements about particular language techniques used in the text. *Hint: Refer back to the annotations on the article for help with this task; many of the answers are there.*

**a** The writer uses informal expression because the topic appeals to a wide range of r______________.

**b** Time-related c______________s, such as the word 'after', are used by the writer to show the passage of time.

**c** The issue of the ex______________ of cacao farmers is partly supported by a s______________c.

**d** Emphasis is given to some facts through the writer's occasional use of a r______________nt word. For example, 'Every ______________ second, Americans scoff a combined total of 100 pounds … of chocolate.'

# INFORMATIVE TEXT

## Informative article

WRITING SAMPLE

Here is a sample text showing you how to structure and write an informative article.

### The Invisible Circus

The Invisible Circus is a stage show with a difference. It incorporates a variety of acts presented as a traditional circus but with a big twist—all of the performers are invisible to the audience. That doesn't mean they aren't present on stage. It's just that the audience can't see them.

### How?

The technology of ultraviolet (UV) light—commonly called 'black light'—allows the audience to see some parts of a performer's body, while other parts are made invisible using black clothing. When the stage and the room are completely blacked out, the clothed parts simply disappear. The parts you *can* see appear white or a fluorescent colour when the UV light is switched on, making them brightly illuminated in the black environment.

The Invisible Circus concept is not dissimilar to a flea circus. A flea circus involves feats that are supposedly performed by tiny fleas, which are too small to be seen from a distance. Of course nowadays there are rarely performing fleas. It's all done through tricks with props and the circus arena itself. In the same way, the Invisible Circus features special tricks and acts that appear to be impossible. But instead of non-existent fleas, the actors work in the dark to perform the stunts and special effects. Can you see the great potential for a circus show using UV tricks?

Plenty of theatrical performers can—and have. Since the dawn of black light technology, which has applications in many fields ranging from nail art to crime solving, UV light has attracted the attention of circus performers and producers. It is used by many dance companies, as it adds an extra 'wow' factor to any production. It is also fairly simple to use.

One of the most popularly known acts to specialise in UV light tricks is the hugely successful Blue Man Group, which specialises in spectacular performance art set to energetic music. But there are others. A show by Cirque du Carousel involves gravity-defying acrobatic manoeuvres that are achieved by hiding additional performers and apparatus in the darkness, so that only the seemingly weightless acrobats appear. *Luminous* is an Australian black light circus-style show featuring live UV body painting, dancing and acrobatics. The Blacklight Circus @ Synphoria takes this kind of production to the next level by providing 3D glasses to their audience, making the already stunning images seem to leap right off the stage.

What will we see next in the magical world of black light theatre?

---

- **Write an attention-grabbing heading that creates interest because it is paradoxical.** How can a visual performance be invisible?
- **Write a brief introduction to the topic of the article.** Colloquial language (such as 'That doesn't mean …') is used to draw the reader in and encourages them to continue. The expression is concise, providing a clear indication of the article's purpose: to convey information.
- **Insert a simple subheading that asks a question and sums up the information to follow.** For example, 'How?'
- **Explain the topic, using jargon and abbreviations to indicate that you are presenting technical information.** Here we see the term 'ultraviolet (UV) light'. Dashes are used to add information in the same way as parentheses. Here we read the common term for UV light. An appropriate image has been included to demonstrate the technical information in this section. This image shows a UV light performance of a hula hoop circus trick, where the performer inside the hoops is invisible.
- **Continue to explain the topic by informing the reader about a similar concept.** This aids the reader's understanding. A contraction—'It's' (for 'it is')—adds to the text's informal style. A rhetorical question is asked at the end of this paragraph to both reflect on what has been said and set up a transition into the next paragraph.
- **Insert a second image to enhance the information being presented.** Here we see an intriguing photo of a performer who would be almost entirely invisible if against a black background. The image helps the reader understand how 'black light' works. Specific examples of fields in which UV light is used are given, to further aid our understanding. An idiom, '"wow" factor', adds to the colloquial nature of the article and makes it accessible to all kinds of readers.
- **Name and briefly describe certain people or specific situations that will help readers connect the information being presented with real-world examples.** One of the acts—Blue Man Group—is very well known around the world and likely to be known to readers; this makes it a particularly useful example. A truncated sentence ('But there are others.') builds interest. Impactful language, such as the adjectival phrase 'gravity-defying' and the evocative expression 'stunning images seem to leap right off the stage', has been used in this climactic section. They help the article close with a bang.
- **Write an open question in place of a conclusion.**

# INFORMATIVE TEXT

## Informative article

## WRITING YOUR OWN SAMPLE

Plan your sample on the lines provided.

- **Write an attention-grabbing heading that creates interest because it is paradoxical.**
- **Write a brief introduction to the topic of the article.** Use concise expression, providing a clear indication of the article's purpose: to convey information. Use colloquial language to draw the reader in and encourage them to continue.
- **Insert a simple subheading that asks a question and sums up the information to follow.**
- **Explain the topic, using jargon and abbreviations to indicate that you are presenting technical information.** Choose an appropriate image to demonstrate the technical information in this section. Employ dashes to add information in the same way as you would use parentheses. In the sample text this is done to provide a common term for UV light.
- **Continue to explain the topic by informing the reader about a similar concept.** This will aid the reader's understanding. Use contractions to add to the text's informal style. Ask a rhetorical question at the end of this paragraph to both reflect on what has been said and set up a transition into the next paragraph.
- **Insert a second image to enhance the information being presented.** Choose an intriguing photo that will attract attention but will also help the reader understand an aspect of the topic. Give specific examples of fields where your topic is relevant, to further aid reader understanding. Use an idiom to add to the colloquial nature of the article and make it accessible to all kinds of readers.
- **Name and briefly describe certain people or specific situations that will help readers connect the information being presented with real-world examples.** Use a truncated sentence to build interest. Use impactful language and an evocative expression in this climactic section to help the article close with a bang.
- **Write an open question in place of a conclusion.**

# NARRATIVE TEXT

## *Literary recount*

**READING WORK**

### Ninety-four years from Fromelles

*This recount is a standalone text. It tells of a special military service in Fromelles, France, commemorating a World War I battle that claimed 5533 Australian soldiers in one night; equivalent to the nation's combined losses in the Boer, Korean and Vietnam Wars. Until recently, 1335 of these men were still 'missing', with no known graves. On 19 July 2010, the ninety-fourth anniversary of the Battle of Fromelles, following a complex series of searches and burials the last of the found soldiers were laid to rest with full military honours at Pheasant Wood Cemetery.*

Yesterday I stood among ribboned wreaths, head bowed, tasting silent tears, as the bugler's last notes echoed over the Pheasant Wood Military Cemetery.

Since we arrived in the pretty village of Fromelles, so many emotions have overtaken us all, even my twin boys, who you'd think, being only ten, wouldn't know what it's all about. Pop's very glad that he decided to risk the journey and has arrived in good health, though the long flight was very tiring. But he says he wouldn't have missed this for the world—the chance to see where his big brother fought and died.

The place is quite transformed now, of course: the muddy Western Front hellholes have given way to a serene carpet of rich green, embroidered with bright roses and studded with white headstones that strike me as freestanding hymnal pages.

Pop has brought along a treasured family letter, sent by Uncle Les from the trenches. I read it at the ceremony on his behalf—at almost the exact spot where it was penned ninety-four years ago.

It reads …

> Dear Mother and Father,
>
> If this letter ever reaches you, you will know that I am thinking of you all back home as I crouch down trying to keep my rifle steady. I don't know how much longer we can hold out. We have only been here in France long enough to dig in, and word has just come along the lines that we will be ordered over the top at 1800 hours. I wonder do you remember the grocery boy, Bobby Mulligan? We two saplings have teamed up, being the youngest pair in the 15th. We've struck a bargain to keep each other's backs as best we can in this place, which is no trifling comfort to us both. All the other chaps are over eighteen and seem to know what they are doing. We try to watch and learn from them, though they mainly just tell us to keep our bally heads down.
>
> I hear the rum jars have woken … some of our boys a little down the way from Bobby and me are starting to take heavy fire, so I will finish now.
>
> I love you Mother and I hope you are proud of me, Father.
>
> Your loving son,
>
> Lester.

Isn't it strange how things work out? I wonder what those young soldiers would think had they known about the connections their two families would have over the decades; that Les's great-niece would marry Bobby's great-nephew and that we'd name our two sons in their honour.

Standing among the resting soldiers in Pheasant Wood close to a century later, I almost felt as if someone had it all planned out from the start.

- The writer doesn't need to explicitly state that this is a military service. The elements listed in the first line **imply** it.
- **Contractions** such as 'you'd' and 'it's are used to keep the style informal and personal.
- A **cliché** ('wouldn't have missed this for the world') is all that is needed to convey the elderly man's feelings about visiting Fromelles with his family.
- The Western Front was a zone in western Europe (mainly encompassing northern France and Belgium) where many horrific World War I battles were fought.
- The writer shifts from literal retelling to a more literary style, using **figurative language techniques** to describe the scene. For example, the cemetery lawn is called a 'carpet'.
- The main text contains a smaller text inside it (a personal letter), making it a **recount within a recount.**
- **Military jargon and expressions,** such as 24-hour time ('1800 hours'), have been used in the letter for authenticity.
- The writer of the letter uses Australian and British **vernacular** and **idioms** from the World War I era (the very early 1900s), such as 'we two saplings', 'the other chaps' and 'keep our bally heads down'. This is a noticeable shift from the main writer's diction.
- After reflecting on the battle that claimed Les's life, the writer **reflects** on the events of the 94 years that followed.
- Like a factual recount, a literary recount ends with a **reorientation** that refers back to the opening lines.

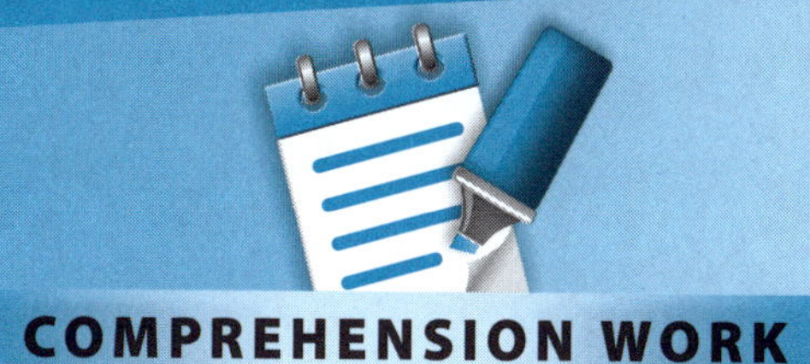

# NARRATIVE TEXT

*Literary recount*

COMPREHENSION WORK

## Literal questions

*Hint: Read the text carefully to locate specific facts and details.*

**1** Who does the writer of the letter think it may never reach? ______________________

**2** In which place did Pop's big brother fight and die? *Hint: This is a literal place.*

**a** Fromelles **b** a hellhole **c** the 15th

**3** What is 'Les' short for in line 24? ______________________

## Interpretive questions

*Hint: These questions require you to combine facts and details to synthesise the meaning.*

**4** To which three senses does the image of 'tasting silent tears' appeal?

**a** sound, taste and sight **b** taste, sight and touch **c** touch, smell and sound

**5** Who has brought the letter to France?

**a** Les's twin boys **b** Les's uncle **c** Les's brother

**6** In line 33 we read the phrase 'we two saplings'. What kind of literary device is this? *Hint: A sapling is a young tree.*

**a** metaphor **b** simile **c** personification

**7** In lines 38–39 we read a sentence linking the phrases 'rum jars' and 'heavy fire'. What do you think 'rum jars' are? *Hint: The term is not a literal one.*

______________________

**8** The writer of the text has twin boys. What are their names? ______________________

**9** In what way are the soldiers at Pheasant Wood 'resting'? ______________________

**10** What type of literary technique is used in line 43?

**a** rhetorical question **b** open-ended question **c** closed question

## Applied questions

*Hint: These questions require you to understand a text's implications to infer meaning from the text.*

**11** A hymnal is a book of sacred songs. Given the situation, why is this an appropriate image in line 22? *Hint: The phrase 'strike me' is an idiom meaning 'seem', 'appear' or 'look like'.*

______________________

______________________

**12** The title of the text could be 'Ninety-four years *since* Fromelles'. Instead the writer has chosen to use the preposition 'from'. What is the effect of this technique on the number 'ninety-four'?

**a** It means both years and place.

**b** It means both years and distance.

**c** It means both distance and speed.

# NARRATIVE TEXT

SPELLING WORK

## List Words

All of the words in the box below appear in the text 'Ninety-four years from Fromelles'.

| | | | | |
|---|---|---|---|---|
| military | wreaths | embroidered | cemetery | hymnal |
| treasured | grocery | trifling | overtaken | headstones |
| soldiers | serene | bargain | eighteen | century |

**1** Answer each of these questions with list words.

**a** Which word, with two letters removed, spells a word without vowels? ____________

**b** Every second letter in this word is the same vowel. Which word is it? ____________

**c** Which three words all feature a *c* pronounced as 'ss' and the same final letter?

____________

**d** Which word has a silent first letter? ____________

**2** Complete each sentence by selecting the correctly spelt word from the options provided. *Hint: Two answers are from the word list; two are not.*

**a** In some countries, millitary / military / militery service is compulsory.

**b** My friend and I struck a bargain / bargin / bargan to look out for each other.

**c** We opened the hymnal to search for a particular sacerd / scared / sacred song.

**d** World War I took place at the beginning / beggining / begginning of the twentieth century.

**3** Unshuffle these letter groups to form list words.

**a** limitary ____________ **b** netrucy ____________

**c** strewha ____________ **d** eerens ____________

**e** tankerove ____________ **f** flirting ____________

The term **typo** is short for 'typographical error' and refers to a typing (or texting) mistake. Rushing, hitting two letters at once, second-guessing a word's spelling, copy-pasting and making small changes are the main causes of typos. The most common typos are switched letters, omitted or added letters, repeated words and incorrect punctuation. These are not always spelling errors per se: our typos often involve words we know how to spell.

**4** There are twelve typos in this passage. Write the affected words correctly on the lines provided. *Hint: Many words in the passage appear in the text 'Ninety-four years from Fromelles'; others are not in the text.*

On the ninety-fourth aniversary of the Battel of Fromelles, a speical service was was held at Pheasant Wood Cemetry to unveil two hunderd-and-three new headstones. These mark the finall resting place of Austrailan soilders whos remains have been found in recent year's in the areaa once known as the Western Front.

____________ ____________ ____________ ____________

____________ ____________ ____________ ____________

____________ ____________ ____________ ____________

# NARRATIVE TEXT

*Literary recount*

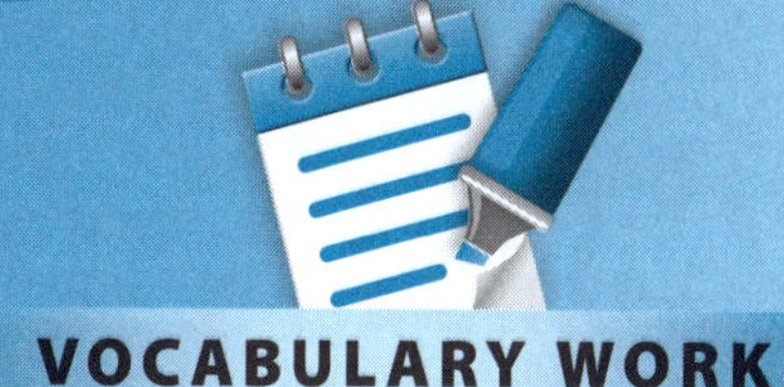

## VOCABULARY WORK

**1** Answer these questions using pairs of words from the word list.

**a** What are the number-related words? ____________ ____________

**b** What are the closed-compound words? ____________ ____________

**c** What are the funeral-related words? ____________ ____________

**d** Which words describe a group and its members? ____________ ____________

**2** Match each list word with its meaning by writing the correct numeral on the line.

| | | | |
|---|---|---|---|
| **a** wreaths | ____ | 1 | embellished with threads |
| **b** embroidered | ____ | 2 | circular arrangements of flowers and foliage |
| **c** serene | ____ | 3 | peaceful and calm |
| **d** trifling | ____ | 4 | pertaining to daily needs |
| **e** hymnal | ____ | 5 | book of sacred song lyrics |
| **f** grocery | ____ | 6 | trivial and insignificant |

As you would have read in the annotations, the writer of the letter in the text 'Ninety-four years from Fromelles' uses Australian and British **vernacular and idioms from the World War I era**; that is, the beginning of the 1900s. These expressions are noticeably different from the diction in the rest of the text.

**3** Re-read these idioms from Lester's letter in their context, then write alternative expressions in your own words. The first one has been done for you as an example.

**a** I wonder do you — *I wonder whether you* OR *I wonder if you*

**b** we two ____________

**c** chaps ____________

**d** bally ____________

**e** saplings ____________

**f** struck a bargain ____________

**g** keep each other's backs ____________

**h** no trifling comfort ____________

**i** a little down the way ____________

**j** I will finish now ____________

**4** Define these expressions, including military and warfare jargon, from Lester's letter. Re-read the letter first.

**a** dig in ____________ **b** the 15th ____________

**c** along the lines ____________ **d** over the top ____________

**5** Complete these two sentences about the formal language usage in the letter that appears inside the text.

The letter's salutation (opening) is very formal: '________ ________ and ________'.

The writer signs off with the description '________ ________ ________' and his full name, ________.

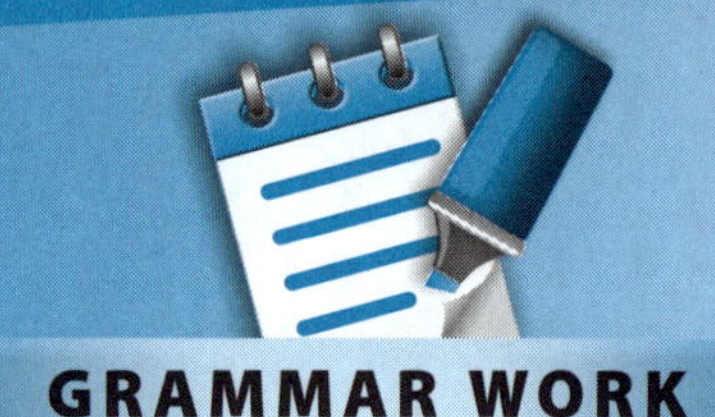

# NARRATIVE TEXT

## GRAMMAR WORK

### *I* or *me*?

We read in Lester's letter the phrase 'Bobby and me' (not 'Bobby and I'). This is not a grammatical error. Contrary to what many people think (and teach), the personal pronoun *I* is not 'more correct' than *me*. The two pronouns are appropriate in different settings. Think about it: we don't say *Please come with I.* A little more on this:

- When the pronoun is the **subject** of a verb, use *I*. For example, *Zali and I* (subject of the verb) *are eating* (verb) *lunch.*
- When the pronoun is the **object** of a verb, use *me*. For example, *The man yelled* (verb) *at Zeke and me* (object of the verb).
- If you're unsure whether *I* or *me* is correct in a sentence, leave out the pronoun's 'friends' and you'll hear the answer. You may also need to alter the verb. If you're still unsure, swap the pronoun (*I* for *me* or *me* for *I*). For example, the first sentence above becomes *Me am eating lunch.* The second sentence becomes *The man yelled at I.* Both are clearly incorrect so we know the other pronouns must be right.

**1** Test your understanding of the above information by inserting *I* or *me* into these sentences.

**a** Bobby and _____ think it's very sad that the pretty village of Fromelles has been bombed into oblivion.

**b** Before the ceremony even began, Pop, the boys and _____ started crying.

**c** Re-reading Uncle Les's letter is always a bittersweet experience for Pop and _____.

**d** Once Bobby and _____, along with our whole unit, got the order to go over the top, we knew it was the end.

**2** Find these partial sentences in the text 'Ninety-four years from Fromelles' and complete them by adding the missing adjectives.

**a** I stood among ______________ wreaths, head bowed, tasting ______________ tears, as the bugler's ______________ notes echoed …

**b** Pop has brought along a ______________ family letter, sent by Uncle Les from the trenches.

**c** Pop … has arrived in ___________ health, though the ___________ flight was very ______________.

**3** Complete the same partial sentences as in Question 2, but this time use any new adjectives of your choice.

**a** I stood among ______________ wreaths, head bowed, tasting ______________ tears, as the bugler's ______________ notes echoed …

**b** Pop has brought along a ______________ family letter, sent by Uncle Les from the trenches.

**c** Pop … has arrived in ___________ health, though the ___________ flight was very ______________.

**4** This brief passage is based on the text. Identify the part of speech of each highlighted word in the passage by writing *N* for noun, *V* for verb, *ADJ* for adjective, *ADV* for adverb, *P* for preposition or *C* for conjunction.

When we **arrived** ____ **in** _____ lovely **Fromelles** _____, we were surprised and **humbled** _____ when we were met at the town square and **greeted** _____ **warmly** _____ by local **councillors** _____. Pop was overwhelmed, **because** _____ this was not his first **trip** _____ to **Northern France** _____ for the sake **of** _____ his brother. It was, however, his first **successful** _____one: Les would be buried at last **and** _____ given his due honour.

# NARRATIVE TEXT

## PUNCTUATION WORK

### Pauses

In every text featuring full sentences, we find **pauses** created by different punctuation marks, including:

- , comma
- : colon
- ; semicolon
- ... ellipsis
- — dash
- ( ) parentheses

The full stop, exclamation mark and question mark are not pauses; they are terminal punctuation marks.

**1** Explain why the semicolon has that name. *Hint: Refer to the colon in your answer.*

______________________________

**2** Re-read the final sentence in the box above. What do you think the phrase 'terminal punctuation marks' means?

______________________________

**3** In the text 'Ninety-four years from Fromelles' we note some different punctuation marks that create pauses. In each extract below find the pause-creating mark, write its name on the line and then complete the statement about the effect or function of the pause. *Hints: Find a different mark in each extract. Ellipsis is not one: it is used here to show partial sentences.*

**a** … who you'd think, being only ten, wouldn't know what it's all about.

Punctuation: ________ This pair of pauses allows the narrator to tell us the twin boys' ____________.

**b** I read it at the ceremony on his behalf—at almost the exact spot where it was penned ninety-four years ago.

Punctuation: ________ This pause conveys the amazement of the ____________ at being in this place.

**c** The place is quite transformed now, of course: the muddy Western Front hellholes …

Punctuation: ________ This pause splits the ____________ and leads into a ______________ of the war zone.

**d** … the connection their two families would have over the decades; that Les's great-niece …

Punctuation: ________ This pause comes before the ______________ between the families is ____________.

**4** To answer these punctuation questions, look back at the text. In the text:

**a** what punctuation marks present the letter as a piece of direct speech? ______________

**b** which two hyphenated compound words denote family relationships? ______________

______________

**c** what punctuation mark follows the letter's salutation? ______________

**d** what is the function of the ellipsis just before Lester's letter? ______________

**5** Circle or highlight the punctuation errors in these slightly altered extracts from the text.

**a** Pop has brought a treasured family letter, sent, by Uncle Les from the trenches I read it at the ceremony on his behalf! At almost the exact … spot (where it was penned ninety four year's ago).

**b** The place is quite transformed now: of course the muddy Wes-tern Front hell-holes have given way, to a serene carpet—of rich green embroidered with bright rose's.

# NARRATIVE TEXT

Literary recount

**WRITING WORK 1**

## Literary recount

A **literary** or **imaginative recount** has features in common with a factual recount. Both recount types provide details about the 'who, what, when and where' of events, and may also touch on their result or aftermath. The events and characters in a literary recount can be either real or fictitious. Rather than offering only facts, as a factual recount does, a literary recount can do some or all of the following things:

* retell at least one key event (made up of a sequence of smaller events)
* describe at least one character's feelings about and reactions to the event
* describe a setting and actions in detail
* record dialogue between characters
* encourage the reader to experience an emotional connection—a literary recount, especially a personal one like the text in this unit, offers a far greater emotional connection between the narrator and the reader than a factual recount does.

**1** What is the main event described in the text 'Ninety-four years from Fromelles'?

______________________________________________

**2** Quote two phrases or brief sentences in the text that encourage an emotional connection in the reader.

______________________ ______________________

**3** Which of the text forms listed below can also be types of recount? Tick the appropriate boxes.

- ☐ short story
- ☐ picture book
- ☐ visual advertisement
- ☐ biography or autobiography
- ☐ personal letter or diary entry
- ☐ fable, myth or legend
- ☐ television documentary voice over
- ☐ poem or song in the ballad genre
- ☐ procedure
- ☐ anecdote

## Structure of a literary recount

To be classed as a literary recount, a text must contain these **structural features**:

* a title or a heading, which can be literal or creative
* an orientation (the first paragraph)
* a description of the setting, introductions to the characters and background information (the first and/or second paragraph)
* a sequence of events in the body of the text, usually chronological, but possibly also non-linear (not in a straight timeline), as in the text 'Ninety-four years from Fromelles', where the events include a letter that is a flashback to World War I
* a reorientation (the final paragraph), where the sequence of events ends and the reader is pointed back to the beginning of the recount.

**4** The title 'Ninety-four years from Fromelles' is more creative than literal. Explain why.

______________________________________________

Both sample texts in this unit contain a smaller text inside the main recount: in the Reading Work section on page 41 it is a personal letter, and in the Writing Sample section on page 49 it is an entry in a reference book. This structural technique aids reader engagement and also provides essential information required for understanding the main text. The structure of the text 'Ninety-four years from Fromelles', our main study in this unit, makes it a **recount within a recount**.

# NARRATIVE TEXT

## *Literary recount*

### What does a recount 'recount'?

A recount retells past events. In the text 'Ninety-four years from Fromelles', the narrator tells us that one of these events occurred 'yesterday'. Other events are described in the letter inside the recount; these happened around the time of the Battle of Fromelles. Despite some of the events being factual and historical (such as the battle), this recount is **literary** because the characters and the letter are all fictitious. Therefore this recount is also in the historical fiction genre (fiction based on or inspired by historical events).

**5** **a** Which elements of the text 'Ninety-four years from Fromelles' are true? *Hint: Your answer should contain more than the main events in the recount.*

______________________________

**b** Which elements of the text 'Ninety-four years from Fromelles' are made up?

______________________________

### Language features of recounts

Some **language features** and techniques that writers of recounts commonly use are:

- first person narration
- past tense mode
- descriptions of feelings or impressions (for example, 'I almost felt as if someone had it all planned')
- emotive language (for example, 'tasting silent tears')
- action verbs (for example, 'stood' and 'strike').

**6** Two examples of action verbs from the recount are given in the box above. Give another two examples from the text.

______________ ______________

**7** Write an extra sentence that could be inserted in the text after the first sentence. You will need to use your imagination to build on the scene described by the narrator. Appeal to at least one of the five senses.

______________________________

In a literary recount, the **tone** (or voice) created by the writer is important. This is because the writer's attitude about the subject is revealed by the language they use. When choosing words and using language features that contribute to a text's tone, a writer also considers the purpose and audience of the text.

**8** **a** Write three adjectives or adjectival phrases to describe the narrator's tone in the text 'Ninety-four years from Fromelles'.

__________ __________ __________

**b** Write three adjectives or adjectival phrases to describe Lester's tone in the letter in the text. *Hint: You will need to re-read Lester's letter carefully before answering.*

__________ __________ __________

**9** Evaluate the effectiveness of incorporating the letter from a soldier into the text. *Hint: In your answer you need to give specific reasons for your evaluation, referring directly to the text.*

______________________________

______________________________

# NARRATIVE TEXT

## *Literary recount*

**WRITING SAMPLE**

Here is a sample text showing you how to structure and write a literary recount.

### Archimedes and me

✱ **Write a title that is literal and names the two characters who will be featured in the recount.**

The day when Archimedes and I became friends is boldly imprinted in my memory.

✱ **Write the recount in the first person.** The narrator is the 'me' in the title.

I opened the narrow wooden door and set up my chair in the doorway. I half-closed the door so that he wouldn't be tempted to escape and leaned close to where he was perched. I made soft noises to the owl and slowly held my hand out towards his brown-and-white speckled chest. His wings were folded neatly towards his back and striped with dark brown feathers. A curved, sharp, black beak contrasted impressively against his pure white throat. Two black stripes served as eyebrows, making him look quite stern. He watched me calmly with deep, golden eyes ringed by circles of tiny, light-brown feathers. There were two little tufts of feathers on top of his head that looked like horns or pointed ears.

✱ **Write in the past tense.** This is because a recount reflects on past events. We don't learn that Archimedes is an owl until part way through the second paragraph. A very detailed description of the owl character is provided by the narrator, creating a vivid image of him in the mind of the reader. Comparative language, such as 'two black stripes served as eyebrows', provides extra detail and makes the owl seem almost human.

I shone my torch onto the open book in my lap and scanned the index … 'great horned owl'. I flipped to the page and was greeted by a creature that looked similar to my new friend but was far less handsome. There was a box of information about horned owls under the picture. It read:

✱ **Include action verbs in the narration.** Action verbs, such as 'shone', 'scanned' and 'flipped', describe small events that are part of the key event (making friends with the owl). A text transition is set up in the narration.

> The horned owl belongs to the family Strigidae. Found in most regions of North and South America, the horned owl and great horned owl occupy a range of habitats, from suburban reserves to semi-arid areas. They feed on living prey, mainly small rodents and reptiles. These owls are two of the most popular species exported from the United States, primarily because they can adapt their life patterns to suit a range of habitats. In South America, for instance, the owls often hunt during daylight hours—usually early morning and late afternoon. They are not strictly nocturnal, as is commonly believed of all owls, but do prefer to spend the midday period sleeping. These owl species live well in captivity. Breeding programs in the USA export chicks to many countries.

✱ **Insert a text into the recount at roughly the halfway point.** It is a reference book extract about owls, which is indented to distinguish it from the main recount. The minor text contains important information about the owl. The narrator refers to this when the main recount text resumes. The language in the minor text is more formal than the rest of the recount; for example, 'They are not strictly nocturnal, as is commonly believed of all owls.'

Needless to say, I was delighted to discover that he could leave his cage twice a day! His natural hunting times permitted it. I cautiously stroked his soft, mottled chest feathers. He didn't seem to mind, and bent his head to look down at my hand.

Now that I was getting to know him, I was certain about a name. I told him in a very serious voice, 'I will call you Archimedes. I hope you like that name. It's the name of a very intelligent man who gave the world a lot of important knowledge.'

✱ **Mention the inserted information and point out its significance in the narration.** We learn that '… he could leave his cage twice a day because his natural hunting times permitted it.' The writer uses contractions to make the narrator's expression informal and candid; for example, 'He didn't seem to mind.' A line of dialogue serves two functions: it adds to the authenticity of the text and it provides exposition about the name given to the owl by the narrator.

I knew immediately that he understood everything I was saying. I knew, too, that we would become firm friends.

✱ **End the recount with a brief reorientation.**

Plan your sample on the lines provided.

- **Write a title that is literal and names the two characters who will be featured in the recount.**
- **Write the recount in the first person.**
- **Write in the past tense.** This is necessary because a recount reflects on past events. Save a secret or important fact about one character until part way through the second paragraph. Give a very detailed description of the same character, creating a vivid image in the mind of the reader. Use comparative language to provide extra detail.
- **Include action verbs in the narration.** These describe small events that are part of the key event. Set up a text transition in the narration.
- **Insert a text into the recount at roughly the halfway point.** Ensure that the minor text contains important information about the subject, to which the narrator can refer when the main recount text resumes. Use more formal language in the minor text than in the rest of the recount.
- **Mention the inserted information and point out its significance in the narration.** Use contractions to make the narrator's expression informal and candid (open and honest). Include a line of dialogue, both to add to the authenticity of the text and to provide exposition about a character or event.
- **End the recount with a brief reorientation.** In other words, refer back to the opening lines.

UNIT 6

# NARRATIVE TEXT

## *Prose fiction*

**READING WORK**

### Excerpt from *The Jungle Book*

*Rudyard Kipling was an English journalist and fiction writer. He composed poems, novels and many short stories. Probably his most famous work is* The Jungle Book, *which has inspired at least nine major film productions on the big and small screen. The book is essentially a collection of short stories, each of which can stand alone, but they can also work together as one whole text. As such we can analyse* The Jungle Book *as an episodic novel. Each episode is a fable, featuring anthropomorphic (humanlike) animal characters and offering moral lessons. In this section of Chapter 1, a pack of wolves discovers a human baby in the jungle just outside their cave home.*

The Law of the Jungle, which never orders anything without a reason, forbids every beast to eat Man except when he is killing to show his children how to kill, and then he must hunt outside the hunting grounds of his pack or tribe. The real reason for this is that man-killing means, sooner or later, the arrival of white men on elephants, with guns, and hundreds of brown men with gongs and rockets and torches. Then everybody in the jungle suffers. The reason the beasts give among themselves is that Man is the weakest and most defenseless of all living things, and it is unsportsmanlike to touch him. They say too—and it is true—that man-eaters become mangy, and lose their teeth.

The purr grew louder, and ended in the full-throated 'Aaarh!' of the tiger's charge.

Then there was a howl—an untigerish howl—from Shere Khan. 'He has missed,' said Mother Wolf. 'What is it?'

Father Wolf ran out a few paces and heard Shere Khan muttering and mumbling savagely as he tumbled about in the scrub.

'The fool has had no more sense than to jump at a woodcutters' campfire, and has burned his feet,' said Father Wolf with a grunt. 'Tabaqui is with him.'

'Something is coming uphill,' said Mother Wolf, twitching one ear. 'Get ready.'

The bushes rustled a little in the thicket, and Father Wolf dropped with his haunches under him, ready for his leap. Then, if you had been watching, you would have seen the most wonderful thing in the world—the wolf checked in mid-spring. He made his bound before he saw what it was he was jumping at, and then he tried to stop himself. The result was that he shot up straight into the air for four or five feet, landing almost where he left ground.

'Man!' he snapped. 'A man's cub. Look!'

Directly in front of him, holding on by a low branch, stood a naked brown baby who could just walk—as soft and as dimpled a little atom as ever came to a wolf's cave at night. He looked up into Father Wolf's face, and laughed.

'Is that a man's cub?' said Mother Wolf. 'I have never seen one. Bring it here.'

A Wolf accustomed to moving his own cubs can, if necessary, mouth an egg without breaking it, and though Father Wolf's jaws closed right on the child's back not a tooth even scratched the skin as he laid it down among the cubs.

'How little! How naked, and—how bold!' said Mother Wolf softly. The baby was pushing his way between the cubs to get close to the warm hide. 'Ahai! He is taking his meal with the others. And so this is a man's cub. Now, was there ever a wolf that could boast of a man's cub among her children?'

'I have heard now and again of such a thing, but never in our Pack or in my time,' said Father Wolf. 'He is altogether without hair, and I could kill him with a touch of my foot. But see, he looks up and is not afraid.'

From *The Jungle Book* by Rudyard Kipling, 1894

- In this text, which was written in the Victorian era, 'Man' means 'mankind' or 'people'. It does not mean 'a male human'. In this era, it was very common to refer to people in general terms using this word.
- The narrator uses **very simple expressions and ideas** like this one to explore what it might be like to live in the world of the jungle and reason like an animal. For this same reason, Kipling often adopts the animals' perspective when telling the story.
- This is a **phonetically spelt** piece of dialogue that represents the tiger's roar.
- Shere Khan is a powerful, intimidating tiger in the story. 'Shere' means 'tiger' in some Indian dialects, and 'khan' is a term for a chief or ruler.
- Tabaqui is a jackal, and the only friend (also the messenger and spy) of Shere Khan.
- The author lets the **characters' dialogue create most of the suspense**, as we see demonstrated here. In fact a lot of this excerpt is written in the form of dialogue.
- A 'thicket' is a dense cluster of bushes or trees.
- The narrator often **addresses the reader directly** using the second person. This technique is common in Victorian literature (particularly children's stories); it draws readers into the world of the story by placing us directly on the sidelines of the action.
- 'Checked' here means 'paused to correct or make a change'.
- Throughout his stories, Kipling seems to be teaching the reader about things in the jungle world he has created. Sometimes this takes the form of **didacticism** (moral teaching) and sometimes we are taught about Nature.
- This word is an exclamation of surprise.
- The animals refer to the baby boy as 'a man's cub' because this is how they understand him as a fellow creature.
- The wolves are so astonished at the boy's lack of fur that they call him 'Mowgli', which is a jungle term for 'frog'. This name denotes his hairlessness.

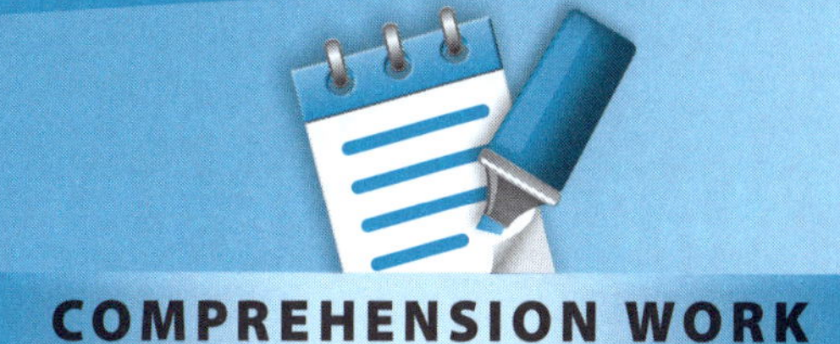

# NARRATIVE TEXT

*Prose fiction*

**COMPREHENSION WORK**

## Literal questions

*Hint: Read the text carefully to locate specific facts and details.*

**1** When does the Law of the Jungle allow a 'beast to eat Man'?

**2** Who discovers the baby boy in this excerpt?

**a** Mother Wolf **b** Father Wolf **c** Shere Khan **d** Tabaqui

**3** What kind of howl does Shere Khan make?

**a** an untigerish howl **b** a full-throated howl **c** a purring howl **d** a mumbling howl

## Interpretive questions

*Hint: These questions require you to combine facts and details to synthesise the meaning.*

**4** Why is it unsportsmanlike to touch Man?

**a** Man is the weakest and most defenseless of all living things.

**b** It leads to the arrival of white men on elephants.

**c** Man-eaters become mangy and lose their teeth.

**d** Everybody in the jungle suffers.

**5** The baby's actions prompt Mother Wolf to say 'how bold!' Quote a line where his bold actions are described.

**6** Why is so much emphasis placed on the baby's nakedness? *Hint: From whose perspective is the story being told?*

**7** Whose arrival in the jungle seems to present the biggest threat?

**a** any men **b** white elephants **c** brown men **d** tigers

**8** What comparative device is used to describe the baby in lines 38–40? *Hint: Read the paragraph carefully.*

**a** metaphor **b** personification **c** simile **d** analogy

**9** Why do you think Rudyard Kipling has used so much dialogue to tell the story?

**10** Quote one example of the narrator interrupting himself. *Hint: Look for dashes.*

## Applied questions

*Hint: These questions require you to understand a text's implications to infer meaning from the text.*

**11** Re-read the first paragraph. Who do you think makes 'The Law of the Jungle"?

**a** man **b** animals **c** man and animals **d** nobody

**12** Kipling never visited the kind of jungle in which this story is set. How does this come across in the excerpt?

# NARRATIVE TEXT

Prose fiction

SPELLING WORK

## List Words

All of the words in the box below appear in the text 'Excerpt from *The Jungle Book*'.

| | | | | |
|---|---|---|---|---|
| rustled | mumbling | lose | haunches | savagely |
| accustomed | full-throated | twitching | atom | purr |
| mangy | arrival | muttering | uphill | unsportsmanlike |

**1** Give a list word that is in the same family as each word below.

**a** mumbler ________________ **b** savagery ________________

**c** rustling ________________ **d** sportsman ________________

**e** arrive ________________ **f** atomic ________________

**g** purring ________________ **h** lost ________________

### Syllable division rules

- Each syllable must contain a vowel or a vowel sound (for example, *man–go; ba–by*)
- A divider must come before a single middle consonant (for example, *o–pen*)
- Double consonants must be divided (for example *let–ter*)
- Any compounds or affixes (prefixes or suffixes) must be divided between the constituent words or affixes (for example, *hand–bag, un–tie, teach–er*)

**2** Break these list words into syllables, applying the rules outlined in the box above.

**a** twitching _____–_____ **b** atom _____–_____

**c** uphill _____–_____ **d** mangy _____–_____

**e** muttering _____–_____–_____ **f** savagely _____–_____–_____

**3** Answer these questions using words in the word list:

**a** Which word contains a silent letter *t*? ________________

**b** Which word is a hyphenated compound? ________________

**c** Which word, with the letter *a* removed, means 'intuitive feelings or guesses'? ________________

**d** Which four-letter word is an example of onomatopoeia? ________________

**e** Which word has a prefix that means 'not'? ________________

**4** Rewrite these sentences from the text using contractions (such as *don't*) to make them sound more modern.

**a** But see, he looks up and is not afraid.

________________________________

**b** Then, if you had been watching, you would have seen the most wonderful thing in the world …

________________________________

________________________________

# NARRATIVE TEXT

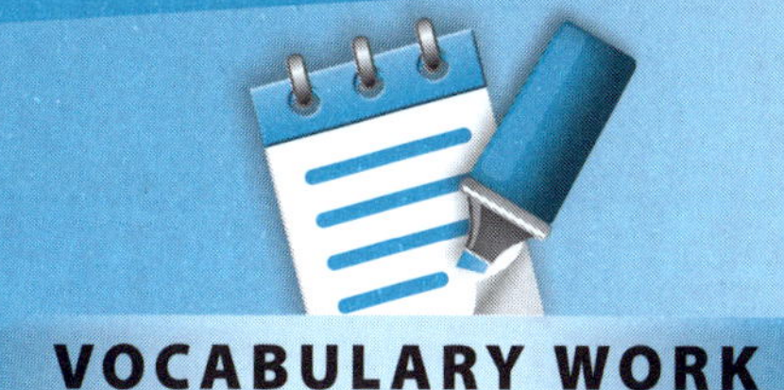

## VOCABULARY WORK

While there is very little setting (place) description in the text 'Excerpt from *The Jungle Book*', Kipling paints the world of the story by providing **detailed descriptions of action** and complementing this with dialogue between the animals.

**1** Flesh out the setting description in these sentences from the excerpt by adding appropriate details about the cave and the jungle outside. *Hints: Use mainly adjectives. Write more than one word in each space for the second and third questions.*

**a** The ____________________ bushes rustled in the __________________ thicket.

**b** Father Wolf ran out a few paces along the ________________________________ ground and heard Shere Khan muttering and mumbling savagely as he tumbled about in the ____________________________ scrub.

**c** … as soft and as dimpled a little atom as ever came to a ____________________________ wolf's cave in the ______________________________________________________ jungle.

**2** This time create completely original descriptions of the settings by writing full sentences. *Hints: Your sentences don't need to slot into the text anywhere in particular. Try using simile or metaphor.*

**a** Describe the light inside the wolf family's cave.

______________________________________________________________________________

**b** Describe the jungle slope mentioned in line 26 of the text ('uphill').

______________________________________________________________________________

**c** Describe the tree where the baby is found 'holding on by a low branch' in line 34 of the text.

______________________________________________________________________________

Some words and phrases used by Kipling in *The Jungle Book* stand out because they sound **old-fashioned**. These expressions were commonly used in his era. For example, we read in the annotations that 'Man' means 'mankind' or 'people'. This term is used to distinguish humans from animals. It does not mean only 'a male human'.

**3** Show your understanding of some of these idioms used by Kipling by inserting them into new sentences. *Hint: You may need to re-read some words in the story to understand their meaning.*

| man | man-killing | unsportsmanlike | the fool | checked | altogether | but see |
|---|---|---|---|---|---|---|

**a** He may be a little scruffy, ___________ ____________, he is every bit the gentleman.

**b** ________________________ and beast can co-exist in peace.

**c** 'It is a dangerous thing to encourage ________________________ among the Pack,' warned Father Wolf.

**d** 'I do not care whether it is ________________________: I enjoy hunting Man!' grinned Shere Khan.

**e** ___________ ____________ has no concept of the danger that he is in at this very moment.

**f** Mother Wolf ________________________ herself just before growling at the snarling Tabaqui.

**g** A situation where wolves raise a human child is ________________________ strange.

# NARRATIVE TEXT

## GRAMMAR WORK

### Different types of verbs

All verbs indicate actions or states of being. There are three main **types of verbs**:

- action verbs, which express movements, gestures, thoughts and feelings (for example, *eat, take, walk, love, think*)
- verbs that show ownership (for example, *have, possess*)
- linking verbs, which don't express a direct or specific action on their own (for example, *feel, get, were*)
- auxiliary or 'helping' verbs, which help the main verb in a phrase and give it meaning (for example, *is, be, do, have*).

**1** Underline all the verbs in these sentences from the text 'Excerpt from *The Jungle* Book', including any auxiliary verbs.

**a** They say too—and it is true—that man-eaters become mangy, and lose their teeth.

**b** He made his bound before he saw what it was he was jumping at, and then he tried to stop himself.

**c** 'I have never seen one. Bring it here.'

**2** Choose antonyms by matching the verbs in the list below with verbs from the text.

diminished giving began save cooled pulling retreat launching

| Word from the text | Antonym from the list | Word from the text | Antonym from the list |
|---|---|---|---|
| **a** grew | ______ | **b** ended | ______ |
| **c** charge | ______ | **d** kill | ______ |
| **e** burned | ______ | **f** landing | ______ |
| **g** pushing | ______ | **h** taking | ______ |

**3** Show whether these words from Question 2 can be used as past tense, present tense or future tense verbs by ticking the appropriate boxes. *Hint: Some of the verbs work as both present and future tense words.*

| | Past tense | Present tense | Future tense |
|---|---|---|---|
| **a** grew | ☐ | ☐ | ☐ |
| **b** ended | ☐ | ☐ | ☐ |
| **c** charge | ☐ | ☐ | ☐ |
| **d** kill | ☐ | ☐ | ☐ |
| **e** landing | ☐ | ☐ | ☐ |

**4** Change the tense of words from Question 2 to fit into these sentences.

**a** grew — My aunt always comments on how much I seem to ______ each year.

**b** taking — Last week the trip ______ four hours.

**c** ended — Tonight's farewell party ______ our twelve years in this town.

# NARRATIVE TEXT
## *Prose fiction*

**PUNCTUATION WORK**

### Possessive apostrophes

It is easy enough to use an **apostrophe** to show **possession** (or ownership) for a singular noun, but you might not know as much about this punctuation feature as you think. Read the points below to learn or refresh.

* The rule to show possession for a singular noun is: place an apostrophe after the owner, then add *s*. For example, *Jon's car*; *the choir's music*. Notice how the second 'owner' is a group, but still a singular noun.
* The rule to show possession for a plural noun is: place an apostrophe after the owners. For example, *the writers' conference*; *the athletes' bus*.
* What about singular nouns ending in *s*? Modern practice is to add an apostrophe plus *s* regardless of whether the singular form of the noun ends in *s* or not. However, many writers prefer to omit the *s*, particularly for nouns ending in two consecutive 's' or 'z' sounds, because it looks neater this way. For example, *Moses' robe* is less untidy on the page than *Moses's robe*. The additional *s* also affects pronunciation. For example, *Moses's* has one more syllable than *Moses'*—this can become awkward with some words. Still, the choice is yours.
* When there are two or more owners, place an apostrophe and an *s* after only the last owner. For example, *Peta, Kat and Rahma's apartment overlooks the sea.*

**1** The phrases below come from the text 'Excerpt from the *Jungle Book*'. *Hint: Re-reading the phrases in context may help.*

**a** woodcutters' campfire — Who owns the campfire? ____________________

**b** the tiger's charge — Who is making the charge? ____________________

**c** a man's cub — Who owns the cub? ____________________

**2** Rewrite each of these phrases with a correctly placed apostrophe, based on the ownership information provided.

**a** the white mens guns (The white men own the guns.) ____________________

**b** the man-eaters teeth (The man-eaters own the teeth.) ____________________

**c** the wolf packs lair (The wolf pack owns the lair.) ____________________

**3** Add apostrophes to the sentences below to show possession where necessary. *Hint: You do not need to add or change any other punctuation marks.*

The Jungles natural law exists for good reasons, and its main function is to keep the animals sanctuary free of men and their weapons. As such, Jungle beasts are forbidden to eat humans except for the purpose of their childrens education, and then, the pack or tribes hunting grounds are not appropriate places for such killings.

**4** Rewrite this biographical information about Kipling, adding any necessary punctuation marks, including possessive apostrophes. *Hints: Capital letter are already included. Plural numbers do not need apostrophes.*

The late 1800s saw Kipling become friends with Australias beloved AB 'Banjo' Paterson The two writers shared an affinity for the outdoors most of Patersons works feature the bush its beauty and its power and many of Kiplings tales also celebrate Natures wonders The mens friendship lasted until Kiplings death in the 1930s

____________________

____________________

____________________

____________________

# NARRATIVE TEXT

## *Prose fiction*

**WRITING WORK 1**

### Prose fiction

As mentioned in the annotations provided for the text 'Excerpt from *The Jungle Book*', this book can be analysed according to two different text categories: short story or episodic novel. Both text forms are types of **prose fiction**, which:

- is made-up (fictitious), either entirely or with small elements of fact included, like historical people or events
- consists of a plot (storyline) that includes an orientation, a complication, events, a climax and a resolution
- features a certain setting: the time and place of the story
- follows the actions and relationships of one or more characters (the main character is called the protagonist)
- explores themes and sometimes messages or morals.

**1** What is meant by the term 'episodic novel'? *Hint: Refer back to the annotations if you need to.*

**2** What do we **not** know about the setting of *The Jungle Book* from reading the text?

**3** The complication of the story in this unit has already occurred before the excerpt begins. What is this complication likely to be? *Hint: A complication is a key event that prompts all ensuing events in a story.*

**4** Having read the excerpt, who do you think is most likely to become the protagonist as the story continues?

### Connectedness in an episodic novel

There are two main reasons why we can refer to *The Jungle Book* as an **episodic novel**.

- The stories in the book refer to each other. For example, the second story in the book begins: 'All that is told here happened some time before Mowgli was turned out of the Seeonee wolf-pack', which is a direct reference to the first story (from which the excerpt in the text has been taken).
- The stories are interspersed with songs, in a similar way to JRR Tolkien's *The Lord of the Rings*. These songs, which can also be read as poems, create a sense of Jungle folklore.

### Epigrams

When a short text precedes a larger text, we call it an **epigram**. Each of the *Jungle Book* stories is bookended by a pair of poems or songs, so essentially there are two epigrams per story. JRR Tolkien's *The Lord of the Rings* is one of the best-known examples of a story that features poems and songs heavily. One purpose of this technique is to create a sense that these smaller texts have been taken from a real parallel world.

**5** In the box above, we read that Kipling uses songs and poems to 'create a sense of Jungle folklore'. What is one other way that this is created in the narrative? *Hint: Re-read the first paragraph of the text.*

**6** Re-read the first sentence in the box above under 'Epigrams'. What does 'bookended' mean?

# NARRATIVE TEXT
## *Prose fiction*

**WRITING WORK 2**

### An author's style

A prose fiction **author's** particular **style** emerges due to the way the story is crafted. Elements and features of this literary crafting can include:

* detailed description of action involving the main character
* the telescoping of time
* non-linear storytelling techniques such as flashbacks
* first person narrative mode
* layers of meaning, created by techniques like foreshadowing, dramatic irony and allegory
* imagery that appeals to the five senses
* emotive and heightened language
* a particular mood, generated by a combination of setting, dialogue, action and emotion
* detailed descriptions of characters
* dialogue through which characters communicate
* figurative language such as metaphor and hyperbole
* tone; that is, the 'voice' of the writer that can be 'heard' by the reader.

**7** Re-read the text 'Excerpt from *The Jungle Book*' and quote examples of stylistic elements from the list in the box on the previous page.

a dialogue: ____________________

b metaphor: ____________________

c imagery that appeals to our sense of sound: ____________________

d a detailed description of action involving the main character: ____________________

____________________

**8** Sum up the tone of the excerpt using adjectives or adjectival phrases; for example, *bitterly sarcastic.*

____________________

### Special features of Kipling's stories

Here are three particular **features** that we find in **Kipling's** *The Jungle Book* which contribute to his style:

* Anthropomorphism; that is, treating animals as though they are human by giving them speech, etc.
* Foreign or made-up names and words. For example, the wolves name the boy in the story Mowgli, a word used among the jungle animals to mean 'frog'. This name describes the human boy's lack of fur.
* Didacticism; that is, moral instruction that is given in or through the narrative. In *The Jungle Book,* Kipling's narrator is didactic in that many references to law are made. For example, the phrase 'The Law of the Jungle' opens our excerpt and is repeated throughout the book. Moreover, Victorian values and Victorian ideas of 'civilised' behaviour are celebrated. In fact, there are more than forty references to law in Kipling's stories about Mowgli (the baby boy in the text).

**9** Complete this statement to show your understanding of anthropomorphism.

Kipling, in both *The Jungle Book* and his *Just So Stories*, presents a____________ characters almost as though they are h____________. Unlike other a____________c animal characters, such as Beatrix Potter's Peter ____________, Kipling's do not wear human ____________, use furniture, and so on. They do, however, have person____________s and show emotions, cleverness and other human t____________s.

# NARRATIVE TEXT

## Prose fiction

WRITING SAMPLE

Here is a sample text showing you how to structure and write a short piece of prose fiction.

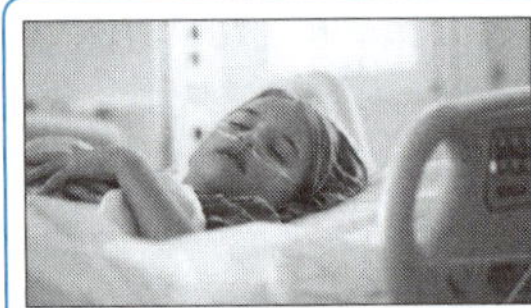

### Inner vistas

**Write an intriguing or symbolic story title.** This title suggests the idea of an interior view or a vision of the world from inside somewhere. As we read on, we learn that Lizzie, the main character and narrator, is in a coma. The 'vistas' created in the story are her experiences while trapped inside her body.

'Has she had her physio today?

'No. That's Thursday mornings. Not today.'

'Oh, really—it's down to once a week now?' I can hear the frustration in her voice.

'Yes … there's been no improvement at all, so Doctor thought it best.'

'Oh, "Doctor thought it best". I see. Sounds like they're giving up on us, Lizzie. But we're not giving up, baby. I'm not; you're not. I know you're still with us. You come back, you hear me? I'll wait for you. As long as it takes.'

I hear you, Mamma—lean down closer to me. That's it. Just hearing your voice helps me fight the panic. Keeps me hoping that you really believe I'm still in here. If I could just touch you … but I … mustn't try to move. Mustn't try, or I'll lose it. I'll go over the edge and into that black pit and I don't know if I'll get out next time. Count down to calm, Lizzie: 5, 4, 3, 2 … 1. That's better. See? You're coming out of this. You're gonna make it. You can make them see you're still here.

'Cuppa, Marian?'

**Write the story in the present tense to create immediacy, which in turn creates suspense.** We wonder whether Lizzie is about to wake up. It also helps the reader empathise. The first person narration is a little unusual because it is really interior monologue—this means that the narrator is revealing her personal thoughts. She is not telling a story in the traditional sense; her thoughts have simply been turned into a narrative. Lizzie's thoughts are interspersed with dialogue. The other three people speaking are Lizzie's mother and two nursing staff. Exposition (that is, revealing important information to the reader) and characterisation (depicting and building characters as the story unfolds) are contained in the dialogue and narration.

Ah, no … The panic is on its way again ... 5-4-3-2-1. 5, 4, 3, 2, 1. 5, 4, 3, 2 … 1. Stay calm. Focus your energy. I'm strong. My mind can overcome this body. Come on. Mamma believes in you. She knows you're fighting.

'No, thanks. I'm heading off for a bit of a walk.'

Meaning you're going off for a secret smoke, right Mamma? When are you going to come clean and admit you're doing it again? I can hear you getting up. Must be one of those vinyl seats: it's making that squeaking noise. See you later then, Mamma. Don't be long. I can't be here on my own for long. Too scared. I'll think about something else till you get back.

**Show the emotion of your narrator in an unusual way.** The narrator shows her panic building and then passing through numbers. She counts, as she did in the previous paragraph; first quickly, then more slowly as she becomes calm. Because the narrator can't see, we are given an image of the room through different senses: here sounds tell us (and the narrator herself) about actions and movement. The writer evokes anxiety by using repetition of the word 'long' to lead in to the truncated line 'Too scared'.

* * *

**Use asterisks to indicate that time has passed.** We are not told how much time.

Ughh, so tired …

Someone's here.

Hey—I know you're there, whoever you are. You're a hospital type, judging by those quiet footsteps and that jingling of keys or ID tags. I wonder what you look like, Mister? Ah—you're that new male nurse, aren't you? Nick always wears that Lynx spray too. You sound like a tall guy. Like my driving instructor. How can I get your attention? If I can just … hey! HEY! I think I did it! I think I moved my finger! HEY, MISTER! LOOK AT MY FINGER! MISTER, PLEASE! LOOOOOOOK!

'What was that? She moved! She's awake! Get somebody—quick! Lizzie's awake!

**Write an interjection to open the final section.** The expression 'Ughh' indicates exhaustion. Throughout the narration, the protagonist (Lizzie) asks questions. These indicate to the reader her thought processes, fears and observations, along with actions of other people (such as her mother going out to smoke). This section provides the story's climax, or turning point. This is reinforced by the use of capital letters, which indicate that Lizzie is 'silently shouting' in desperation. The resolution immediately follows the climax—the protagonist is going to be okay.

# NARRATIVE TEXT

## WRITING YOUR OWN SAMPLE

Plan your sample on the lines provided.

**Write an intriguing or symbolic story title.**

**Write the story in the present tense to create immediacy, which in turn creates suspense.** Use first person narration to tell the story, and style it like an interior monologue. Intersperse the narrator's thoughts with dialogue. Create at least another two characters who will speak in the story. Provide exposition and characterisation through the dialogue and narration.

**Show the emotion of your narrator in an unusual way.** Avoid one of the five senses in the narration in order to emphasise other senses. Evoke anxiety by repeating a key word and following it with a truncated sentence.

* * *

**Use asterisks to indicate that time has passed.** You do not need to tell the reader how much time.

**Write an interjection to open the final section.** It should indicate the narrator's exhaustion, frustration, disgust or any emotion that you choose. Throughout the narration, have the protagonist ask questions. These will indicate to the reader their thought processes, fears and observations, along with the actions of other people. Write the story's climax, or turning point. Reinforce the heightened excitement by using capital letters. Write a resolution immediately after the climax. Reassure the reader that the protagonist is going to be okay.

UNIT 7

# NARRATIVE TEXT

## *Narrative poem*

**READING WORK**

### A Visitor in Marl

*Emily Dickinson was an American poet from Massachusetts. She was born and died in the 1800s and is known for creating a uniquely American voice in her poetry. While Dickinson wrote thousands of works during her lifetime, she did not have her first volume of poems published until after her death. She wrote many poems that personify aspects of nature, including the piece featured in this unit. This is also one of her riddle poems, and it is decoded in the notes that follow the poem.*

**A Visitor in Marl**

A Visitor in Marl—
Who influences Flowers—
Till they are orderly as Busts—
And Elegant—as Glass—

Who visits in the Night—
And just before the Sun—
Concludes his glistening interview—
Caresses—and is gone—

But whom his fingers touched—
And where his feet have run—
And whatsoever Mouth be kissed—
Is as it had not been—

- The **title is the same as the first line**. This is the case in many of Dickinson's poems.
- The frost is **personified** throughout the poem.
- Sculptures that are busts show the head and sometimes the upper body of the subject (the person on whom the sculpture is modelled).
- Like the metaphors 'Marl' and 'Busts', this **simile** ('Elegant—as Glass') creates images. Marble, statues and glass are all hard and cold, like ice. The first two are also usually white.
- The frost is shown to be sneaky: he 'visits in the Night' and completes his crime 'just before the Sun' rises. These images of the frost add to his **characterisation**.
- The frost's actions in the final stanza depict him at his most human. This is where the **personification** is at its strongest.
- Like the dashes used throughout the poem, this final dash creates a **fluid (flowing) structure**, suggesting that this natural event will continue to happen in the future.

### Decoding the poem

This riddle poem is an extended metaphor (or more precisely, personification) about frost. You also need to read the annotations above to understand how the poem has been crafted.

- The garden in the poem has a 'Visitor' (the frost) who sneaks in at night and 'influences' (affects) the flowers.
- 'Marl' is a poetic way to say 'marble', which is cold, white and hard, like ice. Many beautiful works of classical art have been sculpted in marble. The frost is personified as an artist who creates natural 'marble' sculptures by freezing the plants in the garden.
- The frost creates beauty by making icy sculptures, but this creation also results in destruction. He makes the flowers 'Elegant—as Glass'. The art of the frost can only come from killing the flowers and badly damaging the entire garden. In the last stanza we read that whatever the frost has 'kissed' (touched) 'Is as it had not been' (that is, dead).
- Once the sun rises, the frost's time is up, but the ice still glistens and sparkles on the flowers and grass for some time. The narrator tells us that, just before sunrise, the frost 'Concludes his glistening interview'.

# NARRATIVE TEXT

## Narrative poem

COMPREHENSION WORK

### Literal questions

*Hint: Read the text carefully to locate specific facts and details.*

**1** When does the frost come?

**a** during the night **b** after the night **c** when the sun rises

**2** Complete the following statement correctly by choosing a word to fill the blank.

The poet has made a pattern in the first and second stanzas by using __________ in exactly the same places.

**a** capitals **b** dashes **c** words

**3** What conjunction is used five times in the poem? ______________

### Interpretive questions

*Hint: These questions require you to combine facts and details to synthesise the meaning.*

**4** There is a pattern of syllables in the poem that makes each stanza 'swell' in the middle. How is this done? *Hint: A syllable is a unit of pronunciation containing one vowel sound. For example,* in-ter-view *is three syllables.*

______________________________________________

**5** In what time period are the events of the poem set? ______________________________

**6** What is the problem with the 'elegant' flowers? ______________________________

**7** What are three very human actions the frost is said to be able to do?

**a** run, go and glisten **b** touch, run and kiss **c** visit, just and have

**8** Elegance is linked to glass in the poem. Why? As part of your answer, give an example of an elegant glass object.

______________________________________________

**9** Based on the context, what is the meaning of 'Till' at the beginning of line 13?

**a** to turn or dig soil **b** a cash register or money machine **c** until

**10** In the last line of the second stanza (line 18), what does the phrase '—and is gone—' suggest about the frost? *Hint: Think about the effect of the dashes as well as the words.*

**a** it goes before it comes **b** it comes and goes quickly **c** it is invisible

### Applied questions

*Hint: These questions require you to understand a text's implications to infer meaning from the text.*

**11** Why do we need the final line of the poem to correctly identify frost as the 'Visitor' in this riddle poem?

**a** Without the death of the flowers, the 'Visitor' could be mistaken for dew.

**b** Without the words 'had not been', the Sun might seem to be the 'Visitor'.

**c** Without the events of the last line, the frost might visit the garden and never leave.

**12** Apart from a book of Dickinson's poems, what kind of poetry anthology might include 'A Visitor in Marl'? For example, an anthology of poems about flowers. *Hint: Do not use the example as your answer.*

______________________________________________

# NARRATIVE TEXT

## SPELLING WORK

**List Words** All of the words in the box below appear in the text 'A Visitor in Marl' and the notes beneath it.

| | | | | |
|---|---|---|---|---|
| uniquely | personified | riddle | decoded | stanza |
| visitor | influences | elegant | orderly | glistening |
| caresses | whatsoever | icy | affects | damaging |

**1** Match up these word fragments to form six list words. *Hint: Some words need three fragments.*

| | | | | | | |
|---|---|---|---|---|---|---|
| flu | ic | fects | dama | gli | ging | sten |
| af | in | y | ences | ded | deco | ing |

**a** ______________________ **b** ______________________

**c** ______________________ **d** ______________________

**e** ______________________ **f** ______________________

**2** In each of the sentences below, which word correctly completes the sentence? Unscramble the letters of both words provided and write the correct word in the space. *Hint: All of the words in this question appear in the list.*

**a** A ____________ poem is fun to read, because it must also be solved. dedlir delyror

**b** A verse of a poem is called a ______________. storivi zatnas

**c** In the poem 'A Visitor in Marl', the frost is ______________. taffces edionfipers

**d** An ______________ person is graceful and well presented. entgale stiengling

**3** Transform the list words in the table into other words from the same word family.

| Word from the list | Base or root word | Adjective |
|---|---|---|
| visitor | **a** | **b** |
| influences | **c** | **d** |
| uniquely | **e** | **f** |
| damaging | **g** | **h** |

When **making an adverb from an adjective**, we usually use *ly* at the end. Some words ending in *e* must keep that letter when the suffix *ly* is added. For example, *brave* becomes *bravely*.

**4** Change these adjectives into adverbs using the *ly* suffix and keeping the letter *e* of the original word. *Hint: The first three adjectives are from the list; the rest are not.*

**a** elegant ______________________ **b** icy ______________________

**c** damaging ______________________ **d** false ______________________

**e** absolute ______________________ **f** immense ______________________

# NARRATIVE TEXT

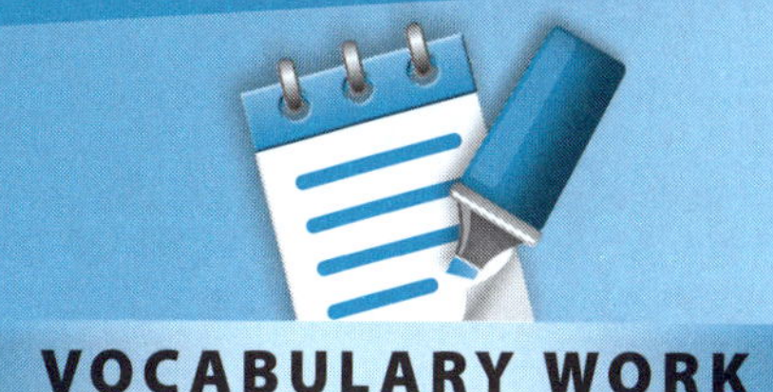

## VOCABULARY WORK

We already know that an **idiom** is an expression used by a particular group of people or in a certain region or era. The key to understanding idioms is that they are not to be read according to the literal meanings of their words. They are a type of figurative language. In the Victorian era, when Emily Dickinson was living and writing, some charming and quirky idioms were in common use.

**1** Can you deduce what these Victorian idioms mean? Draw connecting lines to match the terms and meanings.

| | |
|---|---|
| **a** bags o' mystery | sausages |
| **b** fly rink | feeling morbid or melancholy |
| **c** the morbs | say something utterly preposterous |
| **d** make a stuffed bird laugh | a smooth, bald head that looks like a tiny arena |
| **e** gas pipes | very tight pants |

**2** Add letters to complete the meaning of each Victorian term or phrase as it is used in the text 'A Visitor in Marl'.

**a** Marl m____________

**b** as it had not been as if it n________ e_________d

**c** whatsoever _____y

**3** All of these words are in the text 'A Visitor in Marl'. Define them in full—don't just give synonyms. *Hint: Since some words will have a range of meanings, your answers must be based on their use in the poem.*

**a** glistening ________________________

**b** visitor ________________________

**c** busts ________________________

**d** concludes ________________________

**e** caresses ________________________

**f** before ________________________

**4** Which word in each pair appears in the poem 'A Visitor in Marl'? Tick a box to make your selection. *Hint: Both words are real but only one appears in the poem.*

**a** ☐ flower ☐ flour **b** ☐ feat ☐ feet

**c** ☐ just ☐ adjust **d** ☐ glistening ☐ listening

**e** ☐ he's ☐ his **f** ☐ whom ☐ whose

**5** Choose the real word in each pair by ticking a box. *Hint: This time, one word in each pair is not a word at all.*

**a** ☐ uniquely ☐ uquinely **b** ☐ whichsoever ☐ whatsoever

**c** ☐ interview ☐ interfew **d** ☐ gawn ☐ gone

**e** ☐ tuched ☐ touched **f** ☐ binn ☐ been

**g** ☐ they ☐ thay **h** ☐ before ☐ before

# NARRATIVE TEXT

## Narrative poem

GRAMMAR WORK

### Connectives

As you know, **connectives** are words or phrases that join parts of sentences or text sections. They can also create transitions. Refresh your knowledge of these important language features by reading these notes carefully.

- Connectives link ideas to create a logical, orderly flow.
- Sometimes connectives create a comparison or show a similarity. At other times they show contrast.
- Some connectives show time (such as *before, while* and *whenever*). Others show cause and effect.
- In Dickinson's poetry, punctuation marks—particularly dashes—are often used in place of connectives.

Identify the connectives in the sentences below. *Hint: A connective can be a word or a phrase.*

1 a Emily Dickinson led a fairly isolated life. Ironically, her poems unite people around the world.

b In contrast, Dickinson favours the dash for punctuating her poems.

2 Below, circle each word that can be used as a connective.

| since | the | therefore | at | meanwhile |
|---|---|---|---|---|
| further | because | similarly | no | |

Unless lower-case letters and capital letters are used in an unusual way for impact (as we see in product names such as *iPhone*), **proper nouns** must be given a capital initial letter (for example, *Emily, Massachusetts*). Emily Dickinson uses capital letters very freely; this is one of the distinguishing features of her poetry. When she uses a capital initial letter, it is not always clear why—one reason we know of is to create a proper noun from a common noun, verb or adjective.

3 These phrases contain nouns. Rewrite all of the phrases, changing the initial letter of any proper nouns to a capital letter. *Hints: Some of the phrases do not need a capital letter anywhere—they are already correct. In some proper nouns not every word needs a capital initial letter; for example,* the River Nile.

a the planet earth ______________________ b earth (dirt/soil) ______________________

c your mother's honda ______________________ d star wars ______________________

e the rio olympics ______________________ f a local courthouse ______________________

A **verb** generally describes an action of some kind. Verbs can be literal and observable, or they can refer to a process or state of being. Show your knowledge of this key part of speech by completing the statement below.

4 In the text 'A Visitor in Marl' verbs tell us that, like a person, the frost is able to v__________ someone's house, i______________ flowers and m________ things orderly.

5 Change these words into verbs. *Hint: They do not come from the text 'A Visitor in Marl'.*

a rainy ______________________ b flight ______________________

c agelessness ______________________ d waiter ______________________

# NARRATIVE TEXT

## Narrative poem

**PUNCTUATION WORK**

### Dickinson's punctuation

Dickinson's poems are known for their unique style of **punctuation**. The following points explain why.

- Most of the punctuation marks in Dickinson's poems are dashes (—), rather than the traditional combination of full stops and commas. The dash was commonly used by writers in this era, but Dickinson is possibly the only poet to rely upon it.
- On many occasions, a dash acts as a bridge between sections of a Dickinson poem. Dashes also indicate where pauses should come when reading the poem aloud.
- In the text 'A Visitor in Marl', which is a nature-themed poem, each line ends with a dash, including the final line. This reflects the unending cycles and processes of nature.
- Dickinson has used capital initial letters inside lines, not just in first words. No-one is quite sure why, apart from when some key aspects of nature are personified and written as a proper noun (such as 'Night' and 'the Sun').
- Different versions of the same Dickinson poems have been printed, because the poet's intricate shorthand can be interpreted in different ways. This applies to both punctuation and words.

**1** What are two traditional punctuation marks used in poetry?

**2** What are two functions of dashes in a poem like 'A Visitor in Marl'?

**3** From its use in the final dot point, what do you think 'shorthand' means?

**4** These three sentences contain no punctuation. Punctuate them correctly.

**a** emily dickinson lived in the victorian era and wrote many many poems

**b** it isnt clear why riddle poems were so popular in the 1800s but theres no doubt they were

**c** a visitor in marl is a brief but dense poem containing personification metaphor and sound devices

**5** As mentioned, dashes are used throughout the text 'A Visitor in Marl'. Complete the table below by suggesting other punctuation marks to use in their place. Give each mark's name and symbol. *Hint: There is only one correct answer in each case.*

| Dash in context | Replacement punctuation mark | Name of punctuation mark |
|---|---|---|
| Concludes his glistening interview — | **a** | **b** |
| and is gone— | **c** | **d** |

**6** Which of these uses of the dash could be removed from the text 'A Visitor in Marl' and not be missed?

**a** Who influences Flowers—

**b** and Elegant—as Glass

**c** be kissed—Is as it had not been

# NARRATIVE TEXT
## *Narrative poem*

WRITING WORK 1

### Narrative poems
Poetry is usually classified as either **narrative, lyric or dramatic**. One of the fascinating things about Emily Dickinson's poetry is that she blurs the boundaries between these types. 'A Visitor in Marl' is a good example of this. The poem is both narrative and lyric: it features a short sequence of events but it also offers sensory experiences and observations of nature. On top of all this it is a riddle poem. Riddles were popular in the Victorian period. Lewis Carroll makes fun of their immense popularity in *Alice in Wonderland.*

### Features of narrative poetry
Narrative poems can be identified by particular common features. These include:
- a narrator or speaker—it is not correct to call the speaker in a poem *the poet,* because, even if the poet is writing about personal experiences, he or she adopts a voice or persona to use in the poem
- a literal title or one that is the same as the first line—most of Dickinson's poems are known by either a number or the first line (she only gave titles to around ten of her poems—and she wrote more than 1800!)
- a basic plot or a progression of events over time (either a short or a long period)
- one or two main characters—in the poem 'A Visitor in Marl' the main character is the personified frost; secondary characters are flowers and the Sun
- stanzas (verses), usually of equal length—the three stanzas of 'A Visitor in Marl' each contain four lines
- third person address (that is, traditional storytelling mode).

**1** Is it correct to call the speaker in a poem *the poet* if the poem is about personal experiences? ____________

**2** Name the three characters in 'A Visitor in Marl'.

____________ ____________ ____________

### Language features of Dickinson's poems
Here are some **language features and poetic devices** seen in many Dickinson poems, including 'A Visitor in Marl':
- sound devices, including assonance, near-rhyme and alliteration
- personification and anthropomorphism (treating non-human things as though they are human)
- simile, metaphor and symbolism
- regular meter and rhythm
- dashes as bridges and other punctuation structures.

**3** Unscramble the letters at the end of each line to complete each statement correctly. *Hint: The answers all come from the notes on and about the text 'A Visitor in Marl'.*

**a** Emily Dickinson wrote poems with a uniquely American ____________. evoci

**b** Many of Dickinson's poems have a ____________ that is also the first line. telit

**c** The poem 'A Visitor in Marl' is an extended piece of ____________. tiononificapers

Dickinson liked to use language in **original and unusual ways**, changing the regular meaning of many words.

**4** Write definitions or explanations to show how each of these words is used in the text 'A Visitor in Marl'.

**a** influences ____________ **b** mouth ____________

**c** interview ____________ **d** orderly ____________

# NARRATIVE TEXT

## *Narrative poem*

**WRITING WORK 2**

**5** In the text 'A Visitor in Marl', Dickinson has used certain language features, including a number of poetic devices. Complete the table below with examples and effects of these features from the poem. Some hints are provided in the table but there are no set answers for most of the questions, particularly for effects.

| | Feature or device | Example | Effect |
|---|---|---|---|
| **Structural elements** | Equal stanzas | Three verses of equal length are used to tell the story of the frost. | **a** |
| | Stressed syllables | Sets of three stressed syllables are contained within each line, despite the line meters or rhythms being slightly different. | **b** *Hint: The example provided suggests the effect.* |
| | Dashes | Who visits in the Night—<br>And just before the Sun— | **c** *Hint: Look in the Punctuation Work section on page 66 for the answer.* |
| **Elements of sound** | Fricatives (repeated 'f' sounds) | **d** *Hint: Look in the first stanza.* | The 'Visitor' seems to breathe out ice. The fricative sounds are like the icy breath of the frost as it touches and softly kills the plants. |
| | Sibilance (repeated 's' sounds) | **e** *Hint: Sibilance is used throughout the poem but it is easiest to find in in the second stanza.* | **f** |
| **Elements of imagery** | Personification | **g** | It creates a main character for the poem and its short narrative.<br>A possible deeper meaning is a warning about giving up control to create a beautiful love affair. This action could result in the death of joy and freedom. |
| | Human verbs (actions and processes) | **h** *Hint: Look in the Comprehension Work and Grammar Work sections on pages 62 and 65 for answers if you need to.* | **i** |

# NARRATIVE TEXT

## Narrative poem

WRITING SAMPLE

Here is a sample text showing you how to structure and write a narrative poem.

### The match

**Write a title that specifies the subject.** The subject matter of this poem is a 'match'. From the very beginning of the poem ('Bowl 'im out, mate!') we can clearly see it is a cricket match.

'Bowl 'im out mate! Bowl 'im out!'
The Sunday crowd gives out the shout.
'Blimey, can't you bowl 'im out?
Aagh nah, nah, not that way!
With that delivery he's in to stay!
Bowl 'im out mate! Bowl 'im out!
That's closer, that's better, aaw no!
Ump, can't you see he's gotta go?

**Write the first stanza, using the same number of lines for each main stanza.** This is a structure common to many poetic forms. The two main stanzas in this poem contain eight lines each. The poem tells the story of a cricket match; the poet does this almost entirely through direct speech. The crowd says all of these words, making this group of people like a single main character. Many exclamation marks are used in the poem to express the emotions of the crowd at the cricket. The main technique used in the poem is repetition. This is appropriate as the shouts and comments from the crowd at a cricket match are very repetitive.

'Bowl' im out mate! Bowl the bludger out!
Get up those Poms, Warne, take this bout!
Flip 'im, York 'im, just get 'im out!
Agh, don't give 'em another four!
Give us a reason to cheer 'n' roar!
Ya bowled 'im out mate! Ya bowled 'im out!
Not a bad innings, we agree …
Pity 'bout Gillespie's knee.'

**Repeat the poem's first line to open the second stanza.** This reminds the reader of the repetitive nature of cricket and provides an image of the bowlers running in again and again. The whole poem has a fairly consistent rhythm of four stressed syllables per line. This was established in the first stanza but it is broken in the first line of the second stanza to show the crowd's frustration that no wickets are falling. Idioms and slang terms are used, such as the derogatory term for English people, 'Poms', which is often used in a sporting context. The word 'bout' here means 'fight'.

Tomorrow's game is left to Fate.
New crowds will pour through the hallowed gate.
Then the cries will come from those who 'know'—
'Yer batting's off and the outfield's slow!'

**Write a third stanza made up of two rhyming couplets.** This stanza is a kind of epilogue—it is a follow-up to the main story of the poem. Most of the final stanza is not in direct speech. Instead the narrator finishes the story; this is done to make fun of the crowd. They are called 'those who "know"', which actually means those who *think* they know. Direct speech is brought back in to close the poem. This creates a neat ending and connects the rest of the poem to this pair of couplets.

*Colleen Hodges*

**Write your name at the end of the poem.**

# NARRATIVE TEXT

## *Narrative poem*

**WRITING YOUR OWN SAMPLE**

Plan your sample on the lines provided.

- **Write a title that specifies the subject.**

- **Write the first stanza using the same number of lines for each main stanza.** In your poem use no more than eight lines. The other main stanza will also contain eight lines. Establish a rhythm of four stressed syllables per line. Tell a brief story using a lot of direct speech. Use exclamation marks and other punctuation in your lines of direct speech to express the emotions of the characters. Use repetition as a main technique; think about why this is appropriate in your poem.

- **Repeat the poem's first line to open the second stanza.** Keep the rhythm fairly consistent throughout the poem by using four stressed syllables per line—you should have established this in the first stanza. Break it here in the first line of the second stanza for impact. Use idioms and slang terms.

- **Write a third stanza made up of two rhyming couplets.** This stanza should work as a kind of epilogue—it should be a follow-up to the main story of the poem. Ensure that most of the final stanza is not in direct speech. Instead let the narrator finish the story. Bring back direct speech to close the poem to create a neat ending and connect the rest of the poem to the final lines.

- **Write your name at the end of the poem.**

UNIT 8

# NARRATIVE TEXT

## Monologue

**READING WORK**

### Seeya mate

*This is a standalone humorous script for a solo performer. It includes stage directions at the beginning and throughout the piece. The first stage directions give character details, a scenario (situation) and costume ideas. The remaining stage directions indicate how the actor should move and how certain lines should be delivered.*

*Warwick ('Wokka'), in his early forties, gives the eulogy at the funeral for his mate Thomas ('Perks'). He is making an attempt at formality with an ironed flanno, clean jeans and a sports jacket. He has a dignified mullet. Avoiding further caricature in costume, hair and movement is advised, as the vernacular is already exaggerated.*

Righto. Well, as youse all know, I'm a man of few words, folks; but I been arksed today by Chook to give a bit of a spool so, yeah. Today weez are all honouring the late Thomas P Perkins … *(leans in close to the microphone and uses a very deep voice)* and no, that wasn't a stutter. Ha ha ha. *(Explaining his joke)* It's his … middle name starts with … *(trails off)*. Well, since youse didn't laugh at me stutter joke, I won't try and make a joke about his bad breath. I was gunna, but.

Anyway, 'Perks' … 'Perkins Paste' … 'Perkster' …. 'Chalky' … 'Steak' … 'Gob' … as he was known to his mates, was a man of great mortality and inner well-being and so on and so forth. Yep, people could always lean on him in troubled times and whatnot, and, being partial to the old *(mimes drinking and whistles)* … he'd end up leanin' on us too, most times. Y'know? *(Laughs awkwardly.)*

But Perkle must have been best remembered for—Jacko, you can back me up here—his yarns. *(Gunshot laughs)* Ah yep, old Chalks could keep us amused for hours up the pub goin' on about his shearin' days out in Whatsername, and all them *(slight pause for impact)* laydeez … and all that. Won't get too pacific. *(Forgetting himself and becoming very amused and excited over a past incident)* Oh mate, I'll never forget that barney Jacko and him had over that ute. Got pretty aggro, eh? He's bangin' on his window at 3 am and screamin', 'Jackohhhhh! Ya dogged me! Ya dogged me!' and Jacko comes out with this bow and arrow and he's in his jocks and he goes, *(shouting very loudly and posturing, trying to reconstruct the scene)* 'Did I dog ya, did I? How'd ya like me ta put an arrow in ya …' *(trails off, realising he's about to say something inappropriate)*.

Aw yeah, Gobba Perks. He was one of a kind, alright, wonnee. Rool family man, he was, too. Didn't leave home till uh, forty-five, when he died. And he loved his mum, dinnee. Too right. *(Peers into audience and points)* Ah yeah, there she is, Mumma Perks … oh … looks like she's dropped off.

But yeah, youse and me … weeze … we'll never miss him … *(corrects himself)* we'll never forget him, I mean. Never forget old Perkapants … and his gammy leg, and his bung foot, and all that. It's a real pity he had that industeral deafness, y'know, 'cause he didn't know what hit him when that semi clocked him out on the A4 *(with a suddenly reflective expression he sniffs and gets serious)*.

Yeah, so may he be forever treasured and fossilised in his parents' home, in his mates' hearts, and—o'course —now, Gaz, don't you start losin' it on me, alright, mate? *(Starts to cry)* You'll get me goin'. And, o'course, down the pub. *(Suddenly recovers at the mention of the pub)*.

Speakin' of, there'll be a pig-on-a-spit and a few beers at the Crown after this. *(Looks for confirmation from someone nearby)* That's right, isn't it Joolz? Yep, see youse there then. Righto.

---

- The **title** of the monologue indicates both the subject matter (a highly informal eulogy or funeral speech) and the strong vernacular of the character speaking ('ocker').
- The **stage directions** indicate both the scenario (a funeral) and how the performer should dress. They also tell us that 'the vernacular is already exaggerated': the 'ocker' (broad Australian) language in the script is very strong.
- From the first word, we can see that the character is speaking very informally in what is normally a formal and solemn setting.
- **Transitional words and phrases**, such as 'Anyway', are used to begin sections of the eulogy.
- Miming the action of drinking is an Australian and British **euphemism** for drinking too much alcohol. This is sometimes accompanied by a whistling sound.
- 'Pacific' is a **malapropism** here (misused word). The speaker should say 'specific'.
- The speaker recounts an incident but realises that it is not an appropriate story for this occasion, so he cuts it short.
- The speaker continually uses different names for the deceased man ('Chalks', 'Gobba Perks', 'Perkapants'). This **makes fun** of the social phenomenon of nicknames by giving an exaggerated number of them to one person.
- **Exposition** about the many physical ailments of the deceased is gradual and, as a result, humorous.
- 'Industeral deafness' is a **mispronunciation** of 'industrial deafness', which is gradual hearing loss caused by a very noisy workplace.
- The **highly informal expression** 'that semi clocked him out on the A4' can be translated as 'a truck hit him on the highway'.
- Other **characters** feature in this monologue, despite being invisible and silent: Chook, Thomas Perkins, his mother, Jacko, Gaz and Joolz.
- The eulogy begins and ends with the same word: 'Righto' (meaning 'alright' or 'very well, then'). This is a highly casual expression that tends to be used as a **filler** when the speaker is nervous.

# NARRATIVE TEXT

## Monologue

COMPREHENSION WORK

### Literal questions

*Hint: Read the text carefully to locate specific facts and details.*

**1** What do the stage directions at the beginning say that Wokka's costume indicates?

**a** He is making an attempt at fashion.

**b** He is making an attempt at formality.

**c** He is making an attempt at ironing.

**2** What is the dead man's middle name?

**a** we are not told **b** Thomas **c** Perks

**3** In line 14 of his speech, Wokka jokes that something he just said sounds as if he stuttered. What is it?

______________________________

### Interpretive questions

*Hint: These questions require you to combine facts and details to synthesise the meaning.*

**4** Where did Thomas Perkins spend 'his shearin' days'?

**a** a town called Whatsername **b** a place Wokka can't remember **c** the Pacific

A **malapropism** is a word used incorrectly, often because the speaker or writer misunderstands its meaning.

**5** In line 18 of the text, the word 'mortality' is a malapropism. Which word does Wokka probably mean?

______________

**6** What is ironic about Wokka accidentally describing his friend as 'a man of great mortality'?

______________________________

**7** What is the correct translation of these phonetically spelt words from lines 33–35: 'wonnee', 'rool' and 'dinnee'?

**a** Ronnie, reel, deny **b** wasn't he, real, didn't he **c** wand, rule, dinner

**8** What is meant by the word 'arksed' in line 11 of Wokka's eulogy?

**a** asked **b** Ark **c** arched

**9** Re-read lines 38–40. What three factors probably led to Thomas being 'clocked' by a 'semi' (hit by a truck)?

______________________________

**10** What is 'the Crown' in the final paragraph? ______________________________

### Applied questions

*Hint: These questions require you to understand a text's implications to infer meaning from the text.*

**11** Which word in the last line of the opening stage directions best describes Wokka as a type of character?

______________

**12** Apart from humour, what does the writer of this monologue want to create?

**a** stereotypes **b** sarcasm **c** satire

# NARRATIVE TEXT

## Monologue

**SPELLING WORK**

### List Words

All of the words in the box below appear in the text 'Seeya mate'.

| | | | | |
|---|---|---|---|---|
| funeral | forties | eulogy | mortality | posturing |
| scene | caricature | incident | folks | dignified |
| whatnot | vernacular | partial | reconstruct | inappropriate |

**1** The speaker in the monologue uses many abbreviated words. Most of these contain apostrophes. Expand each of the abbreviations below to its full form, removing the apostrophes and adding the correct missing letter or letters. *Hint: Some answers will remain single words and others will become phrases.*

**a** shearin' shearin__ **b** goin' goin__ **c** screamin' scream____

**d** o'course o__ course **e** y'know y____ know **f** losin' los_____

**g** 'cause ___cause **h** speakin' spea______ **i** how'd how w________

**2** The contractions below are commonly used in colloquial speech anywhere. Write the full words on the lines. *Hint: Some contractions represent more than one phrase so base your answers on the specific use of the words in the text.*

**a** it's __________ **b** wasn't __________ **c** we'll __________

**d** you'll __________ **e** he'd __________ **f** that's __________

**3** Complete these list words by adding the missing chunks from the box below.

| prop | fort | art | post | dent | mortal | hat | construct | log |
|---|---|---|---|---|---|---|---|---|

**a** p _____ ial **b** ______ ies **c** ________ ity

**d** ______ uring **e** w _______ not **f** re __________

**g** ina _______ riate **h** incid ________ **i** eu ______ y

**4** Circle or highlight all of the spelling errors in the passage below. It is based on the text 'Seeya mate'. *Hint: Most of the errors are not list words.*

Oure mate is best remmembered for—and anyone of his friends can back me up—his yarns. Yes inndeed, he use to keep us amused withall his shearing storeys. Heed set the scene allright, waving his arms bout and reconstructing events drammatically. Think he might of missed his calling as an acter. Wooden you agree, fokes?

Australians are well known for their love of **nicknames**. These special terms of reference can be affectionate pet names or derogatory names intended to put a person down. Nicknames are often corrupted versions of a person's real name. This is the case with some of Thomas Perkins's nicknames. Other names that Wokka calls him in the eulogy have no relationship to his real name but may be based on aspects of his appearance or behaviour.

**5** List all of the nicknames Wokka uses for his mate Thomas Perkins in the text. *Hint: You will need to check back through the entire text.*

________ ________ ________ ________ ________

________ ________ ________ ________ ________

# NARRATIVE TEXT
## *Monologue*

**VOCABULARY WORK**

The first three questions in this section relate directly to language features contained in the text 'Seeya mate'. You will need to refer back to the text to complete the questions correctly.

As mentioned earlier, **malapropisms** are misunderstood or incorrectly used words. The text 'Seeya mate' features a few.

**1** **a** Which word in the fourth paragraph (line 39) is mispronounced, making it a malapropism?

______________________

**b** What is the word that Wokka means to say? ______________________

**c** Wokka uses another malapropism in line 42 : 'fossilised'. Why do you think he says this?

______________________________________________

**2** These expressions are spelt according to Wokka's pronunciation. Translate them into real words and phrases.

**a** seeya ______________________ **b** gunna ______________________

**c** rool ______________________ **d** laydeez ______________________

Certain idioms and slang are part of the **Australian vernacular** (the local speech/language). The broadest (that is, the strongest and often the most vulgar) Australian vernacular is known as 'ocker'. This word itself is a slang term.

**3** Match these 'ocker' terms and meanings using connecting lines. There are two separate sets to match up.

**Set 1**

| Term | Meaning |
|---|---|
| **a** mullet | large truck |
| **b** semi | underpants |
| **c** clocked | flannelette shirt |
| **d** jocks | struck very hard |
| **e** flanno | hairstyle with a short front and a long back |

**Set 2**

| Term | Meaning |
|---|---|
| **a** barney | fallen asleep |
| **b** gob | mouth |
| **c** aggro | exaggerated stories |
| **d** yarns | angry and vicious |
| **e** dropped off | fight |

**4** Use each group of list words in a single sentence in any order. The first one has been done for you as an example.

**a** inappropriate, posturing, scene

The seagulls' **inappropriate** strutting and **posturing** at the beachside wedding created a comical **scene**.

**b** funeral, mortality, folks

______________________________________________

**c** eulogy, dignified, incident

______________________________________________

**d** forties, partial, vernacular

______________________________________________

# NARRATIVE TEXT

## Monologue

GRAMMAR WORK

### Pronouns

A **pronoun** takes the place of a noun in a sentence. There are many different types of pronouns, some of which are not easy to spot or define. They are listed below.

- personal pronouns (for example, *This one is for* ***you****.*)
- indefinite pronouns (for example, ***Everybody****'s doing it.*)
- possessive pronouns (for example, *Is this about* ***his*** *comment or* ***your*** *ego?*)
- relative pronouns (for example, *Of all the shoes in the shop, this is the pair* ***that*** *I like best.*)
- demonstrative pronouns (for example, ***These*** *cake recipes were collected by Grandma.*)
- interrogative pronouns (for example, ***Who*** *saw the thief running from the store?*)
- reciprocal pronouns (for example, *Let's hold on tight to* ***each other****, just in case.*)
- reflexive pronouns (for example, *We took care of the car repairs* ***ourselves****.*)
- intensive pronouns, also called emphatic appositives (for example, *The President* ***himself*** *wrote back to me.*)

**1** Re-read the first bullet point. What are another three personal pronouns? ________ ________ ________

**2** Re-read the sixth bullet point. Why do you think this type of pronoun is called 'interrogative'?

______________________________________________

**3** Find the following pronouns in the text and interpret them into correct English.

**a** ya ____________ **b** me ____________ **c** youse ____________

**Interjections** are one of the nine parts of speech. They include words like *yes, well, wow, please* and *oh.* Such words can be used in isolation or as fillers in direct speech. When the direct speech in a text is not fictional and has been transcribed word-for-word, fillers may be left where they are or omitted. This is left to the discretion of the text's writer. When the direct speech is fictional, fillers can be added to make the speech sound authentic. We see this technique used heavily in the text 'Seeya mate'.

**4** In the list of words below are some fillers used in the text. Circle them.

| | | | |
|---|---|---|---|
| uh | whosoever | too right | if |
| and whatnot | and so on and so forth | why oh why | and all that |

**5** In the text we read the erroneous expression 'I was gunna, but'. Complete this statement about it.

'Gunna' is one problem with this sentence but possibly worse is that it ends with a

c____________, a part of speech that only functions ____________ a sentence.

**6** Very informal storytelling or anecdote language often lapses into the present tense by accident. Correct these present tense lines from the monologue by rewriting them in the past tense. Don't make any other changes.

**a** He's bangin' on his window at 3 am and screamin' …

______________________________________________

**b** Jacko comes out with this bow and arrow and he's in his jocks and he goes …

______________________________________________

# NARRATIVE TEXT

*Monologue*

## PUNCTUATION WORK

### Commas, apostrophes and parentheses

Three punctuation marks appear with great frequency in the text 'Seeya Mate': commas, apostrophes and parentheses. First let's recap the function of each.

- A **comma** ( , ) marks a pause or break in a sentence and separates items in a list.
- An **apostrophe** ( ' ) indicates ownership or missing letters.
- **Parentheses** (often mistakenly called brackets, which are actually these square marks: [ ]) are pairs of curved lines enclosing text. Parentheses is the plural form—one of these marks is called a parenthesis. The material contained inside parentheses is also called a parenthesis.

In the text 'Seeya mate' commas and apostrophes help create the 'ocker' speech of the character. Commas indicate pauses and stammers, while apostrophes abbreviate words. These features build the speaker's accent.

**1** The commas and apostrophes have been removed from these phrases from the text. Write *C* (for Comma) or *A* (for Apostrophe) to show which punctuation has been deleted. Write *CA* if it is both. *Hint: You may need to check back with the text.*

**a** Well as youse all know folks ______ **b** till uh forty-five when he died ______

**c** yknow cause he didnt know ______ **d** And he loved his Mum dinnee ______

**e** goin on about his shearin days ______ **f** Yeah so may he be forever treasured ______

**g** hed end up leanin on us ______ **h** well never miss him ______

**2** Commas and apostrophes have been placed incorrectly in these sentences. Move them to their correct locations. *Hint: The sentences contain the correct number of commas and apostrophes; they simply need to be moved.*

**a** At my cousins funeral there was' no eulogy. I'guess, he didnt have, many friends. Well he was a lawyer.

**b** The thing with funeral's, is that if the foods great at the familys' house afterward's you cant pig out.

**3** Insert commas below, following the instructions. No other punctuation needs to be added. *Hint: In most lists no comma is needed before* and. *This is the Australian rule; British and American usage varies.*

**a** Make a list: We're all going to the show: Liam Liam's friend a friend of Goran's and me, of course.

**b** Make a list that includes an interruption: Please buy a baguette croissants and if they have them bagels.

**c** Show uncertainty and pauses: Well I'm not actually sure where we are so um could you pass the map please?

**4** Now insert apostrophes according to the instructions given. No other punctuation needs to be added.

**a** Show all owners: We'll use Dads car and the twins cars to transport the family members.

**b** Show missing letters: Once weve reached the town, youve got to see this café Ive found. Its so cute.

**c** Show abbreviations: Are we goin to go in, or what? Im not waitin round forever.

Remember that **extra information** in texts is often contained in parentheses.

**5** **a** What is the main function of parentheses in the text 'Seeya mate'? ______________________

**b** Quote an example to back up your answer to Question 5a. ______________________

______________________________________________

# NARRATIVE TEXT
## *Monologue*

**WRITING WORK 1**

### Monologues

A **monologue** is a set of lines for one performer. Many monologues involve retelling or acting out a story, but even monologues that don't seem to have a plot are still telling a story: the story of the speaker. Their character is revealed and sometimes develops or changes as they speak.

- The single character addresses at least one listener. This person may be present onstage, particularly if the monologue is a part of a larger play. If the monologue is a standalone text, however, the listener is usually the audience. This is the case with the text 'Seeya mate': the audience passively adopts the role of a group of mourners at a funeral.
- Sometimes the speaker will simply tell a story, like a narrator in a book, but there is much more to most monologues than that. For example, the speaker's thoughts about a particular event or experience are articulated in the text and often the character will inadvertently reveal their faults to the audience.

**1** What type of monologue often has an 'audience' who is present onstage?

______________________________

**2** What do a monologue's character and a book's narrator have in common?

______________________________

### Monologue, dialogue or duologue?

As it is easy to confuse these terms, they are each explained below.

- A **monologue**, as defined above, is a script (or an excerpt from a larger one) written for one speaker. There are various types of monologue and many crossover or blended types. Two key types are comic and dramatic (this term is also given to a type of narrative text called a persona poem).
- **Dialogue** is the general term for any direct speech in texts like plays. Where some people get confused is that dialogue, or conversation, is not necessarily between just two people (that's duologue).
- **Duologue** is a passage of dialogue for two people (a duo) only.

**3** Since 'Jacko' is another character in the text 'Seeya mate', can the text also be classed as a duologue?

______ Why/Why not? ______________________________

**4** What is another name for the text form 'dramatic monologue'? ______________________________

### Purposes of monologues

Here are three key **functions of a monologue**.

- It can reveal a character's experiences and opinions in a play or film (or as a standalone poem). This can happen during the main action or as a voice over.
- It can reveal a character's most personal thoughts, emotions and motivations, with no intended listener. Common in Shakespeare's plays, this type of monologue is called a soliloquy. To avoid confusing it with other monologue types, remember that a soliloquy is truly solo: nobody is meant to be listening.
- It can display the skills of an actor in a theatrical audition. Often, two or three monologues of different kinds will be prepared for an acting audition to show off an actor's versatility and range.

**5** Three contexts in which monologues can appear, listed in the box above, are: p____________ ,

f____________ and a____________________.

# NARRATIVE TEXT

## Monologue

WRITING WORK 2

### An aside …

Special information shared with the audience of a play is called an **aside**. Like a soliloquy, the other characters 'can't hear' what is said. This mini-monologue is another dramatic feature often used by Shakespeare.

### Language features of a monologue

The text 'Seeya mate' is an example of a crossover text form, that is to say it is both narrative and informative. It has elements of informative recount but because it is fictitious, tells of events in a person's life, is narrated by a character, features exaggerated diction and has a climax, it is essentially a narrative text. Let's break down those features:

* Elements of informative recount: The monologue informs listeners about Thomas P Perkins, a man who has recently died.
* Fictitious: This text is entirely made-up.
* Tells of events: While it does not contain a traditional plot, the monologue does contain and retell events.
* Narrated by a character: A stereotypical ocker man (the speaker, Wokka) narrates the 'story' of his mate.
* Exaggerated diction: As noted in the stage directions at the beginning of the text, the words used by the speaker can be called exaggerated vernacular. They echo real speech but in a heightened way.
* Climax: The monologue builds to a high (or turning) point, as we see in a short story or novel.

**6** Define the term *diction*. ______________________________

**7** Circle or underline the words in the list below associated with the text 'Seeya mate' viewed as a type of narrative. *Hint: Not all correct words appear in the bullet points in the box above and some words above are not correct here.*

| | | | | | |
|---|---|---|---|---|---|
| stereotypical | climax | novel | character | action | fiction |
| directions | events | setting | height | traditional | retell |

**8** What do you think is the climax of 'Seeya mate'? Give at least one reason for your answer.

______________________________

**9** Complete the table below by adding examples of language features from the text 'Seeya mate'. *Hint: Use the annotations on the text to help you.*

| Language feature | Example from the text |
|---|---|
| malapropism | **a** |
| direct speech (quoting another character) | **b** |
| interruption inside dashes | **c** |
| awkwardness indicated by ellipses | **d** |
| a list | **e** |
| second person address | **f** |

**10** Do you think the text 'Seeya mate' would work as a monologue if it was not full of exaggerated vernacular? Explain your reasons.

______________________________

# NARRATIVE TEXT

## Monologue

**WRITING SAMPLE**

Here is a sample text showing you how to structure and write a monologue.

### A real nightmare

**Write a title that has an obvious meaning but can take on a second meaning as the monologue continues.** This title is a colloquialism for 'a very frightening situation'. As the story unfolds, it takes on a second meaning: the recurring nightmare being described is a true memory.

I'm dreaming. I dream that I'm standing on the beach watching the water. It's a glorious, baking February Saturday: very bright, very warm … the sea is sparklingly inviting. As I stand there, I can feel my thongs throbbing with the blazing heat of the sand … *(Looks around at eye level)* What's that? I spot a smooth grey fin breaking through a wave. There's another, and another! *(Excitedly)* There's a pod of dolphins playing in the surf. They're so close, right there in the white water!

**Include only a few stage directions in the script.** Interpreting the script and adding more stage directions is a task for the performer during rehearsals. The present tense mode is enhanced by phrases that are even more immediate, such as 'What's that?' Contractions (such as 'I'm', 'they're', 'it's' and 'there's') help make the language colloquial. This helps the audience relate to the character.

I quickly strip off to my swimmers and run right in. I start striding out toward the dolphins, hoping my splashy swimming won't scare them away. I want to try to touch one, if I can. Crazy thought, right, but they are really that close. I stop swimming and lift my head to get my bearings … there's a fin—less than a metre away. With a sick feeling, the realisation hits: this isn't a dolphin.

**In your script imply that the character both describes the action and performs it.** Ellipses are occasionally used (for example, 'to get my bearings … there's a fin') to create suspense and uncertainty. The revelation that 'this isn't a dolphin' is written as a type of serious punchline. The line leads into a transition.

*Transition: the actor quickly moves to a sitting/half-reclining position as the dream comes to an end.*

**Describe an important transition in italicised stage directions.** How it is achieved is up to the actor or director.

I wake up in a tangle of sweaty sheets and fumble for the light switch beside my bed. Relief breaks over me like a cool wave as I regain consciousness from my nightmare. I'm safe in my room; safe from the water, the white water, the weapon-like teeth.

**Write a simile that involves an appropriate reference to a key image or theme in the script.** 'Dream' is renamed 'nightmare', pointing the reader back to the title. Alliteration ('water', 'white water', 'weapon-like') is used to link and emphasise images related to the attack.

*(Reaches for phone and checks it)* 4.40. Always the same. It's just so bizarre. Every single time I have this dream, I wake up at 4.40 am on the dot. How long does the dream last in real time: a minute? A few seconds? Maybe it begins and ends at 4:40. Anyway, it seems like time stops when I'm inside it.

**Provide a detail then repeat it with a little more information added.** The second time '4.40' is mentioned, we learn that it is very early in the morning. Questions show the confusion of the character. Time is the theme from this point until the end of the text.

Once I'm back in the waking world, I always have to face the same horror. Always takes a good couple of minutes until I remember. Usually it's when I feel a phantom itch or when the cat jumps on the empty lower third of my bed and my body doesn't move.
My legs are gone.

**Omit some articles, prepositions and other small words to heighten the colloquial language.** For example, 'Always takes a good couple of minutes …' A clue ('phantom itch') precedes an alarming surprise and a simple, truncated sentence delivers the surprise ('My legs are gone').

Unfortunately this is no ordinary recurring dream: it's a memory. After three massive strikes from a Great White just off Bolsin Beach, a pod of dolphins sheltered me as I somehow dragged myself to shore. I needed nearly a hundred stitches around my abdomen alone … dozens more across my chest. I've had four bone shard removal surgeries on my wrist and hand, and who knows how many hundreds of hours of physical therapy.

**Shift from the present to the past tense as the speaker moves further into reality.** This occurs here from 'After three massive strikes …' to the end of the paragraph. This is an unusual approach to showing time in a text. Specific details here contrast with the questions and uncertainty about the memory or dream earlier in the text. The clarity emphasises that this is the speaker's reality.

Three years, seven months, two days. When will I stop reliving the day I was nearly killed by a shark?

**Omit some words to increase the impact of the details.** For example, 'It's been' has been omitted from the first sentence of this paragraph.

# NARRATIVE TEXT

## Monologue

## WRITING YOUR OWN SAMPLE

Plan your sample on the lines provided.

- **Write a title that has an obvious meaning but can take on a second meaning as the monologue continues.**
- **Include only a few stage directions in the script.** Enhance the present tense mode by using phrases that are even more immediate. Include contractions to make the language colloquial. This helps the audience relate to the character.
- **In your script, imply that the character both describes the action and performs it.** Use ellipses occasionally to create suspense and uncertainty. Deliver a revelation as a type of punchline; the line can lead into a transition.
- **Describe an important transition in italicised stage directions.**
- **Write a simile that involves an appropriate reference to a key image or theme in the script.** Alter a key word to point back to the script's title. Use alliteration to link and emphasise images related to the main event or events.
- **Provide a detail then repeat it with a little more information added.** Use this technique to reveal something to the audience. Use questions to show the confusion of the character. Allow one theme to take over until the end of the text.
- **Omit some articles, prepositions and other small words to heighten the colloquial language.** Write a clue to precede a surprise and use a simple, truncated sentence to deliver the surprise.
- **Shift from the present to the past tense as the speaker moves further into reality.** Include specific details here to contrast with questions and uncertainty earlier in the text and to emphasise that this is the character's reality.
- **Omit some words to increase the impact of the details.**

### Kennedy Space Center

https:/ /www.the attractionattraction.com/ksc-review

Home | Search our site | Search the web | Who are we | Contact us

**The Attraction Attraction**—*Be in the know before you go!*
Comprehensive reviews of tourist attractions and landmarks of all kinds.

**Kennedy Space Center**

The Kennedy Space Center (KSC) at Cape Canaveral, Florida, boasts amazing exhibits that offer hands-on fun and learning. The past, present and future of space exploration are on show, and NASA's launch headquarters features heaps of great attractions for you to make some explorations of your own.

The yawn factor is pretty close to zero at KSC! This is a great day out. For a start there are some MEGA-HUGE rockets—we're talking ten storeys high. And don't miss taking a virtual journey into orbit with the Shuttle Launch Experience. Visitors (all except very young kids) are invited to strap themselves into a simulator and experience the sights, sounds and thrills of a real launch, which is pretty boss! There's even a briefing from a veteran shuttle commander who takes you step by step through the launch.

Other highlights you'll definitely want to squeeze into your day:

- The launch pads (unlike much of the KSC, you're allowed to take snaps here)
- A peek inside Mission Control
- A tour of NASA's massive rocket assembly building

There's a list as long as your arm of ways to 'enhance your experience' for a pretty penny. I guess, if astronomy is your thing, then you might be getting sweaty palms just reading the phrase 'enhance your experience'. Go for it. But if you're just a regular armchair space spectator, keep your cash in your pocket.

As with most tourist attractions, the food is forgettable and overpriced. But you'll work up a good appetite just walking around the place, so you'll probably be happy enough with a chewy hot dog or a vacuum-sealed salad. Hey, you don't come here for fine dining, so whatever.

**Admission:** $50 adult $40 child (ages 3 to 11) Ask for group rates
Includes: Visitor Complex, Cape Canaveral, International Space Station Center, Observation Gantry, Apollo/Saturn Visitors Center



Okay, now keep in mind that these are actually working facilities, meaning that tours can be altered or cancelled. This can be a bummer because tickets are non-transferrable and non-refundable! They also add that nasty little *prices are subject to change without notice* disclaimer, but that's not a regular thing.

Note: For the Shuttle Launch Experience, you need to be in reasonably good health and agree to participate at your own risk. That makes it sound scarier than it is, but just FYI.
So is KSC worth the effort? In short: absolutely!
In NASA-speak: we are go, Flight!



**Coming attractions at The Attraction Attraction**

✔ Universal Studios, Orlando, Florida (USA)
We revisit an old fave to see what's become of it since Harry Potter and his broomstick-brumming buddies landed: Pluses: some super-exciting new rides, including what is seriously one of the best dark coasters anywhere in the world, Diagon Alley … and, of course, BUTTERBEER! Negs: no Hollywood-style backlot or studio tours, since no movies are actually filmed at these 'studios'; also few Hogwarts rooms at this point. Also …
✔ Mt Fuji climbs, central Honshū (Japan)
✔ Australia Zoo, Sunshine Coast, Queensland (Australia)
✔ Orange River rafting, the Richtesveld (South Africa)

- The **name** of the larger website ('The Attraction Attraction'), a **menu** and a **slogan** ('Be in the know before you go!') precede the review.
- The review's **title** is entirely literal and simply states which tourist attraction is being evaluated.
- A number of times in the review, the **abbreviation** 'KSC' is used in place of the full name, 'Kennedy Space Center'. This saves space and keeps the page neat.
- Appropriate **images** related to the KSC enhance the impact of the review and help sell this tourist attraction to targeted readers.
- A sentence featuring **slang** is followed by a simple sentence ('This is a great day out.') 'translating' it.
- In most of the review, the **language is highly informal** (such as 'pretty boss', 'getting sweaty palms', 'MEGA-HUGE') in order to appeal to the reader in a friendly manner.
- The **middle section of the review** features two negative aspects of the KSC (the 'enhance your experience' activities and the food), but these are offset by logical, positive suggestions (simply not buying optional extras and not expecting fancy food).
- **Admission details** are displayed in a small, separated section for the sake of clarity.
- Two small, simple **advertisements** invade the review. These are paid ads and are targeted at the same audience as the website's. Readers are encouraged to click on these links.
- The **opinions of the reviewer are summed up** in a lighthearted way that incorporates a phrase used by astronauts before take-off ('we are go, Flight!').
- Some **other reviews** featured on this website are named at the end of this review, under a catchy subheading featuring a pun and repetition ('Coming Attractions at The Attraction Attraction').

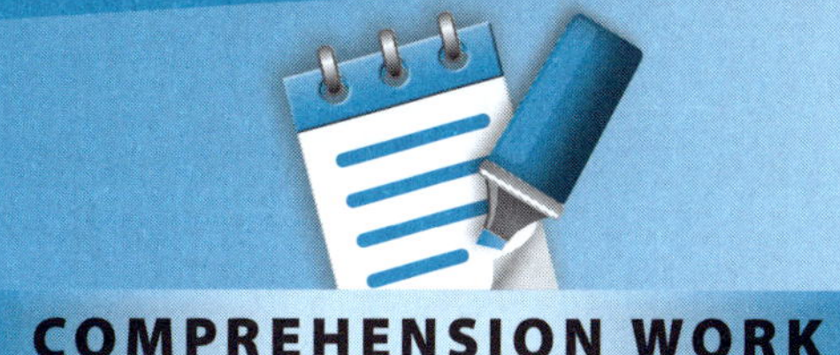

# PERSUASIVE TEXT
*Online review*

COMPREHENSION WORK

## Literal questions

*Hint: Read the text carefully to locate specific facts and details.*

**1** What are the two types of searches that visitors to this website can do?

___

**2** What is the 'nasty little … disclaimer' that applies to admission to Kennedy Space Center?

___

**3** What is 'NASA-speak' for 'absolutely' in line 41? ___

**4** What kind of language feature is 'KSC', which stands for 'Kennedy Space Center'? *Hint: Technically this feature is called an initialism but you only need to give a general term for it here.*

**a** a parenthesis **b** an abbreviation **c** a truncated sentence

## Interpretive questions

*Hint: These questions require you to combine facts and details to synthesise meaning.*

**5** Why might visitors to Kennedy Space Center be happy enough with a chewy hot dog or a vacuum-sealed salad?

**a** They have enjoyed similar food at other tourist attractions.

**b** These products are discounted when patrons buy tickets at a group rate.

**c** They will get so hungry exploring the place that they'll eat anything.

**6** In lines 27–28, what does the reviewer suggest you **not** do when visiting KSC?

___

**7** Which two words sum up the reviewer's thoughts about the food at KSC?

___ and ___

**8** The website's title ('The Attraction Attraction') implies that the site is designed for people who:

**a** are attracted to tourist attractions. **b** act attractively on tours. **c** attract tourists to attractions.

**9** Which catchphrase on this web page sums up the purpose of this review and others on the site?

___

**10** What is the purpose of the second review advertised at the end of the main review?

**a** to evaluate Universal Studios since a Harry Potter attraction was added

**b** to evaluate Harry Potter Studios since it became an attraction

**c** to evaluate Australia Zoo and Orange River Rafting

## Applied questions

*Hint: These questions require you to understand a text's implications to infer meaning from the text.*

**11** What is the most likely reason why a review of Universal Studios in Florida is advertised on this page?

**a** Orlando is in Florida. **b** Harry Potter is in Florida. **c** KSC is in Florida.

**12** What desire do both of the boxed advertisements on this web page appeal to in the reader? *Hint: A desire is something that a person wants or longs for.*

**a** a desire for change **b** a desire for company **c** a desire for money

# PERSUASIVE TEXT

## SPELLING WORK

### List Words

All of the words in the box below appear in the text 'Kennedy Space Center'.

| | | | | |
|---|---|---|---|---|
| astronaut | veteran | briefing | virtual | comprehensive |
| dining | spectator | recreated | reasonably | headquarters |
| tourist | exhibits | simulator | orbit | forgettable |

**1** There is one incorrectly spelt word in each sentence below. Correct it on the line provided. *Hint: All of the misspelt words are either list words or words in the same families.*

- **a** Wow, that space movie had some unforgetable scenes! ______
- **b** The launch commander gave a quick breifing at headquarters. ______
- **c** Even a virtuall rocket launch is an extraordinary spectacle. ______
- **d** We can get a cheap meal at the local dinner. ______
- **e** Florida's turism industry relies heavily on theme parks. ______
- **f** That satellite has been orbbiting for so long, it's virtually grown moss. ______

**2** Some list words contain smaller words. Find the smaller words using the clues below.

- **a** An excuse or justification at the beginning of a list word. r______
- **b** The shortest list word contains an even shorter word meaning 'a little piece'. ______
- **c** A list word meaning 'watcher' hides the rest of the revenge phrase, 'tit for …' ______
- **d** Another word for 'designated living areas' is the second half of a list word. q______
- **e** A memory problem and an eating area join forces in a list word. ______t ______e

**3** Do you know what the roots of some list words mean? Show your understanding by completing the table. *Hint: Answers in the third column should not be simply a list word with s added, or with other small changes.*

| Root | List word with this root | Other words with this root | Root meaning |
|---|---|---|---|
| sim | **a** | simile<br>**b** | **c** |
| re | recreated | **d** | **e** |
| spec | **f** | spectacles<br>**g** | **h** |
| ex | **i** | **j** | **k** |
| orb | **l** | **m** | in the shape of a circle or ring |

**Closed compounds** are compound words made up of two smaller words. They do not contain hyphens. To qualify as a compound, a word's two parts must make sense as words on their own, for example, *raincoat, keyboard, baseball*.

**4** Are these list words closed compounds? Circle *Y* for yes or *N* for no. For each compound write its two parts.

- **a** forgettable Y/N ______ ______
- **b** overpriced Y/N ______ ______
- **c** headquarters Y/N ______ ______
- **d** tourist Y/N ______ ______
- **e** astronaut Y/N ______ ______
- **f** briefing Y/N ______ ______

# PERSUASIVE TEXT

## Online review

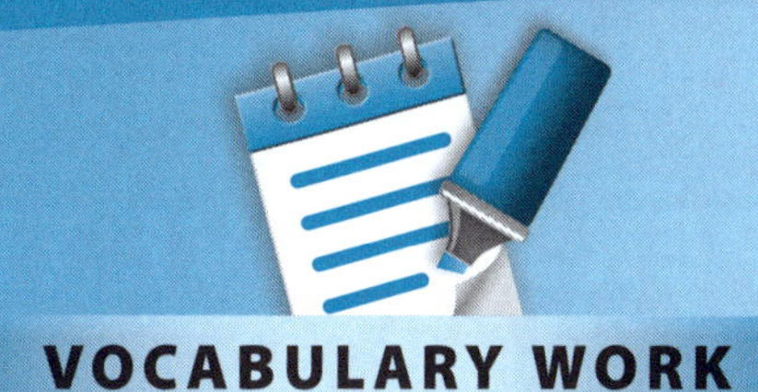

## VOCABULARY WORK

Special terms used in a certain group, profession or field are called **jargon**. Sometimes a word or term has different meanings in different contexts, such as *cutback*, a term used by both surfers and economists. Other jargon exists in only one field, such as *defendant* (law). In the text 'Kennedy Space Center' we read different kinds of jargon.

**1** Which words in the mix below are examples of jargon (any type of jargon, not just space jargon) from the text? Circle them. *Hint: Refer back to the text to check some words in context if you are unsure.*

| | | | | | |
|---|---|---|---|---|---|
| spectator | facilities | NASA | launch pad | dark coaster | Mission Control |
| briefing | highlights | snaps | gantry | virtual | MEGA-HUGE |

**2** Sort these sets of words according to their shared topic in the text. Write the letters in the correct spaces.

| Word set | Topic |
|---|---|
| **a** simulator, pad, commander, step by step, virtual | _____ Universal Studios |
| **b** forgettable, appetite, vacuum-sealed, overpriced | _____ Shuttle Launch Experience |
| **c** dark coaster, recreated, BUTTERBEER, Orlando, old fave | _____ dining |
| **d** group, non-transferrable, cancelled, rates, adult | _____ admission |

**Idioms** are expressions that make sense to a certain group of people. The idioms below are not directly related to space or the Kennedy Space Center, but they do appear in the review of the tourist attraction.

**3** Match each idiom with its closest meaning from the list below. Two meanings in the list are not used.

an interest or hobby | a lot of time | a lot of money | many different items | very well-informed

**a** your thing ____________________

**b** a pretty penny ____________________

**c** a list as long as your arm ____________________

**d** in the know ____________________

Many of the idioms in the text are just one step higher in formality than **slang**.

**4** Divide these slang terms from the review into positive and negative expressions.

fave | bummer | pretty boss | whatever | pluses | yawn factor

| Positive | Negative |
|---|---|
| | |
| | |
| | |

**5** Complete each sentence by selecting the most appropriate word from the options given.

**a** This tourist attraction has some failings but it also has plenty of pulses / pluses.

**b** After the funeral I couldn't find Uncle Lou's orbit / obit in the newspaper.

**c** The site gives a comprehensive / comprehension review of the destination.

**d** Massive queues, rip-off food and irritating kids made this a truly forgettable / unforgettable day out.

**e** The revisited / recreated space scenes are exciting for visitors of all ages.

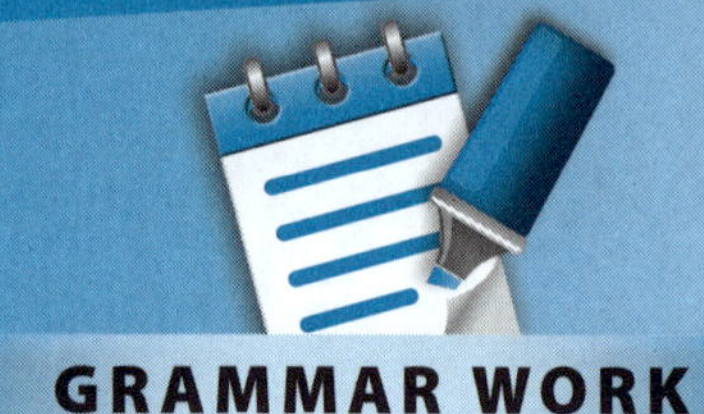

# PERSUASIVE TEXT

## GRAMMAR WORK

**Nouns** (things, places or people) can be **converted into adjectives** (descriptions of nouns) to add detail to our writing. To test whether you have correctly transformed a noun into an adjective (or whether a word is an adjective to begin with), place it before the word *thing*, *place* or *person*—that is, a noun—and see if it works.

**1** Convert these nouns from the text 'Kennedy Space Center' into adjectives.

a health ______________________ b attraction ______________________

c thrills ______________________ d commander ______________________

e visitor ______________________ f day ______________________

**2** Go back the other way: convert these adjectives from the text into nouns.

a sweaty ______________________ b great ______________________

c high ______________________ d exciting ______________________

e scenic ______________________ f young ______________________

A **prefix** is a group of letters at the start of a word. Some common ones are *ex, in* and *mis.* A **suffix** comes at the end of a word. Common suffixes are *ing, est* and *ity.* Understanding prefixes and suffixes helps us decode new words and use known words with confidence. Caution: some word beginnings look like prefixes but are just word roots, often derived from Greek or Latin. Test for a prefix by removing it and checking whether a full word remains.

**3** A list word containing two distinct word roots is 'astronaut'. The roots are both Greek: *astro* means 'stars' or 'outer space'; *naut* relates to a sailor or voyager. Write other words that include these roots.

a astro______________ astro______________ astro______________

b ______________naut ______________naut naut______________

**4** Break apart these closed compound words from the review text and use them to make new compound words. *Hints: There are no set answers. Re-read the information about compound words in the Spelling Work section on page 83.*

a armchair arm ______________ ______________ chair

b backlot back ______________ ______________ lot

c landmark land ______________ ______________ mark

d sunshine sun ______________ ______________ shine

**5** In each set below, which single word can be written on the lines to make six different compound words? *Hint: The word you need for Set 1 is the first half of a compound word in the word list. The word in Set 2 is not from the word list.*

| **Set 1** | | | **Set 2** | | |
|---|---|---|---|---|---|
| fore | ◆______________◆ | line | star | ◆______________◆ | house |
| mast | ◆______________◆ | way | high | ◆______________◆ | weight |
| egg | ◆______________◆ | ache | lime | ◆______________◆ | bulb |

## Capital letters

You know that **capital letters** begin sentences and people's names. Capital initial letters are also used:

- in the names of companies, groups, brands and products (for example, *Microsoft, Green Day, IKEA, iPhone*)
- in the names of countries, geographical features and landmarks (for example, *Germany, the River Ganges*)
- to identify eras, time markers, seasons and days (for example, *the Renaissance, Saturday, April*)
- to identify cultures, religions, movements and events (for example, *Cubism, Judaism, Stockholm Folk Festival*)
- as acronyms—these are formed from the first letters in a name containing multiple words (for example, *NASA*)
- as initialisms—these are abbreviations that do not form a pronounceable word (for example, *KSC*)
- to suggest a strong tone in an informal written text; especially anger, indignation or excitement (for example, *I LOVE it!*)
- in titles of texts—mostly, prepositions and articles in titles are not capitalised (for example, *'Hot in the City'*), although if the title begins with a preposition or article it is capitalised (for example, *In the Line of Fire*)
- to personify a force, element or phenomenon (for example, *Nature, Time, Fate*).

**1** Name three constructed landmarks from three different countries. *Hint: There are no set answers.*

______________________ ______________________ ______________________

**2** **a** Which of the following are acronyms? Circle them.

RADAR PGA NBC UNICEF NATO KSC KFC

**b** Which of the following are initialisms? Circle them.

OTT FYI QANTAS BRB BBC NASA ATM

**3** Identify the tone—anger, indignation or excitement—of each fully capitalised word or phrase below. *Hint: Exclamation marks can create different tones.*

**a** You will NEVER work in this town again! ______________________

**b** I AM GOING TO DISNEY WORLD TOMORROW! ______________________

**c** DO NOT SPEAK TO ME LIKE THAT. ______________________

**d** Go and see this movie. SERIOUSLY. ______________________

**4** Rewrite these text titles with correct capitalisation. *Hints: Two of these are standalone texts (a film and a play) so the titles should be italicised. Two are contained in larger texts (a song from an album and a nursery rhyme) so the titles need to be inside quotation marks.*

**a** the wizard of oz (film) ______________________

**b** the comedy of errors (play) ______________________

**c** livin' on a prayer (song) ______________________

**d** this old man (nursery rhyme) ______________________

**5** How many proper nouns from the text 'Kennedy Space Centre' appear below? Write them out with capital letters correctly added. *Hint: In some proper nouns not every word needs a capital letter. For example, the Kennedy Space Center.*

| | | | | |
|---|---|---|---|---|
| cape Canaveral | shuttle launch experience | virtual | dark coaster | butterbeer |
| disclaimer | nasa | mission control | hot dog | the richtesveld | visitors |

______________________________________________

______________________________________________

### Persuasive online reviews

This type of text is an appraisal of a product, business or activity in which the writer seeks to **persuade** readers to adopt their opinion and act on their advice. An online text based on opinion needs to:

- be written in a persuasive and authoritative manner
- include informative details that will help readers make their own evaluation
- be presented in a format that combines text, headings, graphics and a clear structure
- include interactive elements, such as hyperlinks, video, relevant advertising and site navigation tools, to capitalise on the online context.

**1** What could be added to the text 'Kennedy Space Center' to 'capitalise on the online context'?

______________________________________________

### Authority and authenticity

An online review, like many online texts, may be seen as an **authoritative**, factual source simply because it appears on the internet. This is a dangerous attitude held by many internet users.

- Much of the material we find online is heavily biased, factually incorrect, selective and skewed, poorly researched and/or plagiarised.
- A review can be a personal blog or part of one. The writer might be entirely unbiased and presenting a view simply to be helpful. But how do we know? There may be considerable bias behind the writing.
- A negative review may be written out of spite, as an attack from a competitor or just for the sake of trolling.
- A favourable review may be written for money or by a company employee posing as a customer.
- To safeguard against bias and manipulation, online reviews should be checked for an obvious bias in the writing, fact-checked if a claim seems strange and cross-checked against other reviews.
- The best and most trustworthy reviews will usually present both positive and negative aspects of a product or business. There will be a sense of reason and fairness about the writing. A good writer will also often have a portfolio of reviews to skim-read that will give an impression of his or her authority as a reviewer.

**2** What do these keywords mean in the context of the points in the box above?

a authoritative ______________ b capitalise ______________

c biased ______________ d plagiarised ______________

e blog ______________ f rolling ______________

g safeguard ______________ h portfolio ______________

### Structural features of an online persuasive review

When composing a persuasive review for the online environment we should include basic **visual and structural features** seen on typical web pages. Many of these are:

- page title and banner
- relevant images, captioned if necessary
- menu or navigation bar
- introductory blurb and/or slogan explaining the purpose of the page and the whole site
- brief paragraphs of information
- succinct summary points, marked by bullets or icons
- headings and subheadings
- hyperlinked keywords
- metadata (key information about a web page that helps search engines portray what is on it)
- internal and external site links
- sponsor images/icons and relevant advertisements.

**3** Tick *True* or *False* for each statement about the text 'Kennedy Space Center'. *Hint: The statements refer to the bullet points on the previous page, the review web page and its annotations.*

- **a** Highlights of the Kennedy Space Center are summarised in bullet points. ☐ True ☐ False
- **b** The slogan for 'The Attraction Attraction' site is 'Be in the know before you go!' ☐ True ☐ False
- **c** Internal and external site links are shown in different ways. ☐ True ☐ False
- **d** On a web page, 'menu' is another term for 'banner'. ☐ True ☐ False
- **e** Sponsors of a web page can show their presence with an image, icon or hyperlink. ☐ True ☐ False

**4** How does the writer of the text engage our senses by referring to visual (sight), auditory (sound), gustatory (taste) and tactile (touch) elements in the text? Quote two examples of each. *Hint: Your answers can include negative references that engage the senses, not just positive ones.*

- **a** visual ______________________
- **b** auditory ______________________
- **c** gustatory ______________________
- **d** tactile ______________________

**5** Complete this table of techniques and language features by giving examples from the text. *Hint: Look back at the annotations on the text for ideas, especially regarding effects.*

| Technique or feature | Example 1 | Example 2 | Effect |
|---|---|---|---|
| colloquial language | pretty boss | **a** | **b** |
| concise expression | **c** | **d** | It encourages visitors to the site to read the whole article. |
| truncated sentence | absolutely! | **e** | **f** |
| exclamation | **g** | **h** | **i** |

**6** Apart from the two hyperlinked advertisements on the web page, what are some other links to outside pages? List six. *Hint: Typically, hyperlinks can be identified by an underlined word or phrase; this is called anchor text.*

______________ ______________ ______________

______________ ______________ ______________

Typically, internet users spend a short time on each page when browsing. This means that online text writers must **grab our attention** then hold it for as long as possible. They also need to make their text easy to read.

**7** Which of these web page elements is most likely to capture and/or keep a reader's attention? Circle them.

long sections of text small print red text on a black background small chunks of text bullet points
subheadings key statistics and facts relevant images blaring music a simple navigation menu
digressions and unrelated anecdotes a maximum of three fonts many advertisements and pop-ups
long, complex sentences big words and academic language bold key words a video lecture

# PERSUASIVE TEXT

## Online review

WRITING SAMPLE

Here is a sample text showing you how to structure and write a persuasive online review.

## Book review

*Jane Eyre* by Charlotte Brontë

**Write a literal title for the review.** The persuasion in this text does not extend to the title but it may in other reviews.

First published in 16 October 1847
First published by Smith, Elder & Co., London
Author's pen name: Currer Bell
Genres: bildungsroman, Victorian romance
Available through: Penguin Books

**Choose a suitable image to place directly under the title.** This picture reminds readers of the heroine, Jane, and the child she tutors, Adèle. This evocative image suits the positive review. Adjacent to the image is a series of publishing details about the novel. Included in these details are underlined hyperlinks to appropriate and interesting external sources.

It seems unfair to me but this novel gets a lot of negative reviews from students. Have these haters actually read the book cover to cover? I can understand that it's quite a doorstop but so is *Harry Potter and the Order of the Phoenix*. I can also appreciate that the antique nature of the scenario and some of the language can be barriers, but come on: for 1847 it's very readable. And there's something about the Victorian era that makes a classic romance even headier. Keep a dictionary—electronic or paper (antique!)—handy. If you don't speak French, parts of the Adèle dialogues might confound you but you have heard of Google Translate, right? If you really must you can skip her scenes entirely, but that's just lazy.

**Establish an informal, personal style at the start.** Personal pronouns (such as 'me' and 'I') and colloquialisms (such as 'haters' and 'doorstop') aid this. Some words and phrases are underlined, identifying them as anchor text for hyperlinks to relevant sites. This is done in various places throughout the review. The reviewer addresses the reader directly.

### Two good reasons why it's the goods

There are so many reasons to persevere with this novel, but I'll give you the top two. First it's quite simply a brilliant story. It abounds in complex relationships, tension twists, mystery and, of course, romance. Second it's crafted by a master. The sophistication of the characterisation, description, conflict, motif, allusions—if you don't know what some of these things are, you might need to listen a little harder in English classes—of all those technical and stylistic features of a literary gem are on display.

**Divide the body text under two main subheadings that reinforce the informal style.** Techniques used in the subheadings include repetition, pun ('good'/'goods') and alliteration ('p' sounds in 'practically perfect plot'). Two succinct yet detailed lists sum up a range of reasons to read the novel.

### A practically perfect plot (spoiler-free summary)

Let's return to that magnificent plot. I'll break it down a little to whet your appetite and I'll avoid spoiling it for you (the plot, not your appetite):

- The eponymous heroine (and first person narrator) Jane Eyre is an orphan. She's also plain (i.e. not pretty). I wouldn't have mentioned it but Brontë does, repeatedly, so it's important. When still a baby, orphan Jane is taken in by a kind uncle. In true *Snow White* style the dear man dies and his wife is left to raise Jane along with her own children. This woman's picture should appear in the dictionary next to 'wicked stepmother'. She hates Jane. Her children hate Jane. It seems, at this point, the universe hates Jane. The hatred springs from the fact that the uncle adored Jane and favoured her over his children. So Jane, who was already off to a difficult start in life, suffers badly in this home and later at a boarding school, where there is prejudice against her thanks to good ol' Step-Ma.
- In young adulthood, Jane takes on a job as governess in the employ of the brooding, inscrutable—and often absent—Mr Rochester. Jane tutors and mentors little Adèle, with whom she becomes very close, and things take a big turn for the better. Inevitably love grows between Rochester and our heroine but OF COURSE something has to spoil it. Rochester has a dark and dangerous secret lurking in his very house (it is a very large house though). I'll say no more: it would ruin all the rollicking, romantic Victorian fun.

**Place the second subheading here.** The writer has chosen to summarise the novel's plot in two large bullet points to entice us to read the book. She has avoided 'spoilers' (information that ruins plot twists). A well-known point of reference—*Snow White*—is used to give the reader an idea of one aspect of the novel. Repetition and truncation ('She hates Jane. Her children hate Jane.') are used to both vary the expression and persuade the reader that the story is very engaging. Slang ('good ol' Step-Ma') helps the writer build familiarity with the reader, making it more likely that her opinion will be trusted. A fully capitalised phrase ('OF COURSE') adds a new tone to the review and conveys the writer's enthusiasm for the novel.

You probably have an inkling by now that I ADORE *Jane Eyre*. But please recognise that it hasn't been called a classic for nearly two centuries for nothing. I'm not defending the novel. There's no need. Just read it. ☆☆☆☆☆

**Justify your position at the end of the review.** The writer says 'it hasn't been called a classic … for nothing', and gives the novel five stars, meaning that she thinks it is exceptional.

# PERSUASIVE TEXT

## Online review

Plan your sample on the lines provided.

* **Write a literal title for the review.**
* **Choose a suitable image to place directly under the title.** Adjacent to the image, list a series of publishing or product details. In these details include underlined hyperlinks to appropriate and interesting external sources.
* **Establish an informal, personal style at the start.** Use personal pronouns and colloquialisms to aid this. Underline some words and phrases to identify them as anchor text for hyperlinks to relevant sites. Do this in various places throughout the review. Address the reader directly to build rapport.
* **Divide the body text under two main subheadings that reinforce the informal style.** Use techniques in the subheadings, such as repetition, pun and alliteration, to add interest. Make two succinct yet detailed lists to sum up a range of reasons why this text, product or business is so good.
* **Place the second subheading here.** Sum up the text, product or business in two large bullet points to entice your readers towards it. If reviewing a text, avoid any 'spoilers'. Use a well-known point of reference to give the reader an idea of one aspect of the item being reviewed. Use repetition and truncation both to vary the expression and to persuade the reader. Use slang to build familiarity with the reader, making it more likely that your opinion will be trusted. Write a phrase in capital letters to add a new tone to the review and convey your enthusiasm for the product.
* **Justify your position at the end of the review.** Give the text, product or business a star rating out of five.

# PERSUASIVE TEXT

## *Protest letter*

**READING WORK**

### No power plant!

*This is a protest letter addressed to an MP (member of parliament). Its writer is a citizen who is speaking on behalf of many concerned people on the issue of a proposed coal-fueled power plant in the local area. This kind of text is very similar to a letter to the editor, as you will see in the sample text later in this unit. It also has many features in common with an open letter. The three forms are nearly interchangeable.*

Nevio Georgadis
2 Bright Lane
Tondo Flat NSW 2998
11 October 2016

The Minister for Energy and Resources
NSW State Government
6 Macquarie St
Sydney NSW 2000

**No power plant!**
**Re: Proposed Mitchell Lake development**

To the Minister,

I am writing to strongly and urgently protest against the proposed development of a coal-fired power station at Mitchell Lake. Local and international research has predicted that this dirty development could produce as much as eight million tonnes of carbon dioxide every year. Many of my fellow citizens and I are deeply concerned that your government is about to mindlessly give the green light to this power plant. Has there been no thought given to the massive damage that will be done to the environment if this project goes ahead?

With all of Australia's access to sunlight, wind and waves, WHY are we still using coal to generate so much of our power? In Germany the government's policy is to use only renewable resources for its energy needs. Now Germany's energy needs are met by systems that are nearly 100 per cent environmentally friendly. As a bonus the renewable energy industry has created 250 000 new jobs in recent years—so everybody wins.

If renewable, clean technologies have been proven to work well overseas, why can't Australia follow suit? It is totally unacceptable that we still rely on the burning of fossil fuels in this day and age! With all the information about atmospheric degradation and climate change, why aren't we taking steps now where we can? Rejecting this power plant would be a good start.

Even leaving climate change out of the equation, surely the unnecessary damage that this power station would wreak on the local ecosystem is something to be avoided. Government leaders like yourself have a serious responsibility to protect the environment, public health and your citizens' livelihoods wherever possible.

Stand up for the environment, for health, for jobs and simply for common sense, and show those foreign corporate fat cats that you don't mess with an Aussie with a brain and a conscience. We urge you to do the right thing and vote to reject this proposal for the sake of both our current quality of life and our future.

Yours sincerely,

*N.A. Georgiadis*

Nevio Georgiadis

- The **name and address** of the **sender** precede the recipient's details. Prior to the advent of computers the sender's address was usually written on the right-hand side of the page. Computers and the need to minimise keystrokes introduced the convention of having everything starting on the left-hand side of the page.
- The **date** on which the letter was written follows.
- The **title and address of the recipient** appear next. The recipient is not personally named in this letter. It is equally appropriate here to name the person's role or position.
- The letter is given a **title** that indicates the subject. This particular letter has a dual title that conveys urgency: 'No power plant! Re: Proposed Mitchell Lake development'.
- A **formal salutation** (greeting), 'To the Minister', opens the letter. This is civil and respectful, but it also sounds cold and unfriendly, which sets the tone for the letter as a protest.
- The writer immediately **names the issue**. When read in conjunction with the title, this sentence leaves the recipient in no doubt as to the letter's meaning and purpose.
- **Many questions are posed** by the writer that challenge the MP (member of parliament) receiving this letter. Capital letters and exclamation marks also create a challenging, angry and desperate tone.
- Specific **supporting evidence** about a 'clean energy' country is provided. This evidence strengthens the protest and makes the question that opens the following paragraph sound reasonable.
- The writer tries to reason with the MP, using **qualifying words** that have a subtle strength like 'even' and 'surely'. To support these words, he peppers this section with emotive words like 'wreak' and 'serious'.
- The letter concludes with back-to-back **lists** of specific MP responsibilities as perceived by the public. The second list is more forceful than the first and borders on disrespect.
- The writer **signs off** at the end of the letter.

## Literal questions

*Hint: Read the text carefully to locate specific facts and details.*

**1** Where does the letter writer live?

**a** Mitchell Lake **b** Macquarie St, Sydney **c** Tondo Flat

**2** What does the writer say is 'totally unacceptable'? ______________________

**3** What letter feature appears between the sign-off phrase and the writer's name? ______________________

## Interpretive questions

*Hint: These questions require you to combine facts and details to synthesise the meaning.*

**4** Which of these words is the best meaning of 'Re:' at the beginning of the letter?

**a** reckoning **b** referral **c** regarding

**5** Complete the statement: One function of the first part of the letter's title, 'No power plant!', is:

**a** to inform the MP that a power plant has been proposed.

**b** to demand that the MP know about the power plant.

**c** to sum up the letter in case the MP reads no further.

**6** In line 20 we read the phrase 'dirty development'. What sound technique has been used here and why?

______________________

**7** What two things about Germany's energy production have led to a situation where 'everybody wins'?

______________________

**8** Which of these phrases are intended to be read figuratively (not literally)?

**a** green light, follow suit, fat cats **b** power plant, work well, out of the equation

**c** clean technologies, public health, quality of life

**9** What word towards the end tells us that the power plant is not locally owned? ______________________

**10** What are three things a member of parliament is morally obligated to protect? *Hint: The answers are made explicit in the last two paragraphs.*

______________________

## Applied questions

*Hint: These questions require you to understand a text's implications to infer meaning from the text.*

**11** This letter is addressed to the State Minister for Energy and Resources. Who else could it be addressed to? *Hint: There are many people to whom this letter could be shown but only a few to whom it should be addressed.*

**a** all of Nevio's neighbours **b** the State Minister for the Environment

**c** a TV current affairs show host

**12** Why is 'you don't mess with an Aussie with a brain and a conscience' a backhanded compliment? *Hint: A backhanded compliment is an insult disguised as a compliment.*

**a** The writer is implying that if the MP does not stop the plant, he has no brain and no conscience.

**b** The writer is saying that, on the one hand, the MP has a brain and on the back hand, he has a conscience.

**c** The writer is paying a compliment to all MPs except this one.

# PERSUASIVE TEXT

## SPELLING WORK

### List Words

The words in the box below have been taken from the text 'No power plant!'

| | | | | |
|---|---|---|---|---|
| renewable | degradation | climate | recent | technologies |
| atmospheric | wreak | conscience | ecosystem | environmentally |
| sincerely | policy | proposal | fossil | foreign |

**1** One word in each of these sentences is spelt incorrectly. Write it correctly on the line provided. *Hint: List words are used in most of the sentences, but not all of them are misspelt. Some are used correctly.*

**a** This porposal is going to cause a lot of community outrage. ______

**b** It is our policy to research these issues throughly before voting. ______

**c** Foregin investment has its pluses and its negatives. ______

**d** Currant figures suggest that this plant will earn millions in state revenue. ______

**e** The environmental damage that this power station will reek is scary. ______

**f** The local ecosystem will suffer grately from the pollution. ______

**2** Some list words contain other complete words inside them. Using the clues write these smaller words, along with the list words in which they appear. The first one has been done for you as an example.

| Clue to the smaller word | Smaller word | List word in which it appears |
|---|---|---|
| **a** an object used in a play; starts with *p* | prop | proposal |
| **b** ready, willing and … | | |
| **c** One hundredth of a dollar | | |
| **d** a monarch's time in power is called their … | | |
| **e** from the Latin word for knowledge; starts with *s* | | |
| **f** can mean a piece of wood or a written record | | |
| **g** a commonly used idiom for friend | | |

**Anagrams** are words or phrases that are formed when the letters of another word or phrase are rearranged. Every letter of the original word or phrase must be used—but only once. For example, *team* is an anagram of *mate*.

**3** One list word is an anagram for a word meaning 'middle'.

**a** What is the list word? ______ **b** What is the anagram? ______

**4** Make anagrams from these words. The first three appear in the text.

| | | |
|---|---|---|
| **a** are ______ | **b** life ______ | **c** tarts ______ |
| **d** dads ______ | **e** fist ______ | **f** deaf ______ |
| **g** hate ______ | **h** flee ______ | **i** flue ______ |

**5** Only one word in each trio below is a real word. Cross out the others. *Hint: Each set comes from a list word.*

| | | |
|---|---|---|
| **a** unrenewable | irrenewable | renewdable |
| **b** polic | policies | policitate |
| **c** atmospherical | atmospheres | atmost |
| **d** foreigner | foreignate | foreigned |

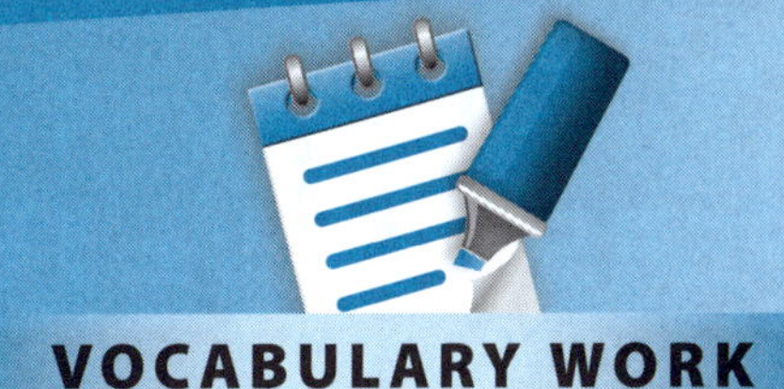

# PERSUASIVE TEXT

## Protest letter

## VOCABULARY WORK

**1** Each of these sentences contains a pair of correctly spelt words but only one works in the context. Circle it. *Hint: The correct words are not necessarily list words.*

- **a** At the heart of this protest is an environmentally / environmental issue.
- **b** Big businesses can recent / resent local citizens standing in the way of development.
- **c** Degradation / gradation of the atmosphere is one of the biggest hazards of this plant.
- **d** In situations like this, an MP must make a conscious / conscience effort to defend the local community.
- **e** We will be sending council representatives to policy / police the site during development.
- **f** The climatic / climactic consequences of worldwide pollution look frightening.

Many **word roots** (segments of words) in English spring from the ancient languages of Latin and Greek. Learning many of these roots can help us expand our vocabulary enormously and decode unknown words.

**2** **a** The issue of acting on one's conscience is raised in the text. The word 'conscience' has its roots in the Latin word *scire,* which means 'to know or understand'. We see the smaller root of this—*sci*—in many English words. Write words (and one phrase) containing the *sci* root by completing the blanks.

sci__________ic (adjective)    neuro__________ce (noun)    disc__________line (noun)

uncon__________us (adjective)    sci__________ fi__________ (noun)

subc__________us (adjective/noun)

**b** The protest letter is addressed to a politician. This word's root—*poli*—comes from the Greek *polis,* meaning 'city' and extending to 'government and society'. Write words (and one phrase) containing the root *poli* by completing the blanks.

p__________cy (noun)    p__________cian (noun)    p__________lly (adverb)

p__________cal (adjective)    poli__________ f__________ce (noun)    metr__________lis (noun)

**3** We use roots when making word families. Complete these word families based on list words.

| | | |
|---|---|---|
| **a** sincerely | si__________ty | ins__________re |
| **b** environmentally | env__________st | en__________ns |
| **c** proposal | pr__________ition | pr__________sing |

**4** The following **idioms** have been used in the protest letter. Do you know what they mean or can you figure out their meanings from the context? Write *True* or *False* for each meaning provided. *Hint: All of these words appear in the letter but are not in the list.*

| Word | Meaning | True or False? |
|---|---|---|
| **a** taking steps | rising sharply | __________ |
| **b** follow suit | do the same thing | __________ |
| **c** green light | approval | __________ |
| **d** fat cats | wealthy obese people | __________ |
| **e** don't mess with | don't make disorganised | __________ |
| **f** out of the equation | mathematical working | __________ |

# PERSUASIVE TEXT

## *Protest letter*

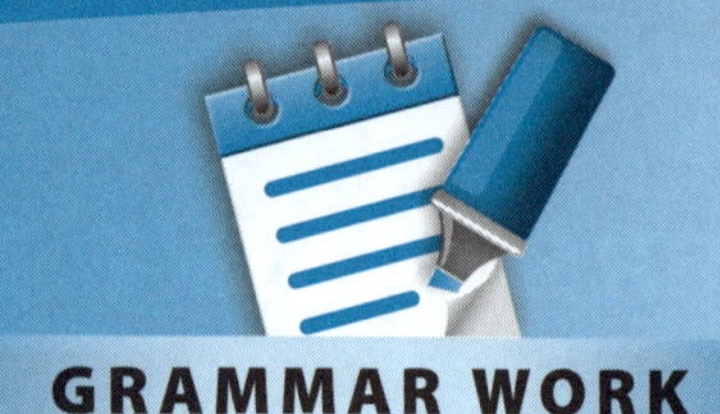

**GRAMMAR WORK**

### Adverb recap

Adverbs **modify**—that is, they change or give extra meaning to—**other words**, including verbs, adjectives or other adverbs. There are adverbs of **place** (giving a general or specific location), **manner** (describing the way in which something is done), **time** (telling when or how often something is done) and **degree** (giving a level or amount). Most adverbs end in *ly*, making them fairly easy to spot. Identifying adverbs without *ly* is much harder. Adverbs of degree and adverbs of manner have been used in the protest letter. They are explored below.

Adverbs of degree:

- tell us the intensity, degree or extent of an action (verb), adjective (noun descriptor) or other adverb
- are usually placed before the word they are modifying; for example, *I am **extremely** tired.*

**1** In the text 'No power plant!', an adverb of degree is used in an exclamatory sentence: 'It is totally unacceptable that we still rely on the burning of fossil fuels in this day and age!'

**a** Which word is the adverb of degree? ____________ **b** Why has it been used? ____________________

______________________________________________________________________

**2** Circle or underline the adverb or adverbs of degree in these partial sentences. *Hint: One of these partial sentences appears in the protest letter.*

**a** we rarely see politicians change their mind based on one protest letter

**b** this issue is extremely important because it affects both our future and our quality of life now

**c** I'm alarmed because the MP seems quite unconcerned about the whole thing

**d** I am writing to strongly and urgently protest against the proposed development

### Adverbs of manner

- Tell us how something (a verb) happens; for example, *Rhett rode **frantically** to Teo's house.*
- Are usually placed after the main verb in a sentence or after the object; for example, *She ate **greedily**.*
- Usually end in *ly*, making them fairly easy to spot.
- Can be tested to confirm what they are by being placed before the word *done.*

**3** Which word in each of these partial sentences is an adverb of manner? Circle or underline it. *Hint: One of these partial sentences appears in the text.*

**a** the letter has been carefully worded to place maximum guilt on the MP

**b** we are cautiously optimistic about the MP overturning the power plant proposal soon

**c** your government is about to mindlessly give the green light to this power plant

**d** the planning has been conducted very sloppily and without really giving the hazards any serious thought

How confident are you in spotting the nine **parts of speech** in passages of text? Begin by looking for the basics: noun, verb, adjective and adverb. Graduate to pronoun, preposition, article, conjunction and interjection. Add one part of speech at a time, identifying each one in texts for practice. Isolating and understanding the functions of the different parts of speech not only helps you in tests but also improves your written expression.

**4** In the two sentences below circle nouns, underline verbs, tick adjectives and draw a box around pronouns. *Hint: These parts of speech all appear at least once in each sentence.*

**a** I must admit this protest is making me stressed and sleepless.

**b** An MP has the moral responsibility to vote with their conscience on behalf of the people.

# PERSUASIVE TEXT

## Protest letter

**PUNCTUATION WORK**

### Punctuating and spelling numbers

Writing **numbers** can be a grey area in composing texts because expressing them as words (rather than using figures or numerals), really comes down to a writer's preference. Punctuating numbers is more standard. There are some generally accepted numeral rules that most writers use. The main ones appear below.

- Spell out numbers used at the beginning of a sentence (for example, *Six o'clock sharp was always dinner time*).
- Using numerals for times in any other part of a sentence is fine (for example, *It's 8.45 already!*). Two exceptions are noon or midday and midnight, which are clearer than numerals.
- For decades expressed in figures you can use the full numeral (for example, *the 1960s*) or replace the first two numbers with an apostrophe (for example, *the '60s*). Either way, there should be no apostrophe before the *s*.
- Hyphenate compound numbers from twenty-one to ninety-nine.
- Hyphenate written fractions that begin with a number (for example, *one-quarter* or *five-eighths* but not *a third*).
- Use spaces or commas in numbers with five or more digits (for example, *15 043* or *15,043*); writers vary in their preference for a comma in numbers with four digits (for example, *1500* or *1,500*).
- After placing the first space or comma (three spaces to the left), separate digits into groups of three with a space or comma (for example, *45 500 000*).

**1** Re-read the fourth point above about decades expressed as figures. When writing a group of years as a figure why should we not use an apostrophe before the *s*?

**a** There is already an apostrophe in the figure.

**b** No plurals or groups need apostrophes.

**c** A hyphen is better.

**2** As noted above, some number expression is simply a matter of personal preference. In the text 'No power plant!':

**a** Why has the writer written '100 per cent' (not 'one hundred percent')?

______________________________

**b** Why is '250 000' more effective than 'two hundred and fifty thousand'?

______________________________

**c** Why is 'eight million' spelt out? ______________________________

Just as we can choose the best type of number expression and punctuation for use in a written context, we may opt to **enhance the impact** of a statement or question in a text by using particular punctuation.

**3** Explain the impact of these punctuation choices made by the writer of the protest letter:

**a** exclamation mark: 'No power plant!'

______________________________

**b** all capital letters for the first word: 'WHY are we still using coal to generate so much of our power?'

______________________________

**c** exclamation mark: 'It is totally unacceptable that we still rely on the burning of fossil fuels in this day and age!'

______________________________

**4** Which of these uses of punctuation are some of the most effective attention-grabbers? Choose three.

interrobang (?!) comma exclamation mark selective italics lower-case letters

# PERSUASIVE TEXT

## *Protest letter*

**WRITING WORK 1**

### Protest letters

A **protest letter**, as the name denotes, is intended to make a strong statement about an issue. This type of letter:

- is a persuasive text designed to bring attention to an issue and make an argument or case
- is a form of non-violent protest
- may be used as an open letter (sent to a particular recipient but also made public)
- may be addressed to one person, multiple people, a business or a governing body.

When writing a protest letter:

- Choose a topical issue. The issue should be of current interest, importance and/or urgency, and it should affect more than a small group of people. Think of your letter as an actual protest. Would you go out and demonstrate in the streets based on this issue? If the issue is protest-worthy, it is certainly letter-worthy.
- Grab attention at the beginning.
- Present and structure it clearly.
- Check your facts and statistics. Make sure that all key details mentioned in your letter are correct. This requires some online fact-checking (using credible sources). Do your homework: don't base your argument on assumptions, sweeping statements, hearsay or few facts.
- Keep it brief.
- End with a punch. Close the letter with a challenge or rhetorical question.

**1** What is the issue raised in Nevio Georgadis's protest letter?

______________________________________________

**2** Apart from protest letters, what are two other forms of non-violent protest?

______________________ ______________________

**3** Re-read the first point above under 'When writing a protest letter …' What is a good synonym for the word 'topical'?

**a** current  **b** tropical  **c** superficial

**4** From the options below, what is the best definition of 'hearsay'?

**a** saying something by ear  **b** a second-hand report  **c** hearing what you say

The forceful exclamation 'No power plant!' and the more formal 'Re: Proposed Mitchell Lake development' are the two parts of a **dual title** that heads the protest letter. Both parts are self-explanatory, but one is more insistent and persuasive. The second part elaborates on the first. Sometimes catchcries like this one are adopted as names for events (such as protests), movements and action groups—and even political parties.

**5** Suggest an alternative title for the protest letter. It does not necessarily need two parts. *Hint: Your suggested title needs to be attention-grabbing, forceful and urgent.*

______________________________________________

Just as it may have more than one addressee, a protest letter may be written by or on behalf of a group of people. Like an open letter, a protest letter can function as a **petition**.

**6** On whose behalf is Nevio Georgadis writing? ______________________

# PERSUASIVE TEXT

## Protest letter

WRITING WORK 2

### Main features of a protest letter

Structural and language features work together in a **protest letter**. The most common ones are:

- an introduction where the topic or issue is clearly identified and an opinion or stance given
- brief, structured points that can be read quickly
- supporting evidence based on research and statistical data (for example, 'eight million tonnes')
- complex sentences that sometimes contain connectives
- occasional transitional phrases (for example, 'Even leaving climate change out of the equation …')
- a brief conclusion that directs a demand or challenge at the recipient.

Persuasive language features used in a protest letter can include:

- emotive language (words that evoke or appeal to emotions)
- commands and demands directed towards the recipient
- strong adverbs (that modify verbs or adjectives) and strong adjectives (that describe nouns)
- rhetorical questions (questions that do not require an answer because it's obvious, or there isn't one)
- moral appeals (requests, pleadings or urgings based on doing what is right).

**7** What is one possible reason why sentences in a protest letter only 'sometimes' contain connectives?

______________________________

**8** What is another persuasive language feature (not listed) that can have an impact in a protest letter?

______________________________

**9** For each persuasive language feature listed above give an example from the protest text 'No power station'.
*Hint: Look back at the Grammar Work section on page 95 for ideas; you may repeat examples from that section here.*

**a** emotive language ______________________________

**b** commands or demands ______________________________

**c** strong adverb ______________________________

**d** strong adjective ______________________________

**e** rhetorical question ______________________________

**f** moral appeal ______________________________

### What makes an open letter effective?

To ensure that an **open letter** is effective in persuading readers about an issue, the writer of the text must:

- address the letter to an appropriate recipient and use appropriate diction for that recipient
- state the issue clearly at the beginning
- support any claims and opinions with authoritative evidence and, preferably, statistical data.

Protest letters can also be given titles, like the letter in the text, to alert the reader about the issue immediately.

**10** **a** What is the letter writer trying to persuade the recipient to understand or realise?

______________________________

**b** What is the letter writer trying to persuade the recipient to do?

______________________________

# PERSUASIVE TEXT

## WRITING SAMPLE

Here is a sample text showing you how to structure and write a protest letter that is also a letter to the editor of a major newspaper.

| Sample | Notes |
| --- | --- |
| To the Editor | **Begin with a simple salutation such as 'To the Editor' or 'Dear Editor'.** In letters to the editor, formal sender and recipient details are not required, and a simple 'To the Editor' or 'Dear Editor' is an adequate salutation. A 'sent' date is optional. |
| **Street View is an invasion of privacy** | **Give the letter an appropriate title.** This title is literal and clearly identifies the issue. |
| I am writing to express my concerns about Google Street View. This 'public service' has been around for years now so why is no one talking about its dangers? | **Fully identify the issue in the first sentence of the letter.** A rhetorical question ends the first section. This question acts as the second half of the issue statement. |
| Street View is a mapping tool that provides 360-degree street-level views of residential areas, including street signs, vehicles, front yards and sometimes also the front doors of people's houses. | **Provide background information to frame the issue.** Here the writer explains what Google Street View is, in case readers are not aware. |
| Many people have expressed concerns that Street View is an invasion of privacy and could pose a safety risk if people's homes and vehicles can now be so easily tracked by any member of the public. Google executives have argued that because they have included a feature that allows people to have certain images removed or blurred, they are acting responsibly in relation to protecting people's privacy. | **Make an argument about the subject of your protest and give a brief counter-argument or justification given by the people you hold responsible.** An argument against this technology is made, along with the counter-argument or justification given by its makers. The writer uses fairly general evidence, in that there are no direct quotes, but it is still appropriate evidence. |
| The problem is, most people do not know what images showing their home or vehicle are out there on the net. Reports have emerged that private roads marked with warnings against trespassing were photographed anyway. There have also been cases where actual individuals have been recognisable in Street View pictures, which is an even more overt example of privacy invasion. | **Elaborate on the problem and give two specific examples of it.** The writer gives two specific examples of the alleged 'privacy invasion' going on. The language is very formal (for example, 'Reports have emerged'; 'actual individuals have been recognisable'), which lends the whole letter an air of authority. |
| My main objection is that people have no say in whether a photo of their house or street is put on the Internet. This tool means that burglars can freely access all sorts of information about who is home alone, when people go out, when people go on holidays, what vehicles they have and where they are stored. Is that not more than a little irresponsible? | **Begin the second-last section with the phrase 'My main objection' to clarify your central protest and also to suggest that you have other objections.** A second rhetorical question is used in the last line of this section to point to the moral aspect of the issue. |
| Being photographed without your consent or even your knowledge is not illegal (why?) but it certainly is immoral! More importantly, I believe—and many people in the community are with me—it is unsafe. | **Ask a question in parentheses to quickly and neatly raise a side issue.** The question here is 'why?' An exclamatory statement ('it certainly is immoral!') shows the writer's indignation. This exclamatory statement is also an appeal to morals. This is a classic persuasive language technique. |
| Elsa King<br>Freeman's Flat, SA | **Write your name, suburb and state to close the letter.** A signature is not required in a letter of this kind. |

# PERSUASIVE TEXT

## Protest letter

**WRITING YOUR OWN SAMPLE**

Plan your sample on the lines provided.

- **Begin with a simple salutation such as 'To the Editor' or 'Dear Editor'.** Formal sender and recipient details are not required. A 'sent' date is optional.
- **Give the letter an appropriate title.** It should be literal and clearly identify the issue.
- **Fully identify the issue in the first sentence of the letter.** Write a rhetorical question to end the first section. This question should act as the second half of the issue statement.
- **Provide background information to frame the issue.**
- **Make an argument about the subject of your protest and give a brief counter-argument or justification given by the people you hold responsible.** You can use fairly general evidence, in that direct quotes are not needed, but the evidence still needs to be appropriate.
- **Elaborate on the problem and give two specific examples of it.** Use formal language to give the whole letter an air of authority.
- **Begin the second-last section with the phrase 'My main objection' to clarify your central protest and also to suggest that you have other objections.** Write a second rhetorical question in the last line of this section to point to the moral aspect of the issue.
- **Ask a question in parentheses to quickly and neatly raise a side issue.** Make an exclamatory statement to show indignation. The same exclamatory statement should also be an appeal to morals. This is a classic persuasive language technique.
- **Write your name, suburb and state to close the letter.** A signature is not required in a letter of this kind.

# PERSUASIVE TEXT

## *Flyer*

READING WORK

## *Yellowfin Seafood Restaurant*

A stunning waterside location and commitment to excellence allows Yellowfin Seafood Restaurant to offer you the perfect dining experience, right on gorgeous Newharbour. With culinary veteran Jai Roney at the helm it's no surprise that Yellowfin was awarded the prestigious title of Most Outstanding Seafood Restaurant again this year at the Restaurant and Catering Awards. You can trust in their promise to source the freshest premium quality seafood available.

Yellowfin's young, dynamic chefs add contemporary flair to our exquisite menu, offering diners a tempting array of dishes—many of them gluten-free—that represent the very best in coastal cuisine. Complementing our fresh local seafood is a carefully chosen wine list showcasing boutique vineyards across Australia and New Zealand. We also carry a selection of French wines for you to explore at leisure.

Our port-side setting presents diners with fabulous views of the Newharbour marina precinct: sparkling waters, luxury yachts, quirky tugs, rustic fishing boats; even the occasional dolphin. The ever-changing vista stretches across one of Australia's most picturesque ports.

As our regular patrons know, the unfailing sea breeze adds a zesty salt tang to your dining experience. Patrons seated waterside by night can enjoy the warmth of gas heaters and ample indoor seating is available. With its unique décor, professional staff and fine-dining menu, Yellowfin offers something for every diner and every occasion.

Whether you desire a romantic setting for an intimate dinner, a versatile space for a lively function or a cosmopolitan venue for corporate events, Yellowfin fits the bill.

Our experienced event manager is available during the day to coordinate and advise about functions and special events.

Call Yellowfin Seafood Restaurant on 1800YFIN or visit our website: newharb.com.au/yellowfin to reserve a table for lunch or dinner and take advantage of this special offer: a 20 per cent discount on a standard main meal (seafood platters excluded) when you mention this advertisement.

Back of flyer:

## *Yellowfin Seafood Restaurant*

*Some morsels from our menu ...*

### *Starters*

*King prawn, rocket and preserved lemon bruschetta* 12

*Baked ricotta with salted sweet potato skins, balsamic vinegar and olive oil* 6.5

### *Entrée*

*Whitebait with a dipping sauce duo (house aioli and jalapeño salsa verde)* 16.5

### *Mains*

*Steamed fish of the day with duck fat potatoes and rainbow salad* MP

*Fruits de mer (platter for two): seafoods on ice with sauces and seasonal salad* 58

### *Desserts (made in-house with fresh ingredients)*

*Chocolate liqueur fondant with cashew ice cream* 9.5

*Mango panna cotta with star fruit and macerated strawberries* 8

newharb.com.au/yellowfin ◇ 1800YFIN ◇ 18009346 ◇ newharb.com.au/yellowfin

---

- The **name of the business being advertised** is shown in larger, bolder typeface than the rest of the text.
- **Second person address** (such as 'to offer you') is used to appeal directly and personally to the reader.
- **Effusive and emotive language**, such as the adjective 'gorgeous', makes the location sound very desirable.
- We are told about **important awards** won by the restaurant.
- The reader seems to be given a **personal guarantee of quality** from the restaurant.
- The fact that many gluten-free options are on the menu is mentioned in passing but **encased in dashes to draw attention to it**.
- There is a **focus on location** in the text. The picturesque area is a big part of the restaurant's appeal.
- 'Regular patrons' are mentioned to inform us that some—perhaps many—people are already **loyal customers**. This suggests that the restaurant must be a good one.
- **Different needs and interests of potential customers** are addressed, to appeal to as wide an audience as possible.
- A free-call **phone number** and a **website** are given.
- An **incentive** (a discounted meal) is offered to readers who act on the advertisement and come to the restaurant.
- This flyer is **printed on both sides** to maximise the advertising opportunity.
- The back of the flyer features a **sampling of dishes** from the restaurant's menu, along with their prices. Appropriately, the majority of dishes include seafood.
- A vegetarian dish is shown to suggest that **vegetarians can be catered for**, despite this being a seafood restaurant.
- A **stylish mode of showing price** (without a second decimal place or dollar sign) is used. This is a popular technique used by restaurants on menus and blackboards.
- A seafood platter is featured to suggest that other platters may also be on offer; also to **encourage diners** to come to the restaurant for an intimate dinner for two.
- The **contact details are repeated at the end** of the flyer, separated by the restaurant's diamond logo.

# PERSUASIVE TEXT
*Flyer*

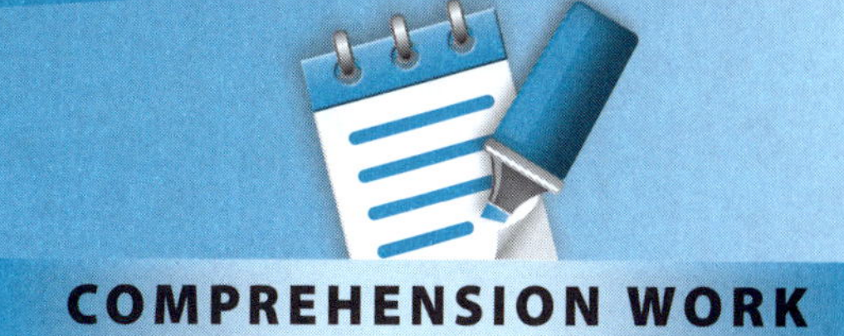

**COMPREHENSION WORK**

## Literal questions

*Hint: Read the text carefully to locate specific facts and details.*

**1** What is unusual about the name 'Yellowfin' as it is printed at the top of both sides of the flyer in the text 'Yellowfin Seafood Restaurant'?

______________________________

**2** What award has Yellowfin Seafood Restaurant won 'again this year'?

**a** Most Outstanding Seafood Restaurant

**b** Most Outstanding Restaurant

**c** Restaurant and Catering Awards

**3** From which countries do the wines at the restaurant come?

______________________________

## Interpretive questions

*Hint: These questions require you to combine facts and details to synthesise the meaning.*

**4** Who runs Yellowfin Seafood Restaurant?

**a** the Newharbour marina **b** Somebody who is not named **c** Jai Roney

**5** Which two location terms have the same meaning in the text? *Hint: Use the letter clues to complete the words.*

p________ - ________ and w____________________de

**6** Based on the context, what does 'vista' mean? ______________________________

**7** What discount on seafood platters is offered to diners who 'mention this advertisement'?

______________________________

**8** What sound technique is used in the subheading at the top of the back of the flyer in the text?

**a** rhyme **b** onomatopoeia **c** alliteration

**9** What does the abbreviation 'MP' stand for in the flyer? *Hint: Consider the meaning of other items in that column.*

**a** market price **b** main part **c** meal platter

**10** What are two dipping sauces mentioned in the menu?

**a** aioli and salsa verde **b** ice and panna cotta **c** whitebait and jalapeño

## Applied questions

*Hint: These questions require you to understand a text's implications to infer meaning from the text.*

**11** The second main dish is 'Fruits de mer'. In this French term, what do you think 'fruits' are?

**a** salad leaves **b** fruit pieces **c** seafood types

**12** Which adjectival term meaning 'on the premises' tells patrons that certain sauces and desserts are made fresh at the restaurant? *Hint: There are two possible correct answers.*

______________________________

# PERSUASIVE TEXT

## *Flyer*

## SPELLING WORK

**List Words** All of the words in the box below have been taken from the text 'Yellowfin Seafood Restaurant'.

| | | | | |
|---|---|---|---|---|
| restaurant | culinary | prestigious | complementing | catering |
| boutique | leisure | precinct | vineyards | yachts |
| ample | décor | coordinate | morsels | rustic |

**1** Form list words by adding these vowels in the right places and writing each word in full: *e*, *a*, *i*

**a** mpl ____________ **b** lsur ____________ **c** ctrng ____________

**2** Form list words by adding these consonants in the right places: *c*, *r*, *n*, *p*, *t*
*Hint: The total number of letters in each word is shown in parentheses.*

**a** deo (5) ____________ **b** oodiae (10) ____________ **c** ei (8) ____________

**3** Select and rewrite the correctly spelt word based on context. *Hint: One word in each pair appears in the text.*

**a** Our seafood comes from the best local sources / sauces. ____________

**b** A fisherman chooses certain bait / baked to target certain fish. ____________

**c** It is a pleasure dripping / dipping a fresh prawn into creamy, zesty mayo. ____________

**d** Straw / star fruit is featured on the Yellowfin Restaurant menu. ____________

**4** Use slashes to separate list words in the letter chains below. Cross out any spare letters at the ends of chains.

**a** SOMORSELSAMPLELEISUREELS **b** MINPRECINCTRUSTICCATERINGSTICT

**c** BOUTIQUEDECORCOORDINATEERION

**d** PEPRESTIGIOUSCOMPLEMENTINGGRIGTIN

**5** Two words in each sentence below are spelt incorrectly. Find the words and rewrite them correctly on the lines. *Hint: Not all of the incorrectly spelt words are from the list.*

**a** Just as a botique clothing shop sells special clothes, a botique vineyard sells special wines. ____________ ____________

**b** We have ampol time to sit and enjoy a long lunchen. ____________ ____________

**c** The marinor precinct is a magnifizent seascape. ____________ ____________

**d** The décor in this esstablishment is extreamly ugly. ____________ ____________

**6** This passage, based on ideas in the text, contains some common spelling errors. Rewrite the entire passage on the lines provided. *Hint: If you are unsure of some words, you may find them in the list and/or the text.*

The appeel of a good seafood restraunt never go's out of date. Many patrens of a fine-dinning bisness like Yellowfin will keep comming year after year beccause seafood is offen hard to get or hard to preppare at home. People enjoi the conveniance of a skild cheff doing the hard work for them.

____________________________________________

____________________________________________

____________________________________________

____________________________________________

____________________________________________

# PERSUASIVE TEXT

## *Flyer*

## VOCABULARY WORK

Employing unique and **specialised words** in a persuasive text like a flyer can greatly enhance the text's authority and appeal. Some of the terms used in the flyer in the text 'Yellowfin Seafood Restaurant' are examples of specialised vocabulary. These terms can, however, be used in other contexts and still have the same meaning.

**1** The word 'seasonal' is an example of specialised vocabulary in the text. Write another two examples below. *Hints: There are many possible answers. Be careful not to give examples that are better described as jargon.*

______________________ ______________________

As you know, **jargon** is technical language that has a particular meaning in a particular field of expertise or special interest. One key to recognising jargon is remembering that words in this category can have different meanings in other contexts. For example, the term *body* has a distinct meaning in culinary jargon (technical terms used in the field of cooking). It relates to the texture or consistency of a mixture or a fluid. Other terms, like *casserole*, are peculiar to cooking and only have meaning there. Culinary jargon has been used in the text 'Yellowfin Seafood Restaurant'.

**2** Which of these words from the text are examples of culinary jargon? Write them on the line. *Hint: Some jargon can have different meanings in other contexts.*

aioli fresh seafood macerated jai fondant salsa verde panna cotta duo

______________________________________________

A boating **pun**—'at the helm'—is used in the text to introduce Yellowfin's manager, as though the restaurant is a kind of ship. Puns are very common in advertising. While often cheesy and irritating, they can be memorable.

**3** Show your understanding by completing puns using words from the list below. *Hint: Only three words will be used.*

seafood shells soft sea stuffed shut small stewed

**a** I was hit by a flying can of soda. Lucky it was a __________ drink.

**b** Teddy bears rarely eat at picnics because they're already __________.

**c** I'm on a __________ diet: I see food and eat it.

**4** Find a list word that means:

**a** bring elements together c__________

**b** small, tasty pieces of food __________

**c** plentiful a__________

**d** old-fashioned but charming r__________

**e** related to fine food c__________y

**f** matching or completing c__________

**g** a designated area p__________

**h** grape plantations __________

**5** Only one word in each pair below is a real word. Tick a box to show which one. *Hint: Most of these words appear in the text.*

**a** ☐ décorét ☐ décor

**b** ☐ picturesque ☐ pixaresque

**c** ☐ marinara ☐ marrinade

**d** ☐ plattar ☐ platter

**e** ☐ indimate ☐ intimidate

**f** ☐ yachting ☐ yachtfest

**g** ☐ cosmopolitan ☐ cosmicpolitan

**h** ☐ alioli ☐ alloy

# PERSUASIVE TEXT

## Flyer

GRAMMAR WORK

### Parts of speech

Depending on who you ask, you will be told that there are eight, nine or even ten different **parts of speech**. The most common number of classifications is nine.

- The main parts of speech in the English language are nouns, pronouns, articles, adjectives, verbs, adverbs, prepositions, conjunctions and interjections.
- Many words can be classed as more than one part of speech, depending on how they are used.
- Some countries use the term 'word classes' instead of the term 'parts of speech'. They mean the same thing.

**1** What is the role of a conjunction in a sentence? *Hint: If you know the meaning of the word 'junction', apply it.*

______________________________

**2** **a** How is a noun different from a pronoun?

______________________________

**b** Show your understanding by writing one or two short sentences featuring a noun and a matching pronoun.

______________________________

**3** Which three parts of speech can the word **cooking** fall into, depending on the context?

__________ __________ __________

**4** Identify the part of speech category that each of the list words below falls under. *Hints: Read the words in context. All of the list words are either nouns, verbs or adjectives. Some words may work as two parts of speech.*

**a** restaurant __________ **b** culinary __________

**c** prestigious __________ **d** complementing __________

**e** catering __________ **f** boutique __________

**g** leisure __________ **h** precinct __________

**i** rustic __________ **j** yachts __________

**k** ample __________ **l** décor __________

**m** coordinate __________ **n** morsels __________

**o** vineyards __________

**5** Change these list words into the part of speech shown in parentheses.

**a** décor (verb) __________ **b** yachts (verb) __________

**c** prestigious (noun) __________ **d** ample (adverb) __________

**e** rustic (adverb) __________ **f** complementing (adjective) __________

**6** Which nouns in the word list only appear in the flyer as proper nouns?

__________ __________ __________

# PERSUASIVE TEXT

## *Flyer*

**PUNCTUATION WORK**

### What mark is that?

How confident are you in identifying and using **punctuation marks**? If you struggle, there are a few steps you can take that are guaranteed to improve your knowledge and skill in this area:

- Read. This may sound a little too simple but it really works. Of course you must choose reading material that is correctly punctuated and you need to read a lot. Any text forms are fine, but texts with long, full sentences are best. Read widely and mindfully, taking note of how the different punctuation marks are guiding you.
- Go over all of your marked pieces of work and correct the punctuation errors if you can. If you can't, ask a teacher for help. You can also look up different punctuation marks online and see helpful examples of their use. Errors that your teacher has already corrected can be rewritten to cement your understanding.
- Check that you have punctuated your own writing correctly by asking someone else to read it. If your punctuation is correct, they will tell you that your writing is clear and that your sentences flow.
- Practise your skills in punctuation games and drills, online or in books like this one.

**1** What does it mean to 'read widely'? ____________________

____________________

**2** According to the third bullet point above, 'If your punctuation is correct … your writing is clear'. Why?

____________________

____________________

**3** Choosing from the box below, place the correct punctuation mark or symbol in each space to mirror how it has been used in the text 'Yellowfin Seafood Restaurant'.

| é | . | ... | ( ) | : | - | / | 💎 |
|---|---|---|---|---|---|---|---|

**a** newharb.com.au__yellowfin

**b** d__cor

**c** some morsels from our menu ____

**d** 6_5 (for baked ricotta)

**e** __seafood platters excluded__

**f** gluten__free

**g** Yell___wfin

**h** take advantage of this special offer__

**4** Try using some of the same marks and symbols from Question 3 in different words and phrases.
*Hint: All of the answers appear in the Question 3 list of symbols but not all of those symbols will be used here.*

**a** Let's meet at the caf__ for lunch.

**b** __but don't tell your mum__

**c** French fries__straw chips are extremely fattening.

**d** You'll need these supplies__

**e** Take your car__ we may want to leave the party early.

**5** Fix this unpunctuated sentence from the text by completely rewriting it with correct punctuation.

our port side setting presents diners with fabulous views of the newharbour marina precinct sparkling waters luxury yachts quirky tugs rustic fishing boats even the occasional dolphin

____________________

____________________

____________________

## Flyers

Since a **flyer** is a visual and written text, the opportunities to grab, impact and leave a lasting impression on readers are greater than those offered by other persuasive text forms. Here are some basic details about flyers.

- This text form is designed to advertise or inform. It is commonly used as a persuasive text format because it offers a compact and densely packed advertising format.
- A flyer is very similar to a brochure but it is much smaller. Usually a brochure is a folded piece of A4 or A5 paper, while a flyer is a single small sheet of A6 size. It is designed to be produced cheaply and handed out quickly.
- Often both the front and the reverse sides of a flyer are used by the writer in order to include the maximum amount of information.

**1** Think about some printed flyers you have seen, both persuasive and informative. Perhaps you have been handed one on the street or in a shopping centre. You have probably seen many in your letterbox (colloquially called 'junk mail'). Suggest some purposes of flyers by completing these sentences using topics of your choice.

**a** A flyer may advertise a business such as ______________________________.

**b** A flyer may promote a community event such as ______________________________.

**c** A flyer may be aimed at raising awareness about ______________________________.

**d** A flyer may be distributed at/around ______________________________ prior to an event such as ______________________________.

## Common features of persuasive flyers

The flyer is a specialised **persuasive** text form. Those who write flyers use a combination of text and visual features to grab and maintain the interest of target readers. The most common **structural features of a flyer** are:

- a banner or masthead, featuring a business or product name or other title
- small chunks of text, such as short paragraphs or bullet points
- a simple, clear layout
- subheadings or other visual text variations
- visual images that complement the text and appeal to readers' senses and emotions.

Look back over the text 'Yellowfin Seafood Restaurant' before answering these questions.

**2** Where would we find the banner or masthead of a flyer? ______________________________

**3** What are two structural features that have been used in the text? Name the features and refer specifically to how or where they are seen in the flyer. *Hint: Refer to the bullet points above for ideas.*

______________________________

______________________________

**4** Comment on the visual impact of the flyer (such as layout and pictures). Is it an effective piece of visual advertising? Is it ineffective? Perhaps you can see good and bad points. Give specific reasons for your opinion.

______________________________

______________________________

# PERSUASIVE TEXT

## *Flyer*

**WRITING WORK 2**

### Eye-catching feature of flyers

When printing a brand or company name in a text, particularly a brief, **attention-grabbing** text like a **flyer**, a composer can draw special attention to the name by using techniques such as these:

- adding a symbol or punctuation to the name (for example, 'Yell💎wfin Seafood Restaurant', *Yahoo!*)
- using incorrect, eye-catching spelling (for example, *Cheez Whiz, Froot Loops*)—this can have effects such as drawing attention to the sounds in words and imitating the shape of a product.
- omitting capital initials (as in *adidas*), moving a capital letter (as in *iPhone*), or writing the whole name in capital letters (as in *IKEA*)
- accompanying the name with a catchy slogan or mission statement (for example, *Nike: Just do it.*)
- presenting the name in the form of a logo (as Apple does) or directly beside one (as Qantas does).

**5** Let's extend the first bullet point. Have you noticed that performers—especially pop stars—often give themselves a brand name? Give two examples of performers with punctuation in their name.

______________________ ______________________

**6** What are some of the connotations (implied images, feelings or ideas) of the symbol in the adapted brand name 'Yell💎wfin Seafood Restaurant'?

______________________

### Language features of flyers

The **persuasive language** used in flyers is aimed at encouraging readers to buy a product. Features include:

- imagery that appeals to the five senses (for example, 'stunning waterside location', 'tempting array of dishes')
- romanticised diction; that is, words that add 'romance' to make things seem more appealing (for example, 'zesty salt tang' created by the sea and alluring food terms like 'rainbow salad')
- emotive language (for example, 'dynamic chefs', 'intimate dinner')
- sound devices including alliteration (for example, 'morsels from our menu')
- repetition (for example, the many references to the seascape outside Yellowfin Seafood Restaurant)
- second person address (for example, 'for you to explore at leisure').

Look back over the text 'Yellowfin Seafood Restaurant' before answering these questions.

**7** List some words or phrases from the text that romanticise the restaurant and/or the location.

______________________

**8** Give an example of tactile imagery (appealing to our sense of touch or skin sensations) from the text.

______________________

**9** Evaluate the language used in the text and its impact. Has language been used effectively to spark interest in the restaurant? Is it effective only in some places? Give specific reasons for your ideas, quoting from the flyer.

______________________

______________________

**10** Describe an additional image that would enhance the flyer's persuasive impact.

______________________

**WRITING SAMPLE**

Here is a sample text showing you how to structure and write a single-sided flyer.

## You'll Love Loch Ness

Famous not merely for its fabled and elusive monster of the deep, Loch Ness is one of Scotland's top tourist destinations. Och, aye! Come see why!

- ❖ The area is abundant with natural beauty and wildlife.
- ❖ The majestic loch (lake) itself is 24 miles long and over 750 feet deep, plenty big enough to hide Nessie all these years!
- ❖ Popular activities include castle tours, trail walking, golf, deer stalking and fishing.
- ❖ The Loch Lodge offers four-star accommodation with fantastic views of the loch from most suites.

**The Loch Lodge** is located in the village of Fort Augustus, right near Loch Ness. It's an ideal place to put your weary feet up after a hard day of monster spotting. Apart from stunning panoramic views, your room at the Loch Lodge offers a queen-sized bed, central heating, private bathroom with spa, television, internet access and 24-hour room service.

One highlight of the picturesque scenery is the ruins of **Urquhart Castle**, well worth a visit.

Other attractions around Loch Ness include the **Clansman Centre**, which records the fascinating history of Highland life, and the **Rare Breeds Croft**—home to a variety of rare and endangered birds and animals.

If our wee Nessie has indeed captured your imagination, you can get a little closer on a **Nessalot Fishing Tour** or even hire your own boat from **Loch Launches** for a better chance of photographing the beast … if you dare!

We'd love to see you at Loch Ness this summer.
Visit us online first, then get packing!

www.lochlodgelochness.uk

---

✸ **Make a banner that features a title appealing directly to the reader.** It does this by using second person address and informal language ('you'll'). The fancy typeface romanticises the location before we have even read any details.

✸ **Use an appropriate or stereotypical exclamation and an appeal to the reader that includes a technique to create a punchy lead-in.** Here a stereotypical Scottish exclamation ('och, aye!', meaning 'oh, yes!') and a rhyming appeal to the reader ('come see why!') combine to create a punchy lead-in to the flyer's details.

✸ **Write bullet points of information about the tourist destination you are advertising.** Bullet points of information are punctuated with tartan-like symbols instead of dots to evoke an image of Scotland.

✸ **Make the flyer's main purpose clear in a brief paragraph: to advertise a tourist destination.** This flyer's main purpose is to advertise accommodation: 'Loch Lodge'. Local attractions are briefly described, showing readers that there is more on offer at Loch Ness than monster-spotting.

✸ **Include at least one image of local scenery and attractions to attract potential tourists.** We see a doctored image of the Loch Ness Monster, which creates a sense of mystery, fun and fantasy in the flyer. In addition, local attractions are briefly described, showing readers that there is more on offer at Loch Ness than monster-spotting.

✸ **Use local vernacular to build on the tone.** We read 'our wee Nessie' (an affectionate term for the Loch Ness Monster) to build on the quaint and friendly tone of the flyer. Drama is created in this tiny extract by an ellipsis, the emotive word 'dare', second person address and an exclamation mark.

✸ **End the flyer with a personal invitation to the reader to visit the area and the added suggestion to go soon.** The flyer ends with a personal invitation to the reader to visit the area and the added suggestion that we go 'this summer'. This imposed timeframe is aimed at urging the reader to travel to Loch Ness and is reinforced by two travel-themed commands: 'Visit us online first' and 'get packing!'

✸ **Give a simple contact detail.** Only one contact detail is offered: a web address. The omission of other contact details has two effects: it prevents the reader from feeling pushed and it suggests that the website contains all the information they will need.

# PERSUASIVE TEXT

*Flyer*

## WRITING YOUR OWN SAMPLE

Plan your sample on the lines provided.

- **Make a banner that features a title appealing directly to the reader.** Use second person address and informal language (such as *you'll*) to do this. Choose a suitable typeface that sets the mood.
- **Use an appropriate or stereotypical exclamation and an appeal to the reader that includes a technique to create a punchy lead-in.**
- **Write bullet points of information about the tourist destination you are advertising.** Punctuate your points with suitable symbols instead of dots to evoke an image of the destination.
- **Make the flyer's main purpose clear in a brief paragraph: to advertise a tourist destination.**
- **Include at least one image of local scenery and attractions to attract potential tourists.** Briefly describe local attractions and show their names in bold type.
- **Use local vernacular to build on the tone.** Create some drama by using an ellipsis, an emotive word, second person address and an exclamation mark.
- **End the flyer with a personal invitation to the reader to visit the area and the added suggestion to go soon.** Reinforce this imposed timeframe by writing travel-themed commands.
- **Give a simple contact detail.** A web address is best. Omit other contact details to prevent the reader from feeling pushed and to suggest that the website contains all the information they will need.

# PERSUASIVE TEXT

## Article

**READING WORK**

## Street cred

*In a little corner of Queensland is a special sanctuary that has come to be affectionately known as Helen's Haven. But who is Helen, what is this place and why is it so urgently needed—in Queensland and all around Australia? Our society and culture editor, Catherine Carr, investigates.*

More than 100 000 people are currently homeless in this country. Many of us are aware of the statistics; aware of the problem. Some of us give it more than a passing thought. Only a few are willing to do something about it. One of these people is Helen Youngberry, Founder and Director of Goodna Street Life Helping Hands Centre in Goodna, Queensland.

Goodna Street Life Inc. (GSL) is a non-profit organisation providing meals, temporary housing, a drop-in respite centre and crisis care for those in need. It is close to a railway station, making it convenient for those without their own transport, and it is a drug- and alcohol-free environment. The practical needs that GSL meets on a daily basis include meals, shower, toilet and laundry facilities, clothing and bedding, and computer access for people seeking employment. Counselling is also on offer for those whose lives are in crisis.

One of the strengths of GSL is its independence. It is run entirely by volunteers and not affiliated with any other group, so no-strings-attached charity drives the whole operation. The downside of independence, however, is a lack of sizeable financial backing. Currently the funds required to maintain GSL's facilities and services are raised by various means: an on-site opportunity shop, monthly markets, public and corporate donations, and rental contributions from those using GSL accommodation for an extended period.

Helen was inspired to establish the charity while volunteering to feed Goodna's homeless on Friday nights over a period of two years. She recalls, 'I heard so many stories of people in need and found that there was often nowhere for homeless people—particularly men—to get help with basic everyday needs like meals and showers.'

Statistics from Homelessness Australia and the Salvation Army reflect Helen's observation that there are high numbers of men in their 30s and 40s in need. Further, those most at risk of poverty and homelessness in Australia are single men over the age of 65, Indigenous Australians and people from non-English-speaking backgrounds.

### Bringing the issue closer to home

Jim Carrey credits his family's homelessness with developing his sense of humour … although he didn't enjoy poverty at the time. Nobody does. Daniel Craig, Dr Phil, Jennifer Lopez and Chris Pratt were all homeless at one point. Some did their time on the streets or in parks; others slept in vehicles or on friends' couches. Mega-director James Cameron lived out of his car until he sold his *Terminator* script for one dollar. At least two Aussie stars were also both homeless in the past: Archie Roach, the much-admired Indigenous musician, and Hollywood actor Sam Worthington.

Of course the potential to become rich and famous does not make some people more deserving of charity than others! But these rags-to-riches cases might just prove to you that homelessness does not and should not define a person. It is a temporary situation; a temporary problem … *if* somebody else will step in and help. While some people do indeed choose homelessness, or prove difficult to help due to addictions and mental health issues, many, many more do not.

Helen says that her most rewarding experience in the brief history of GSL has been 'getting two men off the streets, off drugs, working and housed'. Intervention in the lives of the homeless often means far more than a simple meal or a hot shower: it can mean a new start and restored dignity for those struggling with poverty, unemployment, addictions or family troubles.

Helen wants to make a lasting difference by eradicating homelessness in her community entirely.

It's a big call but if anyone can make it happen, this tenacious, huge-hearted woman can. Will you help her?

If you would like to participate in this excellent cause or simply learn more about Goodna Street Life, queries and donations can be directed to:

**goodnastreetlife@gmail.com** **www.facebook.com/goodnastreetlife**

---

- This type of preamble, often used in an article, is called a **teaser**. This one asks three questions that will be answered in the article: 'who is Helen, what is this place and why is it so urgently needed…?' The teaser encourages us to read on.
- **Second person address** is used a few times in the article. For example, 'Many of us', 'Will you help her?' This is a common technique used in persuasive articles because it allows the writer to speak directly to readers and appeal to them.
- The name of the organisation being introduced in the article ('Goodna Street Life Inc.') is **abbreviated** ('GSL') to make the article's appearance neater and to make it easy to read.
- A list of **factual details** is provided to show the reader what GSL offers to people in need.
- The writer **sums up the motivation** of GSL's volunteers.
- This problem **foreshadows and justifies** the financial appeals that will be made at the end of the article.
- The main person who is the subject of the article, Helen, is **quoted directly** to give readers a sense of where she is coming from and what motivated her to establish a charity.
- References to **statistical data** are made to show that Helen has **authority to comment** on the issue of homelessness.
- The **subheading** 'Bringing the issue closer to home' is both a pun on the word 'home' and a hint about why these people are listed in the next paragraph, which is explained in the following paragraph.
- The writer now takes the text in a **different direction** and gives examples of famous people who were once homeless.
- There are lots of **rhetorical techniques** used persuasively by the writer in this single sentence: repetition ('temporary'), punctuation marks that create an earnest tone (; and …), italics ('if') and an indirect appeal to the conscience of the reader ('somebody').
- A **quote** from Helen returns the article to where it left off before the digression. This brief paragraph sets up the appeal to help Helen and GSL at the end of the text.
- **Colloquial language**, including a contraction ('it's') and an idiom ('a big call'), personalise the appeal being made here ('Will you help her?') and give it added impact.
- Like the question that precedes it, this **final line** is written in the second person to reach out to readers. It tells us how to contact GSL with a query or to donate funds.

# PERSUASIVE TEXT

*Article*

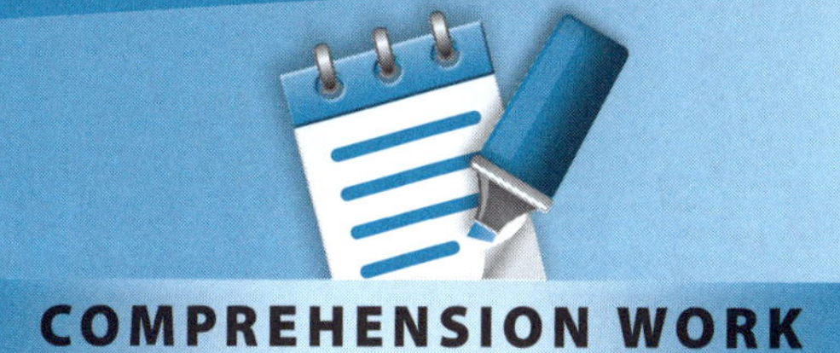

**COMPREHENSION WORK**

## Literal questions

*Hint: Read the text carefully to locate specific facts and details.*

**1** What statistic is presented in line 5?

**a** the estimated number of homeless people in Australia

**b** the estimated number of people who give statistics more than a passing thought

**c** the estimated number of people in Australia

**2** In which suburb is Helen's Haven located?

**a** Queensland **b** Goodna **c** a little corner

**3** What service is offered by GSL to people seeking employment? ____________________

## Interpretive questions

*Hint: These questions require you to combine facts and details to synthesise the meaning.*

**4** Why is GSL's independence both a positive and a negative thing?

____________________

**5** Why is it important that GSL is identified early in the article as a non-profit organisation?

____________________

**6** What do the statistics in lines 25–28 mainly demonstrate?

____________________

**7** What most clearly '[brings] the issue closer to home' in line 33?

**a** Two Aussie stars are mentioned. **b** Sleeping on couches is mentioned. **c** Living in cars is mentioned.

**8** What is the implied meaning of the made-up term 'mega-director', which is used to describe James Cameron?

____________________

**9** What is the intended effect of the structure of lines 50–52?

**a** to highlight the question **b** to highlight the contact details **c** both a and b

**10** In line 32 what does the idiom 'did their time' suggest about homelessness?

**a** It involves watching the clock. **b** It involves having a great time. **c** It can be like a prison sentence.

## Applied questions

*Hint: These questions require you to understand a text's implications to infer meaning from the text.*

**11** Complete the statement: The focus of the article keeps returning to Helen Youngberry because

**a** her achievements prove that ordinary people can make a difference.

**b** she was once homeless herself, so she understands the problem.

**c** her fame and wealth add some glamour and excitement to the cause.

**12** Why might Jim Carrey have developed his sense of humour through the experience of being homeless?

____________________

____________________

# PERSUASIVE TEXT
## Article

**SPELLING WORK**

### List Words

All of the words in the box below have been taken from the text 'Street cred'.

| | | | | |
|---|---|---|---|---|
| homelessness | on-site | charity | sanctuary | dignity |
| temporary | facilities | sizeable | opportunity | affiliated |
| independence | crisis | tenacious | eradicating | accommodation |

**1** Answer each question using list words. These questions test your knowledge of vowels and syllables.

**a** Which word uses the same vowel four times? ____________

**b** Which other word uses the vowel mentioned in Question 1a three times? ____________

**c** In which two-syllable word is a vowel used twice with different sounds? ____________

**d** Two four-syllable words sound more like three-syllable words when pronounced lazily. Which ones?

____________ ____________

**2** Unscramble these nonsense phrases and use the letters to spell list words.

**a** cant use oi ____________ **b** tiny dig ____________

**c** artery mop ____________ **d** a fetid fail ____________

**e** into yurt pop ____________ **f** ray itch ____________

**3** Can you spell other words in the families of list words? In the table make adjectives, verbs and adverbs from the list words shown. Leave the blank cells. *Hint: Some words will not need to change their form at all.*

| List word | Adjective | Verb | Adverb |
|---|---|---|---|
| accommodation | a | b | c |
| facilities | | d | |
| sizeable | | e | f |
| independence | g | | h |

**4** Correct the misspelt words in this passage by rewriting them on the lines beneath. *Hint: Not all of the words are from the word list.*

Currantly the funds required to maintan GSL's facillities and services are raised by verious means, incolluding an onsight opportunity shop and monthly markets. Interveention in the lifes of the homeless often means far more than a simple meil or a hot shower: it can mean a new start and restored diginty for those struggelling with povarty, unemployment, addictions or family troubles.

____________ ____________ ____________ ____________

____________ ____________ ____________ ____________

____________ ____________ ____________ ____________

**5** **a** How many of the fifteen list words end with a consonant? ____________

**b** How many list words begin with a vowel? ____________

# PERSUASIVE TEXT

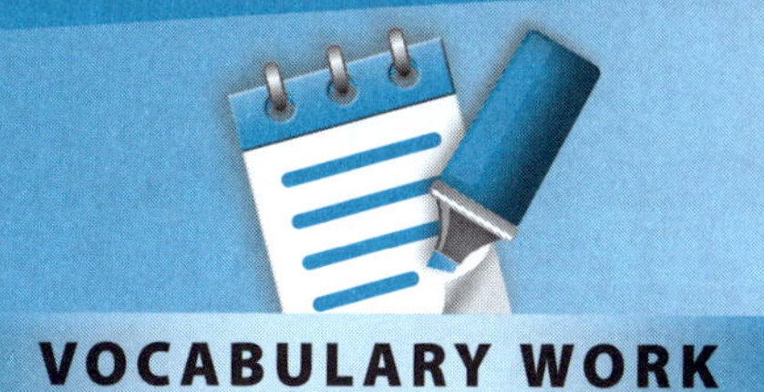

## VOCABULARY WORK

### Improving your vocabulary

When it comes to acing essays, creative writing, job interviews and many other challenges that require you to express yourself clearly, your **vocabulary** can be your best friend. No matter how extensive your vocabulary is right now, it can always be **improved**. One of the best ways to do this is by simply reading. When you come across an article like 'Street cred', don't put it aside because it seems too long and don't skim through it mindlessly. By reading it carefully you will not only be learning about an important social issue but you'll also be improving your vocabulary.

**1** Which list word can be used to complete each sentence? Select one.

| | |
|---|---|
| **a** Everyone wants to live with ____________________. | dignity / crisis |
| **b** Gaining ____________________ can be a scary but rewarding experience. | tenacious / independence |
| **c** Our ____________________ cater to the needs of people with nowhere to live. | on-site /facilities |
| **d** ____________________ poverty should be an aim held by every person. | charity / eradicating |

**2** Which words appear in the text 'Street cred'? Tick boxes to make your selections. *Hint: All of the words are real. Some may be homophones for words used in the article.*

| | | | | |
|---|---|---|---|---|
| ☐ intervention | ☐ crouch | ☐ couches | ☐ Australians | ☐ risk |
| ☐ frisk | ☐ particles | ☐ particularly | ☐ single | ☐ signal |
| ☐ razed | ☐ raised | ☐ faculties | ☐ facilities | ☐ corporate |

**3** All of these words appear in the text 'Street cred'. Define them in full (don't just give synonyms). *Hint: Since some words may have a range of meanings, your answers must be based on their use in the article.*

**a** markets ____________________

**b** needs ____________________

**c** Indigenous ____________________

**d** affiliated ____________________

**e** downside ____________________

**4** Which is real? One word in each pair is not a word at all. Tick boxes beside the real words from the article.

| | | | | | |
|---|---|---|---|---|---|
| **a** | ☐ musican | ☐ musician | **b** | ☐ rentoll | ☐ rental |
| **c** | ☐ humour | ☐ humer | **d** | ☐ voluntring | ☐ volunteering |
| **e** | ☐ define | ☐ definately | **f** | ☐ entirely | ☐ entyre |
| **g** | ☐ whele | ☐ while | **h** | ☐ contrabute | ☐ contributions |

**5** What is meant by these idioms from the text? Draw connecting lines to match the terms and meanings.

| | |
|---|---|
| **a** street cred | a very challenging task |
| **b** a big call | respect from everyday people |
| **c** rags-to-riches | once poor, now wealthy |
| **d** huge-hearted | served a sentence |
| **e** did their time | very generous |

# PERSUASIVE TEXT
## Article

GRAMMAR WORK

### Syntax

This key grammatical concept is concerned with how words are arranged in a sentence. In a persuasive article, **syntax** is shaped and varied to engage and influence the reader. Find out how by reading the points below.

- Adverbs can be used to open a sentence. For example, ***Obviously** this situation needs to change.* In the text 'Street cred', the phrase 'Of course' is used with the same effect.
- Impact words can be used to close a sentence. For example, 'those whose lives are in **crisis**'.
- Sentences can be truncated (cut short) for impact. For example, 'Nobody does'.
- The present and future tenses can be used selectively to convey a vision. For example, 'Helen wants to make a lasting difference by eradicating homelessness'.

**1** Which of these words is an adverb? Circle it. obviously this situation needs

**2** Find two impact words in the text 'Street cred' (apart from 'crisis') and write them on the lines.
*Hints: Impact words can also be emotive words. They do not need to be placed at the end of a sentence.*

______________________ ______________________

**3** What other features of a sentence can have a big impact? Suggest three.

________________ ________________ ________________

**4** Reorder the words in these sentences to make them identical to sentences in the text 'Street cred'.
*Hint: You will need to add the necessary punctuation marks in each case.*

**a** strengths of one of its independence the GSL is

______________________________________________

**b** few only it to do are willing a something about

______________________________________________

**c** can anyone big call but if make it happen can this it's a tenacious woman huge-hearted

______________________________________________

______________________________________________

**d** of the potential course to become rich some people does not deserving make more of charity and famous than others ______________________________________________

______________________________________________

**5** Change these words into adjectives. *Hint: They all come from the text 'Street cred'.*

**a** volunteering ________________ **b** risk ________________

**c** poverty ________________ **d** entirely ________________

**e** need ________________ **f** funds ________________

# PERSUASIVE TEXT

## Article

**PUNCTUATION WORK**

### Why is punctuation so important?

No doubt you have come across memes and grammar jokes at school that try to persuade you to use correct **punctuation** (*Let's eat Grandma!* versus *Let's eat, Grandma!*, for example). But how much do you know about the ways in which punctuation can persuade? Read the notes below to refresh your knowledge—or to gain some.

- Correctly punctuated sentences flow better than poorly punctuated ones. Flowing, well-expressed sentences are important in persuasive writing because their ideas can be clearly understood by the reader.
- Punctuation marks—especially those in the 'impact' category, such as exclamation marks (!), interrobangs (?!) and ellipses (…)—can transform a phrase or sentence from being bland and lifeless to grabbing the reader's attention, setting a challenge or finishing a point with a bang.
- Pauses such as the semicolon (;) can suggest that you as a writer are sensible and thoughtful, and therefore justified in your opinion and message.
- As you know from using emojis and other symbols in electronic communications, messages can be interpreted in many ways—often unintended or offensive ones. When writing a persuasive article, which can evoke strong responses simply due to the issue being addressed, it is vital that you convey your intended meaning clearly so as to keep the reader on side and open to your message.

**1** One function of a semicolon is to create a pause. How else can it function in a sentence?

______

**2** **a** Which 'impact' mark named in the second bullet point does **not** appear in the text 'Street cred'? ______

**b** Suggest a reason for this. ______

______

**3** Using the symbols in the box below, write the correct symbols for these punctuation marks on the lines provided. *Hints: Some answers are given in the bullet points in the box above. Some symbols in the box below will not be used.*

; , — … ( ) ' - _ # ?! ! : /

| | | | | |
|---|---|---|---|---|
| **a** semicolon ___ | **b** colon ___ | **c** ellipsis ___ | **d** slash ___ | **e** dash ___ |
| **f** apostrophe ___ | **g** full stop ___ | **h** parentheses ___ | **i** interrobang ___ | **j** comma ___ |

**4** Which of the punctuation marks in Question 3 do you find confusing or difficult to use in your own writing? Give both the name and the symbol of the mark or marks.

______

**5** Comment on the persuasive impact of punctuation in this sentence from the text 'Street cred':

'It is a temporary situation; a temporary problem … *if* somebody else will step in and help.'

______

**6** This sentence (adapted from the text) has been incorrectly punctuated. Rewrite it correctly.

these rags/to/riches case's might prove to … you that Homelessness does not, define a person

______

______

# PERSUASIVE TEXT

## *Article*

**WRITING WORK 1**

**Persuasive texts** can come in many forms and have many purposes. These can include advertising a product, making a complaint or a protest, seeking votes or promoting a lifestyle. In the case of the text 'Street cred', the writer is aiming to persuade readers to get involved with a charity, Goodna Street Life, and others like it.

### Main features of persuasive articles

**Persuasive articles** can be identified by their common features, some of which are listed below.

- Factual information is presented in a detailed and credible manner.
- Statistics, quotes and other sources back up the writer's points with authority.
- Emotive language and other persuasive language techniques (see the notes on page 118)

**1** What is a feature of the text 'Street cred' not mentioned above? *Hint: Re-read the annotations on the text.*

______________________________________________

**2** Circle the words that are synonyms for the word *persuading*:

urging     influencing     criticising     convincing     overviewing

### Structural features of persuasive articles

Here are some **structural features** used effectively by composers of this type of text.

- Paragraphs: These basic units of structure address one main topic or idea each, making the article easy to follow. This is the same approach taken in an essay.
- Subheadings: These dividers offer an article a change of direction, as we see in the text 'Street cred' ('Bringing the issue closer to home'). They also break up the material, making the article easier to read, and can emphasise or point to the key purpose or message of the text.
- Pull-quotes: See the notes below.
- Teasers: See the notes on page 118, as these are also language features.

### Pull-quotes

- A **pull-quote** is a small extract that has literally been pulled from a larger text and displayed in a prominent place in the text, such as the centre, or in a text box.
- Like all quotes, a pull-quote can be edited to become smaller or easier to read. This can be done without indicating changes to the reader, but the best pull-quotes will show changes, using ellipses or brackets.
- The impact of a pull-quote can be enhanced by presenting it in a different (and usually larger) typeface to the rest of the article.

**3** The pull-quote below has been taken from the text 'Street cred'. It would be effective in a printed or e-zine version of the article. Why is this pull-quote an effective one? Give a detailed answer.

'... homelessness does not and should not define a person. It is a temporary situation; a temporary problem ... *if* somebody else will step in and help.'

______________________________________________

______________________________________________

**4** Suggest another appropriate pull-quote from the article that is much shorter than the one in Question 3 and give a reason for your choice.

______________________________________________

______________________________________________

# PERSUASIVE TEXT
## *Article*

**WRITING WORK 2**

### Teasers

As mentioned in the notes to the text, these features fall into two categories: structural and language. **Teasers** are:

* pieces of promotional text at the beginning of an article that are designed to attract readers
* composed in a way that will 'tease' potential readers
* phrased as either a brief summary, an intriguing question and/or a cryptic or eye-catching comment, often containing popular or topical proper nouns and terms drawn from subjects that are trending online or used as clickbait
* intentionally lacking in detail so that readers will want to read on to find out more.

**5** Re-read the teaser from the text 'Street cred', then circle *True* or *False* for each statement that follows.

In a little corner of Queensland is a special sanctuary that has come to be affectionately known as Helen's Haven. But who is Helen, what is this place and why is it so urgently needed—in Queensland and all around Australia? Our society and culture editor, Catherine Carr, investigates.

| | | | |
|---|---|---|---|
| **a** | The first six words echo the storytelling cliché *Once upon a time.* | True | False |
| **b** | The phrase 'special sanctuary' contains alliteration. | True | False |
| **c** | The first name of the writer of this article is Helen. | True | False |
| **d** | The issue of homelessness falls under the category of society and culture. | True | False |

### Persuasive language techniques

These techniques are common to many kinds of **persuasive texts**, including advertisements and speeches. There are many stylistic devices in this category. Here are four:

* repetition of key words and ideas; for example, 'It is a temporary situation; a temporary problem …'
* selective use of the second person to appeal directly to the reader; for example, 'these rags-to-riches cases might just prove to you that homelessness does not and should not define a person'
* verbs that express opinions; for example, 'Helen was inspired …'
* questions that challenge the reader; for example, 'Will you help?'

**6** Explain what the second and fourth bullet points in the box above have in common.

______________________________________________

**7** Complete statements about the language features of the text 'Street cred'. Unscramble the letters in parentheses and insert the words correctly. *Hint: Re-reading the annotations on the article will be helpful.*

**a** The article has been written in __________ __________ to show that the issue is relevant now.(stenper enset)

**b** The use of ______________ from a key person adds to the credibility of the information. (squeto)

**c** The writer uses emotive language to speak about the issue of ________________. (sleemsohsens)

**d** __________ __________ address helps persuade readers to get involved in charity. (donces snerpo)

**e** Rather than describing only actions, the ________ in the article describe opinions and attitudes. (resvb)

**f** A ______________ is directed to the reader at the end of the article as a personal challenge. (squotein)

# PERSUASIVE TEXT

*Article*

WRITING SAMPLE

Here is a sample text showing you how to structure and write a persuasive article.

## Reconciliation: what's been and what's next

✱ **Write a title that specifies the issue and divides the content into two categories.** Two categories here are past and future.

*Mabo, National Reconciliation Week, Sorry Day, a Prime Ministerial apology ... What is the next step in building reconciliation between Indigenous and non-Indigenous Australians?*

✱ **Write a teaser that functions as a long subheading.** Like the teaser used in the text 'Street cred', this one asks a key question.

We all know that the issue of reconciliation in Australia is a vital one with regard to improving people's lives but not everyone considers that the issue can improve life for *all* Australians, not just First Australians. This is because reconciliation between Australia's Indigenous and non-Indigenous populations is crucial for our progress as a whole nation.

✱ **Write a first paragraph that introduces the issue using indefinite pronouns and inclusive diction.** Indefinite pronouns 'everyone' and inclusive diction 'our progress' are used here. The effect of these words is to involve readers and encourage them to play a part in reconciliation. Italics persuasively emphasise key words (for example, '*all*') and create a sincere, urgent tone.

### A bleak history

At the time of the Anglo-Europeans' arrival, Australia was occupied by many different Indigenous groups. In the beginning, these people and their custodianship over the land were completely disregarded by the invaders, who took land and resources as if Australia was completely uninhabited. After some time, the consciences of people in authority caused them to make some changes to the ownership issue. The Anglo-Europeans believed that the Indigenous people of Australia were British subjects by conquest, and granted them the use of portions of land. Governor Arthur Phillip tried to implement a policy of compensating Aboriginal people for the taking of their lands, but there were problems regarding ownership. Bitter scenes of slaughter ensued, and many Indigenous people became the victims of cruelty and injustice.

✱ **Write a title for the first main section that reflects the type of information that will be presented in the section.** As its title states, the first main section presents historical information about the issue. The historical information is expressed in a detailed and authoritative manner. For example, a key historical figure, 'Governor Arthur Phillip', is named, and his actions are explained. Emotive language, such as 'Bitter scenes of slaughter', helps the writer make a persuasive impact early in the article. It also reinforces the fact that this issue has 'a bleak history'.

The British government was incredibly ignorant in their dealings with the new colony. The racial attitudes of the time placed the white man above all other nationalities. The white supremacy concept was applied to Chinese and Aboriginal people alike, making only one distinction among all races—white and non-white. Astoundingly, this notion persisted in official dealings with all non-white immigrants until the abolition of the White Australia Policy in 1974.

✱ **Include strong adverbs to convey your thoughts and emotions about aspects of the issue.** Strong adverbs convey the writer's shock and disgust at aspects of the highly racist history of Australia and its leaders. For example, 'incredibly ignorant'; 'astoundingly, this notion persisted'. Specific facts and dates regarding government policy add to the article's authority.

### A brighter future?

Western Australia's Minister for Aboriginal Affairs, Joanne Hodges, says, 'The response of the people of Australia to the reconciliation challenge will test their commitment to the ideals of true democracy.' Hodges gave an influential speech at the Western Australia Reconciliation Forum in 2008. Eight years on, she is concerned that saying 'Sorry' has made everything all right in the minds of a lot of Australians. 'Contrary to what many people think,' says Hodges, 'the disadvantaging of Indigenous Australians continues in our society today, affecting their basic human rights, education, employment, housing, health and governance.' A truly fair society cannot become a reality while such injustices persist—and they do persist.

✱ **Write a second subheading to change the direction of the article.** It is phrased as a question, which suggests the unresolved nature of the issue and invites the reader to get involved in improving the situation.

✱ **Incorporate an interview into the article.** The interviewee is a person with authority to speak on the subject. She is quoted directly. The writer closes this paragraph by reinforcing what the interviewee has said, paraphrasing and extending her point.

The government has taken small steps toward reconciliation by acknowledging and apologising for the gross misdeeds of the past, but Hodges argues that this is only due to international pressure. We are seeing some other positive advances, however, including the recent election of Linda Burney to the House of Representatives. She is the first Indigenous woman to hold this Parliamentary position. Joanne Hodges describes the milestone as 'Exciting and refreshing. Let's hope,' she continues, 'that within this generation, as we grow into an increasingly multicultural nation, we will see Australia become a more unified land, determined to provide equal opportunities and justice for all its citizens—real opportunities—not just in speeches and on paper.'

✱ **In the final paragraph, sum up the current situation regarding the issue and look optimistically—but cautiously—to the future.** Inclusive language, such as 'We are seeing some other positive advances', also create optimism and make readers feel included in the solution. The expert interviewee is quoted once more and the article closes in a memorable manner because she has the last word.

Plan your sample on the lines provided.

- **Write a title that specifies the issue and divides the content into two categories.**
- **Write a teaser that functions as a long subheading.** Ask at least one key question here.
- **Write a first paragraph that introduces the issue using indefinite pronouns and inclusive diction.** Involve your readers and encourage them to play a part in resolving the issue. Use italics to persuasively emphasise key words and create a sincere, urgent tone.
- **Write a title for the first main section that reflects the type of information that will be presented in the section.** Present historical information and express it in a detailed and authoritative manner. Use emotive language to give your writing persuasive impact early in the article and reinforce the subheading.
- **Include strong adverbs to convey your thoughts and emotions about aspects of the issue.** Provide specific facts and dates regarding the issue to add to the article's authority.
- **Write a second subheading to change the direction of the article.** Phrase it as a question, to suggest the unresolved nature of the issue and to invite the reader to get involved in improving the situation.
- **Incorporate an interview into the article.** The interviewee must be a person with authority to speak on the subject. Quote this person directly. Close this paragraph by paraphrasing and reinforcing what the interviewee has said.
- **In the final paragraph, sum up the current situation regarding the issue and look optimistically—but cautiously—to the future.** Use inclusive language to create optimism and make readers feel included in the solution. Quote the expert interviewee once more, giving that person the last word.

# TIPS FOR THE SAMPLE TESTS

STUDY TIPS

## Know what to expect

- Find out from your teacher what knowledge and skills will be assessed in the sample test.
- Find out what format is being used for the sample test.

## Revise and rehearse

- Revise the relevant knowledge and skills.
- Write some practice analysis paragraphs about sample texts.

## Read carefully

- Read all instructions on the test paper.
- Note the mark allocations. These indicate how much you should write and how much time you should spend on each answer.
- Read the questions before the texts, so that when reading the texts, you know what to look for.

## Make your answers count

- Use handwriting that is clear (not too large, too small or too cursive).
- Use all of the answer spaces provided.
- Be specific in your answers and don't use padding or repetition to make them look longer.

## Re-read and check

- Once you have completed a response, re-read it to make sure it actually answers the question. This will only take a few seconds.
- Edit quickly and clearly. If you need to, make corrections using single cross-out lines (not scribbles).

## Manage your time

- Write legibly but quickly.
- Ensure you are working through the test efficiently and not spending too much time on each question, or you may not finish the test.
- If you finish early, don't waste the leftover time. Spend that time checking, editing and possibly extending your answers.

## Be ready

- Always study English actively. This means using a pen and paper to make notes. It also involves recording grammar rules, language features and definitions of difficult terms.
- If you have prepared thoroughly for the test, you do not need to be nervous. Tests are not designed to trap you, but to give you an opportunity to show how much you know.

## Part A Reading and comprehension

Read the following texts and answer the questions that follow on page 125.

### Text 1: Informative text—News article

**Danes prove clean energy is no fairytale**

The Danish rural region of Thy—particularly its capital, Thisted—produces clean energy from entirely renewable natural sources, and it's not a new venture. They've been quietly doing this for the past thirty years. The region has implemented a proven model for communities across the globe who are seeking local, workable solutions to their energy problems.

Thy hit two milestones in 2007, achieving selection for Denmark's first official National Park and winning the European Solar Prize for its renewable energy accomplishments. The region is a worthy winner: the capital Thisted produces 100 per cent of its electricity by clean, renewable means and meets more than 80 per cent of its heating needs with renewables also. Because of its position on the windy North Sea, wind power helps serve the needs of the region instead of coal and oil. But wind power is not the only resource that has enabled Denmark's best and brightest to switch from fossil fuels to clean energy.

*Wind farm*

Thisted's biogas plants use two common waste products that everyone wants to get rid of: straw (leftover stalks and stubble from grain crops) and household garbage. This rubbish is collected from farms and residential areas and used to fire power plants. Massive reductions in electricity bills are delivered, with most customers' energy costs slashed by two thirds.

Even more climate-conscious cleverness is on the way for the region. With a recent proposal designed to reduce carbon dioxide emissions from school buses, Thy goes to the top of the class. A bold plan is being developed to stagger school opening times so that the same bus can be used to transport all students in fewer loads. Not content to rest on its climate-saving laurels, Thy is continuing to look for new sustainable resources, with operations under way in solar power, wind energy, garbage recycling, agricultural and forestry waste, tidal energy and geothermal (underground) heat.

Most admirably of all, Thy's governors are keeping energy solutions local. On accepting the European Solar Prize, Mayor Erik Hove Olesen said: 'I am very proud and grateful that we today receive this award. Not we as authorities claim the honour. Our 46 000 citizens [and] … 1700 local companies made the change … They have together made Thy self-sufficient with energy.' This region is living out an object lesson, proving that entirely clean energy is a real and achievable goal for all communities.

Thanks to Hans Christian Andersen, Denmark has long been famous for its fairytales. Thanks to a Tasmanian named Mary, it is also loved by Australians for its royal family. Now the nation has re-established itself on the map for even more important and impactful reasons. The great Danes are showing the world how working together and using good old common sense can bring clean, green power to the people.

## Part A Reading and comprehension

### Text 2: Narrative text—Monologue

**A real nightmare**

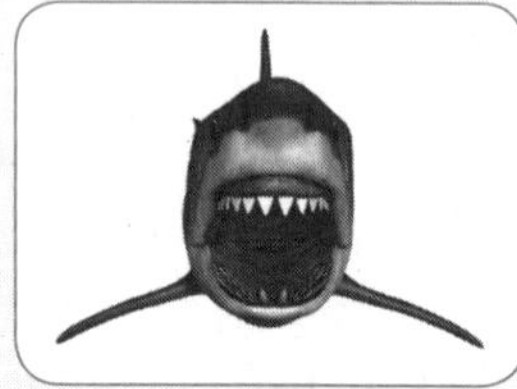

I'm dreaming. I dream that I'm standing on the beach watching the water. It's a glorious, baking February Saturday: very bright, very warm … the sea is sparklingly inviting. As I stand there, I can feel my thongs throbbing with the blazing heat of the sand … *(Looks around at eye level)* What's that? I spot a smooth grey fin breaking through a wave. There's another, and another! *(Excitedly)* There's a pod of dolphins playing in the surf. They're so close, right there in the white water!

I quickly strip off to my swimmers and run right in. I start striding out toward the dolphins, hoping my splashy swimming won't scare them away. I want to try to touch one, if I can. Crazy thought, right, but they are really that close. I stop swimming and lift my head to get my bearings … there's a fin—less than a metre away. With a sick feeling, the realisation hits: this isn't a dolphin.

*Transition: the actor quickly moves to a sitting/half-reclining position as the dream comes to an end.*

I wake up in a tangle of sweaty sheets and fumble for the light switch beside my bed. Relief breaks over me like a cool wave as I regain consciousness from my nightmare. I'm safe in my room; safe from the water, the white water, the weapon-like teeth.

*(Reaches for phone and checks it)* 4.40. Always the same. It's just so bizarre. Every single time I have this dream, I wake up at 4.40 am on the dot.

How long does the dream last in real time: a minute? A few seconds? Maybe it begins and ends at 4:40. Anyway, it seems like time stops when I'm inside it.

Once I'm back in the waking world, I always have to face the same horror. Always takes a good couple of minutes until I remember. Usually it's when I feel a phantom itch or when the cat jumps on the empty lower third of my bed and my body doesn't move.

My legs are gone.

Unfortunately this is no ordinary recurring dream: it's a memory. After three massive strikes from a Great White just off Bolsin Beach, a pod of dolphins sheltered me as I somehow dragged myself to shore. I needed nearly a hundred stitches around my abdomen alone … dozens more across my chest. I've had four bone shard removal surgeries on my wrist and hand, and who knows how many hundreds of hours of physical therapy.

Three years, seven months, two days. When will I stop reliving the day I was nearly killed by a shark?

## Part A Reading and comprehension

### Text 3: Persuasive text—Online review

### Book review

*Jane Eyre* by Charlotte Brontë

First published in 16 October 1847
First published by Smith, Elder & Co., London
Author's pen name: Currer Bell
Genres: bildungsroman, Victorian romance
Available through: Penguin Books

It seems unfair to me but this novel gets a lot of negative reviews from students. Have these haters actually read the book cover to cover? I can understand that it's quite a doorstop but so is *Harry Potter and the Order of the Phoenix.* I can also appreciate that the antique nature of the scenario and some of the language can be barriers, but come on: for 1847 it's very readable. And there's something about the Victorian era that makes a classic romance even headier. Keep a dictionary—electronic or paper (antique!)—handy. If you don't speak French, parts of the Adèle dialogues might confound you but you have heard of Google Translate, right? If you really must you can skip her scenes entirely, but that's just lazy.

**Two good reasons why it's the goods**

There are so many reasons to persevere with this novel, but I'll give you the top two. First it's quite simply a brilliant story. It abounds in complex relationships, tension twists, mystery and, of course, romance. Second it's crafted by a master. The sophistication of the characterisation, description, conflict, motif, allusions—if you don't know what some of these things are, you might need to listen a little harder in English classes—of all those technical and stylistic features of a literary gem are on display.

**A practically perfect plot (spoiler-free summary)**

Let's return to that magnificent plot. I'll break it down a little to whet your appetite and I'll avoid spoiling it for you (the plot, not your appetite):

- The eponymous heroine (and first person narrator) Jane Eyre is an orphan. She's also plain (i.e. not pretty). I wouldn't have mentioned it but Brontë does, repeatedly, so it's important. When still a baby, orphan Jane is taken in by a kind uncle. In true *Snow White* style the dear man dies and his wife is left to raise Jane along with her own children. This woman's picture should appear in the dictionary next to 'wicked stepmother'. She hates Jane. Her children hate Jane. It seems, at this point, the universe hates Jane. The hatred springs from the fact that the uncle adored Jane and favoured her over his children. So Jane, who was already off to a difficult start in life, suffers badly in this home and later at a boarding school, where there is prejudice against her thanks to good ol' Step-Ma.
- In young adulthood, Jane takes on a job as governess in the employ of the brooding, inscrutable—and often absent—Mr Rochester. Jane tutors and mentors little Adèle, with whom she becomes very close, and things take a big turn for the better. Inevitably love grows between Rochester and our heroine, but OF COURSE something has to spoil it. Rochester has a dark and dangerous secret lurking in his very house (it is a very large house though). I'll say no more: it would ruin all the rollicking, romantic Victorian fun.

You probably have an inkling by now that I ADORE *Jane Eyre.* But please recognise that it hasn't been called a classic for nearly two centuries for nothing. I'm not defending the novel. There's no need. Just read it. ☆☆☆☆☆

# SAMPLE TESTS

## PAPER 1

## Part A Reading and comprehension

Answer the following questions:

### Text 1

1 What is the main reason for the Thy region's successful use of wind for energy production? (1 mark)

2 From the information given in the text, define the term 'biogas'. (1 mark)

3 What language technique is employed in the phrase 'great Danes' in the last paragraph of the text? (1 mark)

### Text 2

4 Which four-word line serves as the climax of the monologue, and why? (1 mark)

5 Why is '4.40' repeated? Give at least one reason. (1 mark)

6 What highly appropriate simile describes the speaker's feelings as the nightmare comes to an end? (1 mark)

### Text 3

7 Why are some of the words and phrases in this text underlined? (1 mark)

8 Why might Charlotte Brontë have used a pen name (Currer Bell)? (1 mark)

9 From its use in context, what is meant by the colloquial, size-related term 'doorstop'? (1 mark)

Your Score

/ 9

# SAMPLE TESTS

## PAPER 1

## Part B Language conventions

Answer the following questions:

### Text 1

1 What is the effect of the alliterative phrase 'climate-conscious cleverness' in the fourth paragraph? In your answer you should also comment on the writer's use of the same sound nearby. (2 marks)

### Text 2

2 a What are two clues given just prior to the speaker's revelation, 'My legs are gone'? (2 marks)

b Why has the composer done this?

### Text 3

3 In the section entitled 'Two good reasons why it's the goods', how does the final sentence explain itself? (2 marks)

Your Score

/ 6

## Part C Comparing texts

Answer the following questions:

1 Text 1 and Text 3 are essentially both reviews and both celebrate an achievement, but the texts have very different purposes. Explain. (2 marks)

2 Texts 1 and 3 both refer to fairytales, but for different purposes. What are they? (2 marks)

3 Each text has a unique structure. Comment on each structure below. (4 marks)

a Briefly describe how each text is ordered.

Text 1: ____________________

Text 2: ____________________

Text 3: ____________________

b Which structure do you find the least effective, based on the text's purpose and audience? Why?

____________________

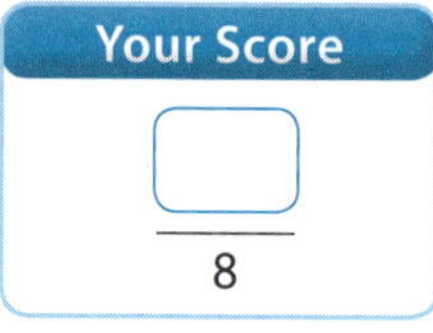


## Part D Themes and meaning

Write a paragraph response to the question in the space provided. Use the number of lines and the allocated marks as a guide to the length of your answer.

1 Choose one of the three texts (1, 2 or 3) and write a paragraph about one or more themes explored by its composer. In your answer refer closely to the text by using brief quotes, paraphrasing, or both. (7 marks)

____________________

____________________

____________________

____________________

____________________

____________________

____________________

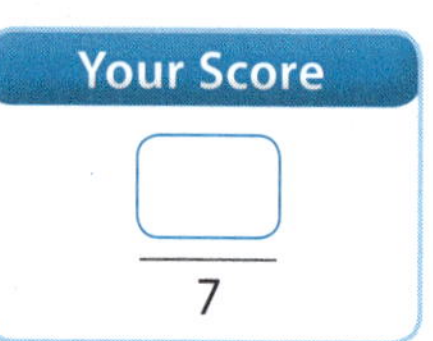


Your Feedback

Part A + Part B + Part C + Part D = 30 = %

## Part A Reading and comprehension

Read the following texts and answer the questions that follow on page 131.

### Text 1: Informative text—Autobiography excerpt

**About time: an ordinary person's autobiography**

The rituals practised in my family seem pretty ordinary at first glance but with a closer look, I guess they're a bit odd. Take Christmas, for example. For us, it's the biggie. I read somewhere that Christmas is the only time of the year when it's acceptable to sit around with other people and eat snacks out of your socks. Yep, strange. What's stranger is that, every year, our Christmas celebrations are virtually identical, despite the fact that we don't enjoy some of them at all! Certain things simply must occur, and in a certain order, or, I don't know … the world might end.

First there's the frenzied and stressful Christmas shopping period, when my parents consistently deny that they intend to buy presents. It's an old gag, but don't they just love it. We all try to spend less each year and find gifts that may actually be of some use but somehow we manage to send ourselves broke on a pile of pointless paraphernalia each time.

Next is the Great Turkey Debate, where my mother asks the family to consider eating 'something different this year', to which our response is always the same: absolute outrage. We refuse to change the tradition of chowing down on a dried-up, tasteless piece of poultry, charred veggies and cloudy gravy, and promptly order the fattest behemoth parrot we can find.

On Christmas Eve, we endure a televised Carols by Candlelight hosted by some TV personality that we love to hate and watch absently while we do some serious snacking to prime our bodies for the following day's overeating. Most of the carol performances are drowned out by our loud criticism of song arrangements, vocal ability, camera work, celebrities' outfits, length of Santa's beard, etc., etc., but we insist on sitting there and whining our way through this apparently unwatchable production until midnight, when we stagger off to bed.

Christmas Day always starts early and, barring a quick cup of tea, presents simply must be opened first. It's also a compulsory ritual between me and my sister to give each other a pair of very loud, preferably very ugly socks and to helpfully label the wrapped package with 'Here are your socks'. A late breakfast is next and it must involve croissants. Then everyone plays with their new toys (yes, we all get them).

Later that day, once we've sufficiently stuffed ourselves on our substandard hot turkey dinner in the blazing heat of summer there's a brief opportunity to have 'outsiders' over, make polite conversation and palm off any presents that can be sneakily regifted. The departure of these visitors is always followed by a celebratory nap before we consume a bizarre casserole of leftovers, drink tepid, flat fruit punch and crack open any surviving choccies. This latter portion of the day is also an ideal time for a good old family argument. That's usually a thing.

Maybe one day we'll come up with some new Christmas rituals that make more sense, are more enjoyable and promote better health but until Santa personally shows up and tells us to do so, I guess we'll stick with the ones we've got.

## Part A Reading and comprehension

### Text 2: Narrative text—Prose fiction

**Inner vistas**

'Has she had her physio today?'

'No. That's Thursday mornings. Not today.'

'Oh, really—it's down to once a week now?' I can hear the frustration in her voice.

'Yes … there's been no improvement at all, so Doctor thought it best.'

'Oh, "Doctor thought it best". I see. Sounds like they're giving up on us, Lizzie. But we're not giving up, baby. I'm not; you're not. I know you're still with us. You come back, you hear me? I'll wait for you. As long as it takes.'

I hear you, Mamma—lean down closer to me. That's it. Just hearing your voice helps me fight the panic. Keeps me hoping that you really believe I'm still in here. If I could just touch you … but I … mustn't try to move. Mustn't try, or I'll lose it. I'll go over the edge and into that black pit and I don't know if I'll get out next time. Count down to calm, Lizzie: 5, 4, 3, 2 … 1. That's better. See? You're coming out of this. You're gonna make it. You can make them see you're still here.

'Cuppa, Marian?'

Ah, no … The panic is on its way again ... 5-4-3-2-1. 5, 4, 3, 2, 1. 5, 4, 3, 2 … 1. Stay calm. Focus your energy. I'm strong. My mind can overcome this body. Come on. Mamma believes in you. She knows you're fighting.

'No, thanks. I'm heading off for a bit of a walk.'

Meaning you're going off for a secret smoke, right Mamma? When are you going to come clean and admit you're doing it again? I can hear you getting up. Must be one of those vinyl seats: it's making that squeaking noise. See you later then, Mamma. Don't be long. I can't be here on my own for long. Too scared. I'll think about something else till you get back.

* * *

Ughh, so tired …

Someone's here.

Hey—I know you're there, whoever you are. You're a hospital type, judging by those quiet footsteps and that jingling of keys or ID tags. I wonder what you look like, Mister? Ah—you're that new male nurse, aren't you? Nick always wears that Lynx spray too. You sound like a tall guy. Like my driving instructor. How can I get your attention? If I can just … hey! HEY! I think I did it! I think I moved my finger! HEY, MISTER! LOOK AT MY FINGER! MISTER, PLEASE! LOOOOOOOK!

'What was that? She moved! She's awake! Get somebody—quick! Lizzie's awake!

## Part A Reading and comprehension

### Text 3: Persuasive text—Article

### Reconciliation: what's been and what's next

Mabo, National Reconciliation Week, Sorry Day, a Prime Ministerial apology ... What is the next step in building reconciliation between Indigenous and non-Indigenous Australians?

We all know that the issue of reconciliation in Australia is a vital one with regard to improving people's lives but not everyone considers that the issue can improve life for *all* Australians, not just First Australians. This is because reconciliation between Australia's Indigenous and non-Indigenous populations is crucial for our progress as a whole nation.

### A bleak history

At the time of the Anglo-Europeans' arrival, Australia was occupied by many different Indigenous groups. In the beginning, these people and their custodianship over the land were completely disregarded by the invaders, who took land and resources as if Australia was completely uninhabited. After some time, the consciences of people in authority caused them to make some changes to the ownership issue. The Anglo-Europeans believed that the Indigenous people of Australia were British subjects by conquest, and granted them the use of portions of land. Governor Arthur Phillip tried to implement a policy of compensating Aboriginal people for the taking of their lands, but there were problems regarding ownership. Bitter scenes of slaughter ensued, and many Indigenous people became the victims of cruelty and injustice.

The British government was incredibly ignorant in their dealings with the new colony. The racial attitudes of the time placed the white man above all other nationalities. The white supremacy concept was applied to Chinese and Aboriginal people alike, making only one distinction among all races—white and non-white. Astoundingly, this notion persisted in official dealings with all non-white immigrants until the abolition of the White Australia Policy in 1974.

### A brighter future?

Western Australia's Minister for Aboriginal Affairs, Joanne Hodges, says, 'The response of the people of Australia to the reconciliation challenge will test their commitment to the ideals of true democracy.' Hodges gave an influential speech at the Western Australia Reconciliation Forum in 2008. Eight years on, she is concerned that saying 'Sorry' has made everything all right in the minds of a lot of Australians. 'Contrary to what many people think,' says Hodges, 'the disadvantaging of Indigenous Australians continues in our society today, affecting their basic human rights, education, employment, housing, health and governance.' A truly fair society cannot become a reality while such injustices persist—and they do persist.

The government has taken small steps toward reconciliation by acknowledging and apologising for the gross misdeeds of the past, but Hodges argues that this is only due to international pressure. We are seeing some other positive advances, however, including the recent election of Linda Burney to the House of Representatives. She is the first Indigenous woman to hold this Parliamentary position. Joanne Hodges describes the milestone as 'Exciting and refreshing. Let's hope,' she continues, 'that within this generation, as we grow into an increasingly multicultural nation, we will see Australia become a more unified land, determined to provide equal opportunities and justice for all its citizens—real opportunities—not just in speeches and on paper.'

# SAMPLE TESTS

## PAPER 2

### Part A Reading and comprehension

Answer the following questions:

#### Text 1

**1** What does the composer mean by the figurative expression 'the fattest behemoth parrot'? (1 mark)

______________________________

**2** What thirteen-letter word beginning with *c* describes the time structure in this text? (1 mark)

______________________________

**3** 'Christmas is the only time of the year when it's acceptable to sit around with other people and eat snacks out of your socks.' This sentence is written in the ________________ person. (1 mark)

______________________________

#### Text 2

**4** What is indicated by the three asterisks (* * *) in this text? (1 mark)

______________________________

**5** Of the five senses, what is the main one used by the narrator to describe the action? Why? (1 mark)

______________________________

**6** Did you notice that a driving instructor is mentioned in the narrative? Six other characters are involved in this text. Some are named, while others (like the driving instructor) are only referred to. Who are they? (1 mark)

________________ ________________ ________________

________________ ________________ ________________

#### Text 3

**7** According to Joanne Hodges in the final paragraph, what has happened 'only due to international pressure'? (1 mark)

______________________________

**8** What is meant by the prefix 'Anglo'? (1 mark)

______________________________

**9** In the text, no real answer is given to the introductory question, 'What is the next step in building reconciliation between Indigenous and non-Indigenous Australians?' Why has it been asked? (1 mark)

______________________________

Your Score

/ 9

# SAMPLE TESTS

PAPER 2

## Part B Language conventions

Answer the following questions:

### Text 1

1 Some highly colloquial idioms are used by the composer in this text. For example, 'chowing down' and 'palm off'. Find two idioms in the second paragraph and give their meaning. (2 marks)

a Idiom 1: ______________________

Meaning: ______________________

b Idiom 2: ______________________

Meaning: ______________________

### Text 2

2 Different rhythms are created in several ways in the text. What are two? Be specific in your answer. (2 marks)

______________________

______________________

### Text 3

3 What is the purpose of the second subheading in the text 'A brighter future?'? (2 marks)

______________________

______________________

Your Score

/ 6

## Part C Comparing texts

Answer the following questions:

Use the number of lines and the allocated marks as a guide to the length of your answer.

1 We know that one purpose of Text 1 is to inform and one purpose of Text 2 is to imagine. What is another purpose of each text? (2 marks)

Text 1: ______________________

Text 2: ______________________

2 Each of the three texts is about conflict. Text 1 is about conflict within one family. Identify the types of conflict in the other two texts. (2 marks)

Text 1: ______________________

Text 3: ______________________

**3** **a** What type of person seems to be targeted by the composer of Text 1? Give evidence. (2 marks)

**b** The target audience of Text 3 is a very wide one. Why? (2 marks)

Your Score ___ / 8

## Part D Themes and meaning

Write a paragraph response to the question in the space provided. Use the number of lines and the allocated marks as a guide to the length of your answer.

**1** All three texts explore personal and public problems. Choose one of the three texts (1, 2 or 3) and write a paragraph about the specific ways in which at least one problem is explored in the text. Avoid repeating ideas from any previous answers. (7 marks)

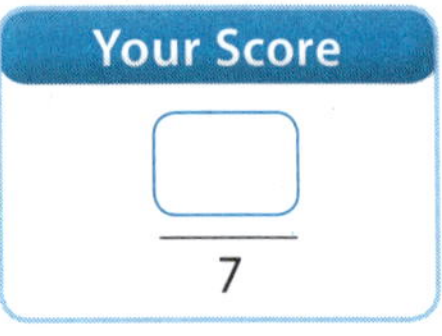


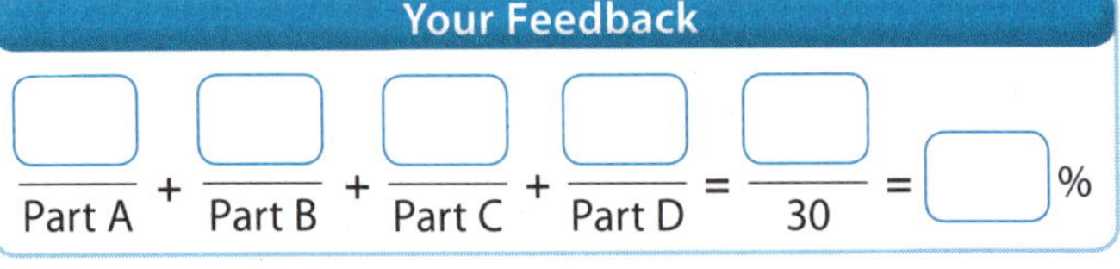

# ANSWERS

## UNIT 1: INFORMATIVE TEXT—NEWS ARTICLE

INFORMATIVE TEXT
### Comprehension Work page 3

**1** **b** This is a **literal** question. In the context of the first paragraph, the word 'conditions' refers to weather, including an extreme heatwave and a lack of rain. We read words such as 'heatwave', 'rainless', 'temperatures' and 'degrees'. All of these words are directly related to the topic of weather. Some of them can also relate to climate but Answer **c** is incorrect because climate is about the general or usual environmental conditions of an area, not specific ones like those mentioned in this paragraph. Answer **a** is incorrect because, in this context, the verb 'moisturises' is irrelevant.

**2** 'With the power of 1500 atomic bombs—enough energy to last Victoria for a year.'
This is a **literal** question. Find line 32 in column 1, locate the phrase 'hurricane of flames', then transcribe the analogy (comparison) given in the line. You could also use the text's annotations as a guide.

**3** 173
This is a **literal** question. We read the keywords from the question: 'the highest number of deaths by bushfire in Australia's history' *(lines 4–7, column 3)*. Immediately after this we read a number: 'A hundred and seventy-three'. The hint is a reminder to look for a number in the text so you answer through a process of eliminating all other numbers in the same paragraph.

**4** The line is used as a caption for the image.
This is an **interpretive** question that may be answered as though it is a literal one. It is interpretive, however, because it relies on knowledge about captions. It is also interpretive if answered from a different angle, as the hint suggests. You could have answered that the line has the purpose of creating drama and evoking emotion, for instance. The most correct answers of this kind also contain a reference to the line as a caption.

**5** Casey Mills is an expert witness because she was both present at the fires and involved in fighting them. As a member of the CFA, Mills is an expert on the subject of this text.
This is an **interpretive** question that requires piecing together information in the annotation (as the hint shows) with the words spoken by Mills.

**6** **a** This is an **interpretive** question. To answer it go directly to the second paragraph, which was specified in the question. You search for the phrase 'particularly lethal' and then knock out the groups of words in Answers **b** and **c** by a process of elimination. In Answer **b** 'vast' refers to the 'desert centre of Australia', not to the wind, and 'drier' is a comparative that makes no sense in the context of the sentence. 'Eternal' doesn't work either. In Answer **c** 'passed' and 'across' make no sense as a continuation of the sentence begun in the question.

**7** **b** This is an **interpretive** question. Focus on the phrase 'natural occurrence' to answer the question. In the first paragraph the natural occurrence of a severe heatwave is named as a main contributing factor to the fires *(lines 8–10, column 1)*. Answer **a** is incorrect for two reasons: it is not a 'natural occurrence' and, as the text states, arson has not been confirmed. Answer **c** is incorrect because it makes no sense as a 'natural occurrence' or in any other way as an answer to the question because it is a figurative phrase.

**8** **c** This **interpretive** question centres on the phrase 'simply unimaginable and undefeatable'. We read this phrase in the text in reference to the 'hurricane of flames' *(line 32, column1)*, which, when combined with the analogy of Answer **b**, 'the atomic bombs', is another way to say 'the power of the flames'. This means that Answer **b** on its own is incorrect. Answer **a** is also related to this answer, but incorrect on its own, as the winds are mentioned at the end of the paragraph, not near the key phrase 'simply unimaginable and undefeatable'.

**9** **b** This is an **interpretive** question. It partly relies on knowledge of the metaphor 'a string of', which refers to connectedness or items in a line. We read in the question that we must go to lines 14–15 in column 3. In that context, with the towns named, the meaning of 'string' in the context becomes more clear. As we read, Answer **c** is easily eliminated because the fact that the towns were picturesque has nothing to do with the other keywords in the question: 'a string of'. Answer **a** is incorrect because this phrase means either 'spread far apart' or 'nervous or stressed'.

**10** Possible answers: solemn, serious, sobering, thought-provoking, grim
This is an **interpretive** question. Skim-read the whole text again and apply your knowledge of tone (the 'voice' of the writer in the text that helps create a mood) then come up with an adjective or adjectival phrase to capture the tone.

**11** **a** This is an **applied** question. Carefully read the whole question then draw a conclusion based on your understanding of the text. The hint only provided a definition; it was not the key to answering the question. The fact that investigators are 'at pains to tell the public that arson has not yet been confirmed' strongly suggests that Answer **a** is

# ANSWERS



correct. Answer **b** is incorrect because it makes no sense with reference to the quote in the question. Answer **c** is incorrect because it is irrelevant.

**12** Suggested answer: There are a number of pieces of evidence in the text for this message, including the opening of the final paragraph (where something 'even more tragic' than the fires is mentioned), the final line, which overtly states the message, and the paraphrased opinion of Casey Mills, the expert witness.
This is an **applied** question. Skim the text again and draw a conclusion based on the ideas being repeatedly emphasised by the writer. Reading the final paragraph's annotation would also help immensely.

## INFORMATIVE TEXT
## Spelling Work
page 4

**1** **a** inferno **b** volunteer **c** picturesque **d** compulsory

**2** **a** weird **b** initial **c** compulsory **d** inferno

**3** **a** ~~SYK~~SKYROCKETED/INITIAL/ARSON~~ICO~~
**b** ~~MWIND~~WEIRD/INFERNO/POTENTIALLY~~ALOT~~
**c** ~~UN~~TRAGIC/COMMISSION/AUTHORITY~~N~~
**d** ~~E~~DELIBERATELY/KILOMETRES/PICTURESQUE~~UE~~

**4** a, o, i

**5** **a** a, i **b** u, o **c** o, e

**6** **a** indescribable, inferno, initial, increasingly, investigators, investigations, including
**b** commission, compulsory

## INFORMATIVE TEXT
## Vocabulary Work
page 5

**1** **a** cruel **b** deliberately **c** tragic **d** weird **e** skyrocketed **f** picturesque

**2** **a** False **b** True **c** True **d** False

**3** **a** kind **b** employee **c** ordinary

**4** **a** thousand **b** not **c** on **d** hot fire

**5** **a** could not believe my eyes
**b** put the pedal to the metal **c** a host **d** surreal

## INFORMATIVE TEXT
## Grammar Work
page 6

**1** hyphenated, closed, open

**2** grandmother, ice-cream, triple-chocolate

**3** **a** township **b** treetops **c** understatement **d** skyrocketed **e** fireballs **f** firestorm **g** bushland **h** heatwave

**4** **a** truly **b** Sometimes

**5** Adverbs: late, nearly, daily. Adjectives: tasty, green, frightening.

**6** impossibly, exceptionally, completely, forever, roughly, particularly, literally, quickly

## INFORMATIVE TEXT
## Punctuation Work
page 7

**1** **a** o **b** i or ha **c** i or ha **d** ha **e** wi **f** ha or woul

**2** **a** can't **b** It's **c** We'd **d** You're **e** You've, you've **f** would've, we'd **g** couldn't, it's

**3** The correct forms are provided in parentheses:
**a** Thered (There'd); crime's (crimes)
**b** welcome (Welcome); Teacher (teacher)
**c** hav'ent (haven't); ARIAs but (ARIAs, but)
**d** costing—us (costing us); fortune? (fortune!)
**e** well all go (we'll all go)

**4** If you live anywhere near bushland, even in a built-up area, bushfires pose a very real threat to your home and your family. Be aware of your bushfire risk, wherever you live. Also, before you can properly protect your property, you'll need to prepare a survival plan.

**5** The information presented in so-called factual news stories is often sensationalised. It's unfortunate that news is tainted by exaggeration and unnecessary drama. Many journalists should be more careful with their words.

## INFORMATIVE TEXT
## Writing Work
page 8

**1** Suggested answer: An alternative image that would be appropriate in this news article is a graphic or weather map from the Bureau of Meteorology showing the areas affected by the fire.

**2** In the news article 'Black Saturday', most of the **lead** section is an interview that provides **evidence** from a **witness** who was there. This part of the report adds **detail** to the main facts of the lead section, and the **statistics** (numbers) provided act as a transition into the **tail** section.

**3** The writer wants to urge the community to work towards improving bushfire safety.

4 Bias means favouring one side of an issue or debate over another, based on personal opinion or prejudice.

5 While Casey Mills's opinion about fire safety is given, it is not a case of biased reporting for two reasons: she was present at the fires and is qualified to recount events; and the writer's own opinion about fire safety issues is not stated.

6 Suggested answers and set answers:
- **a** Suggests that the article is authoritative and the writer can be trusted.
- **b** adjectives
- **c** Provides vivid descriptive detail to help the reader visualise and understand the event.
- **d** impossibly, increasingly, exceptionally
- **e** These bring the text to life with additional descriptive detail. They have a powerful impact on the reader.
- **f** More than 2030 houses and 3500 other structures have been destroyed … half a million square kilometres of land, an area roughly the size of Spain.
- **g** interview, expert witness, Casey Mills's first person recount
- **h** analogy
- **i** personification
- **j** Stronger words than 'fire' are needed to describe the terrible blaze, especially because 'fire' is repeated throughout the article.
- **k** metaphor

## UNIT 2: INFORMATIVE TEXT—INTERVIEW

INFORMATIVE TEXT

### Comprehension Work

page 13

1 **a** This is a **literal** question. Use a process of elimination after locating the three possible answers in the interview. Answer **b** is incorrect because Courtney's point is that malaria is still a major problem around the world, unlike polio, which is 'nearly eradicated'. Answer **c** is incorrect because 'the '80s' refers to a decade in history, which can't be eradicated.

2 outside her/your/one's comfort zone
This is a **literal** question. 'The fourth paragraph' is stated as the place where the answer can be found so you begin there. Finding the key phrase from the question, 'where the magic happens' *(line 40)*, points you to the answer. The phrase 'outside my comfort zone' is correct. Although it is not compulsory to paraphrase, a better answer would be paraphrased slightly, as shown in the answer options above separated by slashes.

3 ten
This is a **literal** question. We read 'So far I have gone to ten different countries because of Rotaract' *(line 39)*. You simply skim-read the interview, looking for the keyword 'countries' to find the answer.

4 Answers could include any four of the following events: she helped start a Rotaract club; she travelled to Serbia and neighbouring countries; she met with international Rotaract clubs; she attended a Conference in Hobart; she ran an Australian trip and participated in the Rotaract Games.
This is an **interpretive** question based on a key phrase ('head-spinningly busy'). As the hint suggests, you need to begin with that phrase. You are not required to use any particular wording in your answer.

5 **b** This is an **interpretive** question. It requires you to find the section of the interview that refers to how Rotaract and Rotary International are connected *(lines 7–8)*. To find this, look back at the questions. The first question names 'Rotary International'. Answer **a** is incorrect because it is the opposite of what the interview says. Answer **c** is incorrect because we also read that 'Inner Wheel is for women only' *(line 11)*.

6 false
This is an **interpretive** question. We read in the introduction that Courtney is 'a citizen of the world' *(line 3)*, but this is not a literal statement. It is an expression that refers to a person who has travelled and seen a lot of the world. You need to understand or make an educated guess at the meaning of this expression. Alternatively you could rely on or deduce the definition of 'dual citizenship', which simply means 'two citizenships'. If Courtney had two citizenships, one in Australia, what would the second country be, since she is a citizen of the whole world? This would help you eliminate 'true'.

7 **c** This is an **interpretive** question. We read all four of the factors influencing Courtney to join the RYE Program *(lines 15–21)*. You only need to make tiny changes to the information in this paragraph to get the answer (such as removing 'HSC Beginners' from the phrase 'studying French'). Answers **a** and **b** alone are incorrect because all four factors mentioned in those options were involved in Courtney's decision.

8 **b** This is an **interpretive** question. Find the key phrase 'That is awesome' in the text. Then find what project is 'awesome'. The answer is obviously contained in the previous paragraph *(line 43)*. Then note that the abbreviation 'RAM' stands for 'Rotaractors Against Malaria', so they are the same

# ANSWERS

thing. This helps you eliminate Answers **a** and **c**. Answer **a** is also incorrect because 'Rotaractors' are people not a 'project'. Answer **c** is also not a 'project': it is the disease that the RAM project is fighting.

**9** **c** This is an **interpretive** question. We read only one answer option, Answer **c**, in the interview *(lines 27–28)* so the key to answering this question is to find this option in the text. Looking for the key phrase 'French people' leads you there. Answer **a** is incorrect because Courtney already knew this. Answer **b** is incorrect because it is not mentioned in the interview. While it may be true, there is not enough evidence to suggest that it is true, nor that Courtney learnt this 'since joining Interact'.

**10** Sample answer: This word suggests that the young people belong to Rotaract (and Rotary); and that they 'act'—that is, they work hard, make a difference and accomplish things.
This is an **interpretive** question. Look for two ideas which suggest the qualities and attributes of the 'Rotoractors'.

**11** **c** This is an **applied** question. The key to answering it is the fact that it is an informative text not a persuasive one. From reading the interview we gather that the interviewer and interviewee share the aim of telling readers about the great and exciting things Rotaractors do. This is a way to 'celebrate Rotaract'. While it may be an aim of both people in the question to 'recruit RAM workers' to fight malaria, this is not suggested from reading the article so Answer **a** is incorrect. Answer **b** is incorrect because polio is 'nearly eradicated' already.

**12** Sample answer: The two main ways in which Rotaractors embrace the world is through charity, which is a kind of symbolic embrace (or hug) and through travel, which is a way to embrace (or experience) the world.
This is an **applied** question. The two-part answer relies on knowledge of the various meanings of the word 'embrace', which you need to apply after reading the article.

## INFORMATIVE TEXT
## Spelling Work page 14

**1** global, organisation, genuinely, disease, sanitation, eradicated, fulfilling, lifelong

**2** **a** Montenegro **b** Serbia **c** Algeria **d** Great Britain

**3** **a** exchange **b** global **c** language **d** combat

**4** **a** globally **b** diseased **c** life **d** combatant

**5** **a** languages **b** organisations **c** mosquitoes **d** diseases

**6** **a** battle **b** worldwide **c** erased **d** swap **e** hygiene

## INFORMATIVE TEXT
## Vocabulary Work page 15

**1** Sample answers:
**a** an imaginary creature or contagious disease that infects a person with a desire to travel
**b** an imaginary place where a person feels safe and comfortable; a place he or she is unlikely to want to leave
**c** cause me to run out of money

**2** from scratch, where the magic happens, stay in touch, follow their dreams, like crazy

**3** **a** I had **b** is not **c** it is **d** you will **e** I will **f** we are

**4** **a** essentially **b** non-profit **c** sanitation

**5** ALGERIA, MONTENEGRO, CROATIA, DENMARK, FINLAND

## INFORMATIVE TEXT
## Grammar Work page 16

**1** **a** bettering **b** giving **c** starting **d** helping **e** wanting **f** working **g** gaining **h** continuing **i** returning **j** trying **k** doing **l** spending

**2** **a** german shepherd, alsatian
**b** movie world, dad
**c** rotary international, third world

**3** **a** Finnish, French, Australian
**b** IRAQI, BRITISH, LEBANESE, ITALIAN

**4** **a** Rotaract Youth Exchange
**b** Rotary Youth Leadership Awards
**c** Higher School Certificate
**d** Rotaractors Against Malaria

## INFORMATIVE TEXT
## Punctuation Work page 17

**1** **c**, **e**, **f**

**2** period, ellipsis, quotation mark

**3** In the past decade, it's become common for students finishing school to opt for a 'gap year' overseas.

Young people enjoy the exposure to the world, the independence, the new friendships, the chance to earn money and, of course, just the adventure of it all! There are benefits of an overseas working holiday but are they outweighed by the risks?

**4** **a** non-profit **b** semi-retired **c** lifelong **d** no-one **e** overseas **f** prevention/resolution **g** head-spinningly **h** fundraiser

**5** **a** its **b** itself **c** it's **d** it's

INFORMATIVE TEXT
## Writing Work
page 18

**1** Sample answer: A closed question is one that requires only a yes or no answer.

**2** short questions, long answers, interesting subject, factual information, structure

**3** Sample answers: **a** a music star, giving information about his or her career and possibly some insights into his or her private life. **b** a remote country or little-understood culture. **c** multiple sclerosis, and share the stories of some people dealing with the disease. **d** a national Olympic or Paralympic Team, including achievements of individual athletes.

**4** **a** Possible answers include: incredible, love it one day, hate it the next, warm (people), follow their dreams, amazing, empower
**b** They should visit one or both of the websites listed at the end of the interview.
**c** Sample answer: a magazine or e-zine aimed at students who go to school and/or university, either a particular institution's magazine or a publication with a wider audience

**5** Correct order of numbers: 6, 7, 8, 2, 1, 3, 5, 4

**6** **a** Rotaractor **b** exchange **c** malaria **d** club **e** president **f** overseas

**7** Sample answers:
**a** formal and factual **b** frustrated and/or amused **c** honest and candid

## UNIT 3: INFORMATIVE TEXT—AUTOTBIOGRAPHY

INFORMATIVE TEXT
## Comprehension Work
page 23

**1** 'Greyhounds'
This is a **literal** question. We read in the first line that the writer's crew 'affectionately called' the ships by this nickname.

**2** 11 000
This is a **literal** question. We read in the ship's 'stats' that its range (that is, the distance it is able to travel without running out of fuel) is '6000 nautical miles (11 000 kilometres) at 18 knots (33 km/h)' *(line 15)*. To answer the question, note the link between the speed and the distance. If you are unfamiliar with the term 'knots', you would still recognise that it is a speed-related term because of the '33 km/h' that follows. You do not need to know the meaning of the term 'range', although this would make answering a little easier.

**3** **a** This is a **literal** question. We read about the 'roles' of these ships in 'combat' and 'warfare' situations. These three words in quotation marks from the question are the keys to answering the question. Locate them in the first paragraph *(lines 9–11)*, then eliminate Answers **b**, **c** and **d**. The keywords from Answer **a** are both given as examples of combat in which these ships have roles. Answers **b** and **d** are incorrect because 'surveillance' and 'reconnaissance' are not direct combat (fighting) roles. Answer **c** is incorrect because 'defence' is a general term that can be used in place of the word 'combat' in the text; it is not a 'type' of combat mentioned in the text.

**4** **a** This is a **literal** question. We read that 'Sea Sparrow missiles and torpedoes' can be launched from one of these ships *(line 19)*. This means that Answer **a** is correct and that Answer **b** is incorrect, because the missiles are called Sea Sparrows—they are not two separate items. Answers **c** and **d** are both incorrect because, while helicopters can be said to 'launch' from the deck of a ship, they are not 'weapons' in the same sense as a missile or torpedo. To get the right answer, read the relevant sentence in the text literally and look for a matching option in the question.

**5** **b** This is an **interpretive** question. Look for 'two fuels' in the 'propulsion' section of the 'stats'. The only two that are fuels in the context of the stats are 'gas' and 'diesel'. Answer **a** is incorrect because 'electricity' is not a fuel mentioned in the text. You may be misled by the diesel engine's maker's name, 'General Electric'. Answer **c** is incorrect because, while 'water' is what the ship moves on and what the propellers move, it is not a 'fuel' for the ship. Answer **d** is incorrect because 'water' and 'electricity' can both be eliminated for the same reasons.

**6** Either quote or paraphrase from this passage: 'Excitingly, they are also in the process of being upgraded with what is arguably the world's best naval defence system for small warships: CEAFAR.

This largely Australian-invented radar and response system decisively proved itself in a recent test off the coast of Hawaii, when the HMAS Perth used CEAFAR to obliterate a US Coyote sea-skimming missile moving at nearly three times the speed of sound.'
This is an **interpretive** question. Follow the key term 'super-ships' to line 25. The most important term in the passage to mention is the acronym 'CEAFAR', which is the name of the 'naval defence system' that is 'arguably the world's best'.

7 **b** This is an **interpretive** question. The keywords in the question are 'enormous cloud of metallic dust', 'line 34' and 'actions'. Once you put these elements together and look in the relevant section, you are able to eliminate Answer **a** because of the nonsense term 'rapidly successful', Answer **c** because 'reflexes' don't describe any actual 'actions' and Answer **d** because 'close-in weapons' are not 'actions'. This leaves Answer **b**, which describes the action of rapidly flicking the four switches, as described in the text.

8 **d** This is an **interpretive** question that involves straightforward elimination. To answer, note that Answers **a** and **b** each include words or phrases that are not 'adjectives', as required by the question, so you can immediately eliminate them. Answer **c** is incorrect because, while 'boiled' can be used as an adjective in some situations, it is not being used as one in this passage, but instead as a verb. Also, the word 'fast', as used in this context, does not indicate that the 'ship is close to sinking'. These eliminations leave Answer **d** as the correct answer, which you can cross-check against the passage.

9 **b** This is an **interpretive** question that tests your vocabulary and understanding of a word's use in context. If you read the word 'minutely' incorrectly, and pronounce 'minute' not as 'my-newt' (tiny) but as 'min-nit' (sixty seconds), you may misinterpret this term as relating to time and incorrectly select Answer **a** or **c**. Answer **d** is incorrect because it is the opposite of 'minutely'. Answer **b** is the only synonym for 'minutely' out of the options supplied.

10 He hears 'five sharp beeps'.
This is an **interpretive** question. The additional words 'a series of' from the text are optional additions to the quote. You are required to interpret the 'five beeps' as representing 'five stars', in reference to the mission. Making a connection between the words 'reassuring', 'welcomed' and 'confirmed' with these 'five beeps' and the 'five-star' result, which all appear in the same sentence *(lines 45–46)*, helps you answer this question correctly.

11 Sample answer: The writer is intimidated by his commanding officer. He wants to impress her and is too proud to celebrate his victory in the combat simulator, so he acts cool and asks 'What's for lunch?'
This is an **applied** question. You are required to draw conclusions about the way the writer stands, moves, gestures, thinks and speaks in order to answer it. Also note his thoughts about how 'intimidating' his commanding officer is and how that relates to his behaviour in front of her.

12 Any three of: stance (the 'jelly legs' of the writer and 'the intimidating presence of [the] commanding officer'); gesture (salute); speech ('Ma'am', 'What's for lunch?'); and facial expression (the commanding officer's 'flicker of a smile').
This is an **applied** question. While the question does not specify that you must give examples of each mode (such as 'Ma'am'), your answer would be enhanced greatly by them. In a similar way to Question 11, you are required to apply your understanding of the writer's attitude towards the CO to the various ways in which he communicates with her. In the fullest possible answer, your examples would be taken from both the writer's behaviour (such as his 'jelly legs' stance) *and* the CO's behaviour (such as her 'flicker of a smile' expression).

INFORMATIVE TEXT
## Spelling Work
page 24

1 **a** surveillance **b** simulator **c** starboard **d** propulsion

2 **a** military **b** surveillance **c** propellers **d** frigate **e** metallic **f** arguably

3 **a** frigate **b** sensors **c** simulator **d** toughest **e** metallic **f** torpedoes

4 **a** propelled **b** sensed **c** torpedoed **d** succeeded **e** argued **f** simulated

INFORMATIVE TEXT
## Vocabulary Work
page 25

1 **a** military **b** surveillance **c** nemesis **d** simulator, toughest

2 **a** simulation **b** strike **c** argument **d** toughness **e** metal **f** sense or sensation

3 **a** watched **b** doomed

4 **a** statistics; numbers, figures or data
**b** when I say
**c** 5.05 pm; five past five in the afternoon

# ANSWERS

**5** Completed puzzle:

| | | | | | | | | | | |
|---|---|---|---|---|---|---|---|---|---|---|
| W | A | R | S | H | I | P | H | M | A | S |
| O | R | U | W | C | K | R | A | M | N | T |
| R | S | A | I | K | E | C | O | M | S | A |
| R | L | O | N | G | R | A | N | G | E | R |
| A | I | O | G | Z | L | Y | F | E | N | B |
| P | T | T | A | A | A | N | V | A | D | O |
| S | R | B | B | U | N | C | D | A | R | A |
| D | N | U | O | H | Y | E | R | G | N | R |
| R | A | N | U | W | S | L | O | W | E | D |
| E | E | E | T | O | Y | O | C | E | D | P |

Catchphrase: run silent and run deep

INFORMATIVE TEXT
## Grammar Work
page 26

**1** **a** My beloved Greyhounds were being upgraded to super-ships! OR My beloved Greyhounds were upgraded to super-ships! OR My beloved Greyhounds have been upgraded to super-ships!
**b** I watch, horrified, as a vertically launched warhead goes streaking … OR I am watching, horrified, as a vertically launched warhead goes streaking …
**c** I know I will have to act fast.

**2** **a** Connectives are crossed out (answers may vary slightly): The missile closed in, ~~still~~ appearing to have us locked in its sights. ~~But then~~ it swung to a minutely different course, slowed for a moment, ~~then~~ acquired a new target—the metallic dust cloud—~~because~~ it was larger than our ship. The explosion rocked the frigate like a toy boat in a washing machine. But she held steady.
**b** Nouns are underlined; adjectives are circled: The missile closed in, still appearing to have us locked in its sights. But then it swung to a minutely different course, slowed for a moment, then acquired a new target—the metallic dust cloud—because it was larger than our ship. The explosion rocked the frigate like a toy boat in a washing machine. But she held steady.

**3** Sample answers: and, as

**4** **a** came **b** wondered or considered
**c** inhaled **d** frowned or scowled
**e** stared **f** released
**g** staying or sitting **h** loosen

INFORMATIVE TEXT
## Punctuation Work
page 27

**1** Check your answer against this corrected passage:
Excitingly, they are also in the process of being upgraded with what is arguably the world's best naval defence system for small warships: CEAFAR. This largely Australian-invented radar and response system decisively proved itself in a recent test off the coast of Hawaii, when the HMAS Perth used CEAFAR to obliterate a US Coyote sea-skimming missile moving at nearly three times the speed of sound. Understandably, I'm a little miffed that, now I've retired, my beloved Greyhounds are being upgraded to super-ships!

**2** Check your answer against this corrected passage:
The Royal Australian Navy boasts eight active warships in the ANZAC class. These ships are called frigates. The writer of the autobiography *Bleeding Blue: A Life in the Navy* says that many Navy personnel call these ships 'Greyhounds'.

**3** Examples and effects may vary.
**a** exclamation mark
**b** 'Full to starboard on my mark!'
**c** italics **d** replaces direct speech neatly
**e** contraction (two joined words with an apostrophe)
**f** they clearly didn't want to go alone
**g** But she held steady.
**h** creates momentum and rhythm **i** colon (:)
**j** My reflexes took over: I snatched
**k** saves words and creates speed
**l** brief suspense and a surprise are created

**4** **a** ellipsis (…)
**b** question mark (?) 'Would this be the last time we called in?'

**5** Answers will vary.

INFORMATIVE TEXT
## Writing Work
page 28

**1** Answers will vary.

**2** dates, names and terminology

**3** Sample answer: An autobiography contains less dialogue than other forms of recount and narrative because it is written in the first person. Also, dialogue is difficult to write in a completely factual text because it needs to be remembered accurately. This is why we usually see more paraphrased or reported (indirect) speech than dialogue (direct speech) in an autobiography.

**4** We find particular jargon, idioms and vernacular in an autobiography because these are the expressions used by the subject, who is also the writer. These language features are a part of his or her natural mode of speech.

**5** **a** I celebrated my victory by doing something highly unusual for a Navy cadet: I took a day off.
**b** Despite turning the ship sharply he still thought she was a sitting duck, but the missile missed them by a hair.
**c** The enemy vessel had their [or the] ANZAC frigate in its sights and he knew that the lives of his crew were all in his hands.

**6** **a**, **d** and **e**

**7** **a** The writer uses understatement to show that a **flicker** of a smile can actually be high **praise**.
**b** An example of **hyperbole** in the text is 'sweat was deluging my face'.
**c** Technical proper nouns in the text include the missile names **Sea Sparrow** and **Coyote**.

**8** **a** Greyhounds, The Machine
**b** the sea boiled, jelly legs
**c** like a toy boat, fire boiled up like lava
**d** Any four of: she or her (frigate), beeps welcomed me back, my nemesis, a clunk and a sigh, wasn't too happy (combat simulator), fire from the belly, crippled ship (enemy destroyer), diesel turbines screamed
**e** caj
**f** Any three of: CEAFAR, ANZAC, HMAS, US
**g** Any three of: jelly legs, tough nut, my nemesis, wasn't too happy, cool as a cucumber

## UNIT 4: INFORMATIVE TEXT—ONLINE ARTICLE

INFORMATIVE TEXT

### Comprehension Work

page 33

**1** **a** This is a literal question. We read the answer in the article directly after the keywords from the question *(line 15)*. Choosing the correct option requires you to locate the word from the question, with its precise spelling, in the second paragraph of the article. Answer **b** is incorrect because an 'axolotl' is a Mexican salamander (often called a walking fish). Answer **c** is incorrect because 'cacao' is the plant from which cocoa comes.

**2** The beans (cocoa beans) are used to make chocolate. OR the seed of the cacao plant
This is a **literal** question. The answer is located in the second paragraph: 'Chocolate is made from cocoa beans—the seed of the cacao plant' *(lines 7–8)*. Locate the key words from the question in the article to get the answer.

**3** Mesoamerican
This is a **literal** question. We read the phrase 'the Mesoamerican Aztec and Mayan cultures' *(line 7)*. To double-check it, you could note that 'Mesoamerican' is a proper noun (with a capital letter), as specified in the question.

**4** **c** This is an **interpretive** question. To answer it, re-read line 18 then eliminate two options. We read the phrase 'the Spanish conquest of South America', and interpret the 'conquistadors' as being Spanish people involved in the 'conquest' mentioned. Answer **a** is incorrect because it is highly unlikely that 'South America' would ever have been partly or entirely 'concreted'. Answer **b** is incorrect because there is no suitable explanation of what or who would have been 'conducted' in South America.

**5** the 17th
This is an **interpretive** question. You could answer 'the 1600s', but the best answer includes the number of the 'century': 17. This answer requires knowledge of how centuries are numbered—that is, the 1600s are also called the 17th century. In line 23 we read the key number, '1689', very close to the keywords from the question, 'milk chocolate'. You need to locate these keys to complete the answer.

**6** Chocolate can affect our brain by giving us a 'mental high' and 'increasing our theta brainwaves', which makes us feel relaxed.
This is an **interpretive** question. We read the two-part answer in the first two bullet points of the text. The question points to the bullet points. Read them and interpret which points refer to brain activity to get the correct answers.

**7** Sample answer: The phrase 'consumers follow their conscience' *(line 30)* means: more shoppers are trying to do the right thing by chocolate producers. In practical terms, this means that more 'Fairtrade' certified cocoa products are being sold, as mentioned in the text.
This is an **interpretive** question. We read in the text that '"Fairtrade" certified cocoa (cocoa bought from farmers for a fair price) is becoming more popular', and the explanation is that 'consumers'—or shoppers—are trying to do the right thing by farmers.

**8** **a** This is an **interpretive** question requiring you to piece together (synthesise) parts of the text, the question and the correct answer. We read in the fifth bullet point *(line 40)* that the 'melting point of chocolate is 30 to 32°', which is only a slight variation of the first part of Answer **a**, and the following phrase, 'just below our regular body temperature', is repeated word-for-word in

Answer **a**. Answer **b** is incorrect because it makes no sense: our hand and mouth are parts of our body. Answer **c** is incorrect because it has nothing to do with 'body temperature'.

**9** **b** This is an **interpretive** question. Carefully re-read the section of the article that explains 'Fairtrade' and interpret Answer **b** as the best description for the word 'trade'. Knowledge of the word 'trade' in general would help you answer. Answer **a** is incorrect because paying for chocolate (as described in the text) is not a case of exchanging a product for a product, but for money. Answer **c** is incorrect because in the context 'trade' is not about swapping types of chocolate, but buying it.

**10** **a** This is an **interpretive** question. A shortcut to the answer is the title, which specifies that the article is primarily about the 'history' of chocolate. Answers **b** and **c** are incorrect because, while some of the 'health benefits of chocolate' and 'the ingredients in chocolate' are mentioned in the text, neither of these is the article's main topic.

**11** **b** This is an **applied** question. To find the answer, apply your understanding of both formal versus informal language and the style of language generally used in 'a reference book such as an encyclopedia', which is formal. As such, the informal style of the article, particularly its last paragraph, would need altering to fit in with such a text. Answer **a** is incorrect because the language is 'informal'. Answer **c** is incorrect because it makes no sense as an option. Being 'uncertain' is a trait that a reader of the text may have; not the text itself.

**12** Sample answer: The purpose of the bullet point section of the article is to present a range of miscellaneous facts about chocolate. These facts are not incorporated into the other paragraphs because they are too brief and too varied to be presented in that manner. One bullet point fact is an event in the history of chocolate's development but it is a random detail that cannot be easily grouped with other content.
This **applied** question requires you to re-read the bullet points and apply your understanding of the range of topics to the question.

INFORMATIVE TEXT
## Spelling Work
page 34

**1** **a** beccause, dellectable, eading
**b** choclate, clasted, shugar
**c** consummers, offen, relise
**d** benofficial, antixodiant
**e** forlow, consense, by

**2** chocolate, confectionery, temperature

**3** Beginnings: rec, temp, ex, con
Endings: ant, tion, ments, able, cial

**4** concoction, consumers, conscience, confectionery

**5** **a** conscience **b** temperature **c** chocolate

**6** Sample answers:
**b** said: bed, head, dead;
mail: fail, pale, hail;
air: fair, pear, bare
**c** pure: manure, fewer, cure;
lure: tour, bluer, sewer;
sure: more, poor, four
**d** goal: foal, mole, bowl;
oar: bore, more, score;
cloak: spoke, joke, oak

INFORMATIVE TEXT
## Vocabulary Work
page 35

**1** **b** By ~~the time~~ the 1600s ~~came~~, chocolate was popular all over ~~and right across~~ Europe.
**c** Dark chocolate is so good ~~and healthy~~ for you that it noticeably improves ~~these~~ aspects of your ~~body's~~ health.
**d** ~~Just~~ eating ~~up some~~ chocolate brings about a stronger~~, more potent~~ high than ~~even~~ kissing ~~does~~.

**2** **a** minor and cocoa
**b** confectionery and consumers
**c** ailments and delectable
**d** beneficial and acquainted
**e** exploited and antioxidant

**3** **a** aroma and inhaling
**b** inventor, relaxed, high, mental and feel

**4** **a** consuming **b** scoff **c** nibbling

**5** **a** consume **b** exploiting **c** acquaintance
**d** conscientious

**6** Stationery is a word for office supplies, while stationary means unmoving.

INFORMATIVE TEXT
## Grammar Work
page 36

**1** **a** in **b** around **c** with
**d** into **e** through **f** from

**2** Aztec, Mayan, Europe, Cadbury, Nestlé, Celsius, Wakefield

**3** brainwaves, Fairtrade, groundbreaking, lifetime's, Mesoamerican

**4** **a** concoct **b** concocted **c** exploitation
**d** exploitative or exploited **e** recreation
**f** recreate **g** ail **h** ailing

INFORMATIVE TEXT
### Punctuation Work
page 37

**1** **a** italics **b** repetition **c** short sentence **d** image **e** italics

**2** **a** France's Marie Antoinette and Napoleon Bonaparte were two famous chocolate fans.
**b** Every single second, Americans scoff a combined total of 100 pounds (45 kilograms) of chocolate.
**c** That's why it can dissolve so quickly in our hand or mouth.

**3** Some answers are samples, as there are many possible answers; others will be the only correct answer.
**a** cocoa beans—the seed of the cacao plant
**b** reduce your risk of heart disease by a third!
**c** Marie Antoinette
**d** 'Fairtrade' certified cocoa
**e** Some delectable *Did you know?* …

**4** dash/comma/inverted comma/period/exclamation mark/apostrophe

INFORMATIVE TEXT
### Writing Work
page 38

**1** Answers must come from the bullet points listed in the panel above the question; for example, 'short passages of information'.

**2** photographs, diagrams, tables

**3** Answers will vary. Sample answers:
**a** An informative article may educate people about a particular country, such as Germany.
**b** An informative article may be useful for students conducting research for a school subject, such as Geography.
**c** An informative article may help raise awareness about an important social issue, such as slavery.
**d** An informative article may be included in a book about a certain subject, such as popular snack foods.

**4** Answers will vary. Sample answers:
**a** subheading, bullet points
**b** A chart or graph showing medical data or statistics would enhance the information in the final paragraph. The chart or graph would support the writer's claims about the health benefits of dark chocolate.

**5** **a** 'Chocolate history, short and sweet'
**b** story about Ruth Wakefield **c** *xocoatl*
**d** creamy off-white **e** cocoa beans and powder
**f** reduce your risk of heart disease by a third

**6** **a** Aztec and Mayan cultures
**b** Marie Antoinette, Ruth Wakefield and Napoleon Bonaparte
**c** plantations of cacao were grown
**d** extracted

**7** **a** readers **b** connectives
**c** exploitation, statistic **d** redundant, single

## UNIT 5: NARRATIVE TEXT—LITERARY RECOUNT

NARRATIVE TEXT
### Comprehension Work
page 43

**1** 'Mother and Father'
This is a **literal** question. We read at the beginning of the letter that it is addressed to 'Mother and Father' *(line 28)*. The very next phrase is 'If this letter ever reaches you'. These two elements are the keys to answering the question. You could also answer: his parents or his family. Answering 'home' is incorrect because the question specifically asks 'who'.

**2** **a** This is a **literal** question. The answer is contained in the second paragraph. We read the name of the place in the second sentence, 'Fromelles' *(line 3)*, and the description of the place 'where his big brother fought and died' *(lines 18–19)*. The key phrase 'big brother' points you to the answer. Answer **b** is incorrect because it is not a literal answer but a figurative expression. The hint reminds you to look for a 'literal place' in the text. Answer **c** is incorrect because it does not answer 'where'. 'The 15th' is the brigade (division or unit) to which Lester and Bobby belonged.

**3** Lester
This is a **literal** question. We read this full name at the end of the letter and we know from the fourth paragraph that Les wrote the letter *(line 42)*.

**4** **b** This is an **interpretive** question. Re-read the phrase 'tasting silent tears' and break these words down into the relevant senses: taste, sight (of the tears) and touch (the feel of the tears on skin). Answer **a** is incorrect because the tears are 'silent' so sound does not apply. Answer **c** is incorrect because, even if the tears had a smell, they have no sound.

**5** **c** This is an **interpretive** question. We read a reference to Answer **c** in lines 18–19; also that he came to France. Later we read 'Pop has brought along a treasured family letter' *(line 24)*. These elements, pieced together, point to the correct answer. Answer **a** is incorrect because, as we read in the second paragraph, the boys belong to the writer of the recount *(lines 14–15)*. Answer **b** is incorrect because Les's uncle is not mentioned anywhere in the text.

# ANSWERS

CHECK YOUR ANSWERS

**6** **a** This is an **interpretive** question. You need to understand the meaning of the three devices then work out the right option based on the phrase 'we two saplings' *(line 33)* and the hint about the meaning of 'saplings'. Answer **b** is incorrect because there are no simile indicators (such as *like* or *as*), meaning that the image is a direct comparison. Answer **c** is incorrect because humans are being likened to trees. Personification works in the opposite way.

**7** Answers will vary but should refer to powerful weapons. The best answers will also refer to the idea that the weapons belong to the enemy.
This is an **interpretive** question. Avoid literal answers, as indicated by the hint. 'Rum jars' was a slang term used in World War I trench warfare to describe very heavy mortar bombs (or 'shells'), whose impact was so powerful that, even without shrapnel, death by concussion or shockwave was instantaneous to anyone nearby.

**8** Lester (or Les) and Bobby
This is an **interpretive** question. We read that the writer of the recount has 'twin boys' *(lines 14–15)*. Later we read 'Les's great-niece would marry Bobby's great-nephew and … we'd name our two sons in their honour' *(line 46)*. Matching up these two sections indicates that the recount writer's twin boys are named after Lester (Les) and Bobby, giving you the correct answer.

**9** The wording of answers will vary but answers must refer to the fact that the 'resting' soldiers are dead, which is implied in the final paragraph of the recount.
This is an **interpretive** question. You interpret the euphemism 'resting' as meaning that the soldiers' remains have been properly laid to rest. The men died nearly a century ago. You may find the introductory paragraph helpful in answering this question but it is not vital to finding the correct answer.

**10** **a** This is an **interpretive** question. Make sure that you understand the three techniques listed then eliminate two options. Also, locate the question in the text by looking for a question mark. A rhetorical question has and needs no answer, making Answer **a** the correct option. Answer **b** is incorrect because the question doesn't invite any answer at all, unlike an open-ended question. Answer **c** is incorrect because a closed question asks for a 'yes' or 'no' answer, unlike the question in this paragraph.

**11** It is an appropriate image because the ceremony is solemn and sacred like a stereotypical church service.
This is an **applied** question. You may have worded your answer in a slightly different way or answered from the angle of the 'hymnal pages' (in reality, gravestones) being dedicated to or written about the fallen soldiers. Apply the definition of 'hymnal' provided, your understanding of the setting or event described in the text and the meaning of 'sacred' in the question to the text.

**12** **b** This is an **applied** question. Apply your understanding of language features or techniques (such as using an unusual preposition) to this situation and to consider purpose and effect. Answer **a** is incorrect because the preposition ('from') prevents the number from adopting a meaning about place. Answer **c** is incorrect because there is nothing in the title to suggest that 'speed' is a relevant idea.

NARRATIVE TEXT
## Spelling Work
page 44

**1** **a** hymnal **b** serene **c** cemetery, grocery, century **d** wreaths

**2** **a** military **b** bargain **c** sacred **d** beginning

**3** **a** military **b** century **c** wreaths **d** serene **e** overtaken **f** trifling

**4** anniversary, Battle, special, was, Cemetery, hundred, final, Australian, soldiers, whose, years, area

NARRATIVE TEXT
## Vocabulary Work
page 45

**1** **a** eighteen, century **b** overtaken, headstones **c** cemetery, headstones **d** military, soldiers

**2** **a** 2 **b** 1 **c** 3 **d** 6 **e** 5 **f** 4

**3** **b** us or the pair of us **c** men
**d** bloody, silly or stupid
**e** young trees, young guys or rookies
**f** made a deal or pact
**g** look out for and help each other
**h** a great comfort or not a small comfort
**i** nearby or in the next trench
**j** I will end the letter here

**4** **a** establish a base (by literally digging trenches)
**b** the 15th unit or group
**c** on the communication lines or down the trenches
**d** over the top of the trench (and into no-man's land)

**5** Completed sentences: The letter's salutation (opening) is very formal: **'Dear Mother and Father'**. The writer signs off with the description **'Your loving son'** and his full name, **Lester.**

# ANSWERS

CHECK YOUR ANSWERS

NARRATIVE TEXT
## Grammar Work
page 46

1 **a** I **b** I **c** me **d** I

2 Missing words in order:
**a** ribboned, silent, last **b** treasured
**c** good, long, tiring

3 Answers will vary. Sample adjectives in order:
**a** elegant, warm, lingering **b** beloved
**c** fine, onerous, taxing

4 Abbreviations for the parts of speech in order:
V, P, N, ADJ, V, ADV, N, C, N, N, P, ADJ, C

NARRATIVE TEXT
## Punctuation Work
page 47

1 Sample answer: The semicolon has that name because it is half of a colon. This is denoted by a dot. The semicolon's pause is 'softened' by a comma. It is not as strong as a colon.

2 'Terminal punctuation marks' means punctuation marks that create a complete stop—or termination.

3 **a** Punctuation: commas. This pair of pauses allows the writer to tell us the twin boys' **age**.
**b** Punctuation: dash. This pause conveys the amazement of the **writer** or **narrator** at being in this place.
**c** Punctuation: colon. This pause splits the **sentence** and leads into a **description** of the war zone.
**d** Punctuation: semicolon. This pause comes before the **connection** between the families is **explained** or **given**.

4 **a** Quotation marks
**b** great-niece, great-nephew **c** comma
**d** Sample answers: It creates a transition; It creates a shift into the past.

5 Corrected passage to check against:
**a** Pop has brought a treasured family letter, sent by Uncle Les from the trenches. I read it at the ceremony on his behalf—at almost the exact spot where it was penned ninety-four years ago.
**b** The place is quite transformed now, of course: the muddy Western Front hellholes have given way to a serene carpet of rich green, embroidered with bright roses.

NARRATIVE TEXT
## Writing Work
page 48

1 A special military service commemorating the lives of Australian soldiers who died in the Battle of Fromelles.

2 Sample answers: 'he wouldn't have missed this for the world'; 'I hope you are proud of me, Father.'

3 All boxes except those for visual advertisement and procedure may be ticked.

4 We can see that this title is more creative than literal because, as explained earlier in the chapter, 'Ninety-four years' is used as a measurement of distance not just time.

5 **a** Answers must include the Battle of Fromelles, the town of Fromelles, the cemetery, and references to trench warfare.
**b** Answers must include the characters, the events directly involving the characters, and the letter.

6 Sample answers: arrived, fought, read, crouch, ordered, marry, standing (there are more possible answers)

7 Answers will be entirely original sentences but they must fit in with the rest of the text, build on the scene and appeal to at least one of the five senses.

8 Sample answers:
**a** solemn, emotional, proud
**b** upbeat, genuine, cautiously optimistic

9 Sample answer: This approach is a highly effective one because it brings the historical event of the Battle of Fromelles to life. When we read in the letter that 'word has just come along the lines that we will be ordered over the top', an order that we know, historically, led to the deaths of thousands of men, we are immediately transported to the World War I trenches. Suddenly the statistics take on more meaning. While the description of the service at the cemetery ninety-four years later is moving and effective, it is far more effective because it is accompanied by the letter.

## UNIT 6: NARRATIVE TEXT—PROSE FICTION

NARRATIVE TEXT
## Comprehension Work
page 53

1 'when he is killing to show his children how to kill'
This is a **literal** question and we read the answer explicitly in the first line of the text *(lines 11–12)*. Locate the key phrases from the question ('the Law of the Jungle' and 'beast to eat Man') in that sentence then simply quote or paraphrase the appropriate part of the sentence as the answer.

2 **b** This is a **literal** question. Re-read or skim the fourth paragraph *(line 35)*. It is clear as we read, following the actions of Father Wolf, that he is the one who finds the baby boy. Answer **a** is incorrect because we see Mother Wolf tell Father to 'bring

[the man's cub] here'. Clearly she has not found the baby boy. Both Answers **c** and **d** are incorrect for the same reason: we read in the text that Shere Khan and Tabaqui are nearby but they do not find the baby boy.

**3** **a** This is a **literal** question. We read this phrase in the second paragraph of the text and can locate it by looking for the keywords from the question: 'howl' and 'Shere Khan' *(line 22)*. Answers **b** and **c** are incorrect because we read that 'the purr grew louder, and ended in the full-throated "Aaarh!" of the tiger's charge' *(line 21)*. This line eliminates both the purr and the full-throated sound. Answer **d** is incorrect because Shere Khan's 'muttering and mumbling' in the same paragraph is not connected to a howl.

**4** **a** This is an **interpretive** question. We read that 'it is unsportsmanlike to touch' Man *(line 19)* appearing immediately after the words quoted in Answer **a**. Note the link between these two phrases, and understand that there are real reasons for the law and perceived reasons—or the animals' ideas about the law. Answers **b**, **c** and **d** are all incorrect because these are real reasons why beasts should not kill Man. They are not, however, reasons 'why' it is 'unsportsmanlike to touch Man'.

**5** There are two possible answers: 'He looked up into Father Wolf's face, and laughed'; or 'The baby was pushing his way between the cubs to get close to the warm hide.'
This is an **interpretive** question. Interpret one of the lines describing the baby's actions as matching Mother Wolf's soft exclamation 'How bold!' Both quotes are equally correct; the first because Father Wolf specifically refers to the baby's action of laughing at him and the second because this action directly follows Mother Wolf saying 'How bold!'

**6** This emphasis is made because we are given the point of view of wolves, who are covered in fur.
This is an **interpretive** question. You will find the hint very helpful in answering it. Once you interpret the perspective as being the wolves', you are able to discern the answer.

**7** **a** This is an **interpretive** question. Re-read the first paragraph and interpret the identity of the 'biggest threat' as specified in the question. Answer **b** is incorrect because it is not a real option but an alteration of the phrase 'white men on elephants'. Answer **c** is incorrect because there is a more correct answer: 'any men'. Answer **d** is incorrect because, while tigers can present a threat, they are not the 'biggest' threat. Also, they are not 'arriving' in the jungle; they are already there.

**8** **a** This is an **interpretive** question. There are two keys to answering it correctly: first we are pointed to the fifth paragraph, where we find only one 'comparative' description: 'as soft and as dimpled a little atom as ever came to a wolf's cave at night.' Second the hint warns us to 'read the paragraph carefully'. This suggests that the comparative device we are looking for may be hard to tell apart from another device. You may be misled by the three uses of the word 'as' in the description of the baby, thinking that they point to a simile. But read the description closely: it does not say 'as soft and as dimpled *as* a little atom'. So Answer **c** is incorrect. Ignore the uses of 'as' and you are left with a metaphor: the baby is being called 'a little atom'. Answer **b** is incorrect because the boy is already a 'person'. Answer **d** is incorrect because an analogy is not merely a description but a more complex comparison of two ideas or systems.

**9** Sample answer: Rudyard Kipling may have used a lot of dialogue to tell the story in order to bring the animal characters to life. If the animals did not speak—and very frequently—it would be difficult for readers to empathise with them and therefore difficult for them to understand the conflicts in the story.
This is an **interpretive** question. You are required to think about the writer's purpose and consider the impact of dialogue.

**10** There are two possible answers: '—and it is true—', or '—an untigerish howl—'
This is an **interpretive** question. Interpret what an 'interruption' might look like in the story and find an example of one. Following the hint is important. It is also vital, however, not to simply quote any phrase including dashes, because only two phrases can be called interruptions. The others don't work as interruptions because the dashes have been used in place of colons. For example, 'the most wonderful thing in the world—the wolf checked in mid-spring.'

**11** **d** This is an **applied** question. The Law of the Jungle is based on instinct and logic. The narrator seems to be suggesting that it simply exists but was not 'made' at all. If anyone can be named as its maker, it is God. Answer **a** is incorrect because Man's arrival in the jungle is one of the outcomes of breaking the Law. Man would not have made a law that works against himself. Answer **b** is incorrect because we read about a 'reason the beasts give among themselves' for the Law *(line 17)*. If the animals 'made' the Law, this statement would not make sense. Answer **c** is incorrect because the Law is about animals versus Man. It is not something that animals and Man have joined together to create.

**12** Sample answer: This comes across in the story by the absence of setting description. Despite the action partly taking place inside a cave there is very little description of the jungle outside, which could suggest that Kipling does not know a lot about it.
This is an **applied** question requiring you to make a judgement about what you have read in the text—and what seems to be missing—based on the information given in the question.

## NARRATIVE TEXT Spelling Work page 54

**1** **a** mumbling **b** savagely **c** rustled
**d** unsportsmanlike **e** arrival
**f** atom **g** purr **h** lose

**2** **a** twitch–ing **b** a–tom **c** up–hill
**d** man–gy **e** mut–ter–ing **f** sav–age–ly

**3** **a** rustled **b** full-throated **c** hunches
**d** purr **e** unsportsmanlike

**4** **a** But see, he looks up and isn't afraid.
**b** Then, if you'd been watching, you would've seen the most wonderful thing in the world …

## NARRATIVE TEXT Vocabulary Work page 55

**1** Answers are based entirely on students' own ideas. Sample answers are given below.
**a** The **dewy** bushes rustled in the **thorny** thicket.
**b** Father Wolf ran out a few paces along the **gnarled, uneven** ground and heard Shere Khan muttering and mumbling savagely as he tumbled about in the **palette of greens that made up the verdant** scrub.
**c** … as soft and as dimpled a little atom as ever came to a **dim, stifling** wolf's cave in the **perspiring, heaving** jungle.

**2** Answers are based entirely on students' own ideas. Sample answers:
**a** The light in the cave was grey but somehow alive with warmth; it had a life in its own right and it gently radiated that life to the wolf family.
**b** Up, up, ever up, but treacherously falling and dipping and hollowing, went the vine-entwined jungle slope.
**c** Like an impossibly tall, impossibly gangly great-uncle, the ancient, ghostly tree lurched bonily in the gloom.

**3** **a** but see **b** man **c** man-killing
**d** unsportsmanlike **e** the fool
**f** checked **g** altogether

## NARRATIVE TEXT Grammar Work page 56

**1** **a** say, become, lose
**b** made, saw, was, was, jumping, tried, stop
**c** have, seen, bring

**2** **a** diminished **b** began **c** retreat **d** save
**e** cooled **f** launching **g** pulling **h** giving

**3** **a** past tense **b** past tense
**c** present tense, future tense
**d** present tense, future tense
**e** present tense, future tense

**4** **a** grow **b** took **c** ends

## NARRATIVE TEXT Punctuation Work page 57

**1** **a** the woodcutters **b** the tiger
**c** a human (a man or woman)

**2** **a** the white men's guns
**b** the man eaters' teeth **c** the wolf pack's lair

**3** The Jungle's natural law exists for good reasons, and its main function is to keep the animals' sanctuary free of men and their weapons. As such, Jungle beasts are forbidden to eat humans except for the purpose of their children's education, and then, the pack or tribe's hunting grounds are not appropriate places for such killings.

**4** The late 1800s saw Kipling become friends with Australia's beloved AB 'Banjo' Paterson. The two writers shared an affinity for the outdoors: most of Paterson's works feature the bush, its beauty and its power, and many of Kipling's tales also celebrate Nature's wonders. The men's friendship lasted until Kipling's death in the 1930s.

## NARRATIVE TEXT Writing Work page 58

**1** An episodic novel is a series of narrative episodes that are brought together to form one long narrative text.

**2** We do not know the time period from reading the excerpt; we only know the place.

**3** The complication is likely to be the baby boy being abandoned or becoming lost in the jungle.

**4** Mowgli (the human baby boy found in the jungle) is the character most likely to become the protagonist as the story continues.

**5** Kipling refers to the Law of the Jungle in the narrative to add to the sense of Jungle folklore.

**6** 'Bookended' means enclosed by or with matching items at each end. To say that the stories are 'bookended' by poems or songs means that a poem or song appears before and after each story.

**7** Answers will vary. Sample answers:
**a** '"A man's cub. Look!"' **b** 'a little atom'
**c** 'the full-throated "Aaarh!" of the tiger's charge'
**d** 'though Father Wolf's jaws closed right on the child's back not a tooth even scratched the skin as he laid it down among the cubs.'

**8** Answers will be based on each student's interpretation of the text. Sample answer: curious and excited.

**9** Kipling, in both *The Jungle Book* and his *Just So Stories*, presents **animal** characters almost as though they are **human**. Unlike other **anthropomorphic** animal characters, such as Beatrix Potter's Peter **Rabbit**, Kipling's do not wear human **clothes/clothing**, use furniture and so on. They do, however, have **personalities** and show emotions, cleverness and other human **traits**.

## UNIT 7: NARRATIVE TEXT—NARRATIVE POEM

NARRATIVE TEXT

### Comprehension Work

page 63

**1** **a** This is a **literal** question. We read in the second stanza that the 'visit' happens 'in the Night' *(line 15)*. Find the keyword 'Night' and check back through the stanza to ensure that you have the right answer. Answers **b** and **c** are eliminated when we read that the visitor is gone 'just before the Sun' comes up.

**2** **b** This is a **literal** question. You need a basic knowledge of capital letters and dashes. Then find them in the first and second stanzas. Dashes are the only features used in 'exactly the same places', as demanded by the question. The annotations reinforce this.

**3** 'and'
This is a **literal** question. You need to know that 'and' is a conjunction (joining word). Then count how many times it is used in the poem: five.

**4** Sample answer: Each stanza has six syllables in the first and last line, and eight in the third line. Because the third line is the longest and contains the most syllables, the stanza seems to swell out and in again.
This is an **interpretive** question. Before answering, read the hint to ensure that you understand what syllables are. Then count the syllables in each line to identify the pattern. Lastly, note that this pattern creates the 'swelling' effect mentioned in the question.

**5** There is one answer but many ways to express it. For example: An unspecified time period OR No time period is stated or suggested in the poem OR The poem's events occur outside of time OR The poem's events are timeless.
This is an **interpretive** question. To answer it, however, simply re-read the poem without imposing a time on it. Claiming that the time period is the Victorian era (late 1800s) is incorrect. Despite the fact that it was written in the Victorian era, we have no way of knowing if Dickinson meant for the events to be trapped in that time. In fact it is unlikely that she did. The events in poems, as in many other literary works, often exist outside time.

**6** The problem with the 'elegant' flowers is that they are dead.
This is an **interpretive** question. Make a connection between the flowers, the 'influence' that the frost has on them and what is meant by the phrase 'elegant as glass'. When the frost touches the flowers, they become like beautiful glass sculptures but this means that they die.

**7** **b** This is an **interpretive** question. The key to answering it is the phrase 'very human' in the question. It helps you eliminate Answers **a** and **c** because to 'glisten', for instance, is not a 'very human' action. Answer **c** can also be easily eliminated because 'just' is not an action.

**8** Sample answer: Elegance is linked to glass because a well-made glass object, such as a vase or champagne flute, should be shapely, in proportion, delicate, graceful and beautiful. A sculpture made of glass is particularly elegant.
This is an **interpretive** question that requires you to make a connection between an adjective ('elegant') and a noun ('glass'). If you try to answer based on why Dickinson made this connection you're thinking too hard. You simply need to show the relationship between elegance and glass, and give an example of something elegant made from glass.

**9** **c** This is an **interpretive** question. You need to know or deduce that 'till' is a variation of the word 'until'. You also need to locate 'Till' in the poem *(line 13)* and check the three options based on the word's use in context. Answer **a** is incorrect because, while this is one meaning of 'till', the question specifies that the meaning must be 'based on the context'. For this same reason, Answer **b** is incorrect.

**10** **b** This is an **interpretive** question. Find the phrase in the question in the second stanza *(line 18)* and look at what the dashes are doing in the line (as mentioned in the hint), which is to suggest that the frost 'comes and goes quickly' (Answer **b**). Answer **a** is incorrect because the frost can't disappear 'before' it appears. Answer **c** is incorrect because throughout the poem the frost is shown to be visible.

# ANSWERS

CHECK YOUR ANSWERS

**11** a This is an **applied** question. Check all of the answer options against the poem to find the answer. It would make sense when we re-read the poem to think of the 'Visitor' as dew, if the last line did not mention that it kills the flowers. Dew does not kill flowers but waters them and helps them live. So, in addition to interpreting the question and the line of the poem, apply your understanding of dew to answer the question. Answer **b** is incorrect because the Sun does not freeze (or water) plants. Answer **c** is incorrect because it has nothing to do with the final words of the poem ('is as it had not been').

**12** Some possible answers: a Victorian poetry anthology; an American poetry anthology; an anthology about forces of nature; a collection of riddle poems; an anthology of extended metaphor poems
This is an **applied** question. You need to know what the word 'anthology' means or glean its meaning from its use in the context of the question. Then think of the main features of 'A Visitor in Marl' and apply at least one of those features to the task of creating an anthology theme or purpose. Using the answer suggested in the question is incorrect; you must come up with your own idea.

## NARRATIVE TEXT Spelling Work

page 64

**1** influences, icy, affects, damaging, glistening, decoded

**2** a riddle b stanza c personified d elegant

**3** a visit b visiting c influence d influential e unique f unique g damage h damaged or damaging

**4** a elegantly b icily c damagingly d falsely e absolutely f immensely

## NARRATIVE TEXT Vocabulary Work

page 65

**1** a sausages b a smooth, bald head
c feeling morbid or melancholy
d say something utterly preposterous
e very tight pants

**2** a marble b never existed c any

**3** a sparkling and shining; reflecting light
b someone who arrives and/or stays somewhere as a guest for a short period of time
c sculptures that feature a subject's head and sometimes torso
d finishes; comes to an end
e gently touches or lands upon
f prior to; earlier than

**4** a flower b feet c just d glistening e his f whom

**5** a uniquely b whatsoever c interview d gone e touched f been g they h before

## NARRATIVE TEXT Grammar Work

page 66

**1** a Ironically b In contrast

**2** since, therefore, meanwhile, further, because, similarly

**3** a the planet Earth
b earth (dirt/soil)
c your mother's Honda
d Star Wars
e the Rio Olympics
f a local courthouse

**4** In the poem 'A Visitor in Marl', verbs tell us that, like a person, the frost is able to **visit** someone's house, **influence** flowers and **make** things orderly.

**5** rain, fly, age, wait

## NARRATIVE TEXT Punctuation Work

page 67

**1** the comma and the full stop

**2** They form bridges between sections and they indicate pauses.

**3** a code or system of abbreviated writing that saves time and space

**4** a Emily Dickinson lived in the Victorian era and wrote many, many poems.
b It isn't clear why riddle poems were so popular in the 1800s but there's no doubt they were.
c 'A Visitor in Marl' is a brief but dense poem containing personification, metaphor and sound devices.

**5** a , b comma c . d full stop

**6** a, b and c (i.e. all three options)

## NARRATIVE TEXT Writing Work

page 68

**1** No

**2** the frost, flowers, the Sun

**3** a voice b title c personification

4 **a** changes or transforms
**b** flower head or petals
**c** interaction with the flowers in the garden
**d** unmoving, still or frozen; staying in their place

5 Sample answers:
**a** The use of repetition creates a rhythm and establishes the power and consistency of the frost.
**b** The rhythm suggests a natural process and/or that this event happens each night.
**c** It points out where pauses should be taken—these pauses build suspense.
**d** influences Flowers
**e** visits just Sun Concludes his glistening Caresses
**f** Connotes crispy, sharp icicles and creates an image of the garden frosting up.
**g** The frost is personified throughout the poem as an artist (and a villain).
**h** influences, visits, concludes [an interview], caresses, gone, touched, run, kissed
**i** Makes the personification of the frost consistent and adds to the mystery of the riddle.

## UNIT 8: NARRATIVE TEXT—MONOLOGUE

NARRATIVE TEXT
### Comprehension Work
page 73

1 **b** This is a **literal** question. To answer it, notice that the exact wording of Answer **b** appears in the text *(lines 7–8)*. Answer **a** is incorrect because no mention is made of fashion in the text. Answer **c** is incorrect because his ironing is a part of his 'attempt at formality'. He is not 'making an attempt at ironing'.

2 **a** This is a **literal** question. Skim-read the second paragraph of the text and note that we are not told the middle name, only its first letter (P) *(line 13)*. Answer **b** is incorrect because we read in the text that Thomas is his first name. Answer **c** is incorrect because we read in the text that Perks is one of his nicknames.

3 the dead man's name: Thomas P Perkins
This is a **literal** question. Immediately after the name in the text we read 'and no, that wasn't a stutter'. The keywords from the question are contained in this statement so you need to locate the keywords in line 14 of the text to find the answer.

4 **b** This is an **interpretive** question. Find the key phrase from the question ('his shearin' days') in the text *(line 24)* and re-read the sentences around it to understand that Wokka says 'Whatsername' because he can't remember the name of the place. In Australian vernacular, the same approach is often taken when a person's name is forgotten.
Answer **a** is incorrect because there is no such town as 'Whatsername'. Answer **c** is incorrect for two reasons: there is no mention of Thomas shearing in a place called 'the Pacific', and 'Pacific' in this context is a malapropism for the word 'specific'.

5 morality
This is an **interpretive** question requiring you to synthesise elements from the text and the question. In the question, the language feature 'malapropism' is defined. This definition helps you see that the word the speaker probably intended to say sounds very similar to 'mortality'. Given the context—a celebration of a man's life—mentioning the man's 'morality' or good character would be appropriate.

6 It is ironic because the man has died. 'Mortality' means 'the condition of being destined to die'. He has literally become 'a man of great mortality'.
This is an **interpretive** question. It tests your vocabulary: specifically, the meaning of the words 'mortality', 'morality' and 'ironic'.

7 **b** This is an **interpretive** question. The best answering method is to test the options in the contexts to see if they fit. Answer **b** offers the only options which do so. Answer **a** is incorrect because nobody named 'Ronnie' is mentioned in the text. If this word was meant to represent a name it would at least begin with a capital letter. Answer **c** is incorrect because 'wand' is an entirely ill-fitting noun in this context. The other words in Answers **a** and **c** are also incorrect but the first words in each set are the most incorrect.

8 **a** This is an **interpretive** question. The word 'arksed' is a straightforward mispronunciation. Anwers **b** and **c** are incorrect because they make no sense when tested in the position of 'arksed' in line 11.

9 The three things that probably contributed to the accident are Thomas's physical impediments: 'gammy leg', 'bung foot' and 'industeral [industrial] deafness'.
This is an **interpretive** question. Locate the section of the text in which the key words 'semi clocked him' *(line 40)* are used and read around that phrase to interpret three likely contributing factors. These are the three impediments specifically mentioned by Wokka. Re-reading the annotation explaining 'industeral deafness' helps you. The annotation that explains the meaning of 'that semi clocked him' may help also, but you are given a reminder of this meaning in the question.

10 a pub / hotel / bar / drinking establishment
This is an **interpretive** question requiring you to link the name 'Crown' in the 'final paragraph' *(line 46)* (as the question indicates) with the word 'pub' in the preceding lines of the text. The most

correct wording is a 'pub' because this is the word used several times in the text itself.

**11** 'caricature'
This is an **applied** question. Knowing the definition of the word 'caricature' helps you in answering but it is not entirely necessary. Applying your understanding of the phrase 'type of character' to the relevant section of the text leads you to the word 'caricature' *(line 9)*. Test whether this word works as the answer by re-reading it in context and applying the advice given by the stage directions to the question.

**12** **c** This is an **applied** question requiring you to infer the writer's intentions from the text. One intention or aim ('humour') is mentioned in the question. To find the correct second intention, call on your knowledge of vocabulary. Answer **a** is incorrect because 'stereotypes' already exist. They are a part of the monologue but are only used by the writer, not created. Answer **b** is incorrect because the tone of the text is not sarcastic. It is lighthearted and satirical, meaning that it makes fun of certain people and situations.

## NARRATIVE TEXT
## Spelling Work page 74

**1** **a** shearing **b** going **c** screaming
**d** of course **e** you know **f** losing
**g** because **h** speaking **i** how would

**2** **a** it is **b** was not **c** we will
**d** you will **e** he would **f** that is

**3** **a** partial **b** forties **c** mortality
**d** posturing **e** whatnot **f** reconstruct
**g** inappropriate **h** incident **i** eulogy

**4** Corrected passage to check against: Our mate is best remembered for—and any one of his friends can back me up—his yarns. Yes indeed, he used to keep us amused for hours with all his shearing stories. He'd set the scene all right, waving his arms about and reconstructing events dramatically. Think he might have missed his calling as an actor. Wouldn't you agree, folks?

**5** Perks, Perkins Paste, Perkster, Chalky, Steak, Gob, Perkle, Chalks, Gobba Perks, Perkapants

## NARRATIVE TEXT
## Vocabulary Work page 75

**1** **a** pacific **b** specific
**c** Sample answer: Wokka seems to associate the word 'treasured' with something that is buried in the ground. Therefore, when he says 'may he be forever treasured', he follows it with another burial-related word ('fossilised') in the hope that it will strengthen what he is trying to say.

**2** **a** see you (later) **b** going to **c** real **d** ladies

**3** **Set 1:**
**a** hairstyle with a short front and a long back
**b** large truck **c** struck very hard
**d** underpants **e** flannelette shirt

**Set 2:**
**a** fight **b** mouth **c** angry and vicious
**d** exaggerated stories **e** fallen asleep

**4** Sample answers:
**b** The **folks** at the **funeral** were reminded of their **mortality**.
**c** The pastor presented the **eulogy** in a **dignified** manner, recalling **incidents** from the deceased's life.
**d** The stout man in his **forties** spoke amusingly, showing himself **partial** to the **vernacular** of his youth.

## NARRATIVE TEXT
## Grammar Work page 76

**1** Possible answers: it, I, me, we, they, she, he, her, him, them, us

**2** Sample answer: This type of pronoun is called 'interrogative' because it 'interrogates' or asks a question.

**3** **a** you **b** my **c** you, all of you, you all

**4** uh, too right, and whatnot, and so on and so forth

**5** 'Gunna' is one problem with this sentence but possibly worse is that it ends with a **conjunction**, a part of speech that only functions **within / inside** a sentence.

**6** **a** He was bangin' on his window at three AM and screamin' …
**b** Jacko came out with this bow and arrow and he was in his jocks and he went …

## NARRATIVE TEXT
## Punctuation Work page 77

**1** **a** C **b** CA **c** CA **d** c
**e** A **f** c **g** A **h** A

**2** **a** At my cousin's funeral, there was no eulogy. I guess he didn't have many friends. Well, he was a lawyer.
**b** The thing with funerals is that if the food's great at the family's house afterwards, you can't pig out.

**3** **a** We're all going to the show: Liam, Liam's friend, a friend of Goran's and me, of course.
**b** Please buy a baguette, croissants and, if they have them, bagels.
**c** Well, I'm not actually sure where we are, so um, could you pass the map, please?

**4** **a** We'll use Dad's car and the twins' cars to transport the family members.
**b** Once we've reached the town, you've got to see this café I've found. It's so cute.
**c** Are we goin' to go in, or what? I'm not waitin' 'round forever.

**5** **a** stage directions
**b** Sample answer: '*(Laughs awkwardly)*'

NARRATIVE TEXT
## Writing Work
page 78

**1** a monologue that is part of a larger play

**2** A monologue's character and a book's narrator can both tell a story.

**3** No. Two reasons: Jacko doesn't speak and there are other silent characters like him (such as 'Mumma Perks'). If Jacko's presence could make the text a duologue, the other characters would stop it from being a duologue.

**4** persona poem

**5** play, film and audition

**6** Diction means word choice.

**7** climax, character, action, fiction, events, setting, retell

**8** Sample answer: The climax of the monologue is the accident that killed Thomas P Perkins. We can identify this as the climax because other information in the text builds to this point. It is also the highest point in the script. Naming this event as the climax makes Wokka the narrator of the story.

**9** Sample answers:
**a** fossilised
**b** 'Jackohhhhh! Ya dogged me! Ya dogged me!'
**c** —Jacko, you can back me up here—
**d** youse and me … weeze …
**e** his gammy leg, and his bung foot, and all that
**f** we'll never forget him

**10** Sample answer: No, because the vernacular is the foundation of the whole piece and the reason for its humour. Without the broad 'ocker' accent coming through, the humour would be lost and language features like malapropisms wouldn't work. The exaggerated vernacular creates a sense of realism in relations to the spaeker and adds humour.

# UNIT 9: PERSUASIVE TEXT—ONLINE REVIEW

PERSUASIVE TEXT
## Comprehension Work
page 83

**1** a search of the site itself (for reviews) and a search of the internet (for attractions they may wish to visit)
This is a **literal** question. The information in parentheses is optional. We read these two search options in the menu bar. Look for the keyword in the question—'searches'—and locate 'search' twice in the text *(line 3)*.

**2** *prices subject to change without notice*
This is a **literal** question. We read the description 'nasty little' and the noun 'disclaimer' *(line 36)*, and the answer appears between them. This question calls on your skills of observation. You need to see that the phrase 'nasty little … disclaimer' is divided in two and brackets the answer in the text.

**3** we are go, Flight!
This is a **literal** question. We read the keyword 'absolutely' *(line 40)*, then the key phrase, 'NASA-speak' directly after. Immediately following this phrase is the answer: 'we are go, Flight!' As the annotations tell us, this phrase is an affirmative response given by astronauts to Mission Control as they prepare for take-off. This information is not required to answer the question but it does reinforce the fact that 'we are go, Flight' means 'yes' or 'absolutely'.

**4** **b** This is a **literal** question requiring a process of elimination to find the answer. One clue to answering it is the hint, where we read 'Technically, this feature is called an initialism.' An initialism is a specific type of abbreviation. Answer **a** is incorrect because a parenthesis is a side comment not an abbreviation. Answer **c** is incorrect because 'Kennedy Space Center' is a name not a truncated sentence.

**5** **c** This is an **interpretive** question. Locating the key phrase 'be happy enough with a chewy hot dog or a vacuum-sealed salad' in the text *(lines 28–29)* is the key. We read a statement that is very similar to Answer **c** directly before the key phrase, which is followed by a statement that reinforces the point: 'Hey, you don't come here for fine dining, so whatever' *(line 29)*. Answer **a** is incorrect because the whole point is that this type of food is NOT particularly enjoyable. Answer **b** is incorrect because no mention of discounted food associated with group rates is made in the text.

**6** 'enhance your experience'
This is an **interpretive** question. You may have used slightly different wording. No specific words

from the question are used in the same form in the text but the question does point you to the specific place where the answer appears. Re-read the fourth paragraph *(lines 23–29)*, looking for something the reviewer suggests NOT to do when visiting KSC. The only thing that fits the description in that section of the text is 'enhance your experience'.

**7** forgettable and overpriced.
This is an **interpretive** question. We read about food in only one section of the text so you need to go there *(lines 27–29)*. Then you are looking for two words only. The food appraisal is summed up in these two words at the beginning of the paragraph. A knowledge of the meaning of the two words would help in answering this question but it is not vital.

**8** **a** This is an **interpretive** question. You are required in this question to cut through the repetition of the word 'attraction' and make sense of what each Answer option is actually saying. Careful reading and re-reading of each option is important. Selecting the correct answer is based on your comprehension of the whole text and the people for whom it is designed. Answer **b** is incorrect because the word 'attractively', while in the word family of 'attraction', has an entirely different meaning in this phrase. It refers to beauty or stylishness. Answer **c** is incorrect because the target site users ARE tourists. They are not attracting other tourists to attractions.

**9** *Be in the know before you go!*
This is an **interpretive** question. You need to understand the word 'catchphrase', which also means 'slogan'. This connection could easily be made with the help of the annotation about the slogan. A catchphrase or slogan is a catchy, brief statement that sums up a company or service and what it offers. This website offers knowledge to help tourists make decisions about attractions that are worth visiting. Another key to answering the question is the phrase 'and others [reviews] on the site'. The fact that the catchphrase refers to other parts of the site leads us to the top of the page as the location where the catchphrase is most likely to be found. It is placed directly under the website title 'The Attraction Attraction' *(line 2)*.

**10** **a** This is an **interpretive** question. First locate the 'second review advertised at the end of the main review' *(line 42)*. This immediately eliminates Answer **c** because it is not about Australia Zoo or Orange River Rafting. Answer **b** is incorrect because it blends the names 'Harry Potter' and 'Universal Studios'. This is a subtle difference from the correct answer but an important one. To confirm Answer **a** as the correct answer, you need to re-read the relevant section and sum up what it is about.

**11** **c** This is an **applied** question but a very simple one. To answer it, you need to recognise that people travelling to Florida for a tourist attraction are highly likely to be interested in other attractions while they are there. KSC and Universal Studios are both in Florida, making them good partners on a review site like this. Answer **a** is a completely irrelevant statement. It states a fact but has nothing to do with the question. Answer **b** is incorrect because Harry Potter himself is not in Florida; a Harry Potter-themed attraction is in Florida.

**12** **a** This is an **applied** question that extends our study of the text to the secondary texts contained within it. The keyword, 'desire', is defined in the hint. Answer **a** makes the most sense when applied to the advertisements: the first ad encourages readers to change the way they travel ('your way') and offers suggestions of how to do this *(line 30)*. The second ad is even more overtly about change, encouraging readers to change careers and work from home *(line 41)*. Answer **b** is incorrect because it is not really related to either ad. The second ad is particularly unrelated, as the reader is being encouraged to leave other people behind and work from home without company. Answer **c** is incorrect because money is not mentioned in the first ad at all. This option works only for the second ad.

PERSUASIVE TEXT
## Spelling Work
page 84

**1** Corrected words:
**a** unforgettable **b** briefing **c** virtual
**d** diner **e** tourism **f** orbiting

**2** **a** reason **b** bit **c** tat
**d** quarters **e** forget, table

**3** **a** **sim**ulator
**b** Suggestions: **sim**ultaneous, as**sim**ilate
**c** similar or appearing to be the same
**d** Suggestions: **re**gain, **re**issue, **re**peating
**e** again or once more
**f** **spect**ator
**g** Suggestions: per**spect**ive, **spec**ulate
**h** to see or look
**i** **ex**hibits
**j** Suggestions: **ex**pel, **ex**it, **ex**tract
**k** out or out of
**l** **orb**it
**m** Suggestions: **orb**, **orb**ital

**4** **a** N **b** Y over, priced **c** Y head, quarters
**d** N **e** N **f** N

# ANSWERS

CHECK YOUR ANSWERS

PERSUASIVE TEXT
## Vocabulary Work
page 85

1 launch pad, dark coaster, Mission Control, gantry, virtual

2 **a** Shuttle Launch Experience **b** dining **c** Universal Studios **d** admission

3 **a** an interest or hobby **b** a lot of money **c** many different items **d** well-informed

4 Positive: fave, pretty boss, pluses
Negative: bummer, whatever, yawn factor

5 **a** pluses **b** obit **c** comprehensive **d** forgettable **e** revisited

PERSUASIVE TEXT
## Grammar Work
page 86

1 **a** healthy **b** attractive **c** thrilling **d** commanding **e** visiting **f** daily

2 **a** sweat **b** greatness **c** height **d** excitement **e** scene or scenery **f** youth or youthfulness

3 Sample answers:
**a** astrophysics, astrology, astronomical
**b** cosmonaut, Argonaut, nautical

4 Sample answers:
**a** armguard, highchair **b** backlog, feedlot **c** landscape, trademark **d** sunburn, shoeshine

5 **Set 1:** head. The compound words created are: forehead, headline, masthead, headway, egghead, headache

**Set 2:** light. The compound words created are: starlight, lighthouse, highlight, lightweight, limelight, lightbulb

PERSUASIVE TEXT
## Punctuation Work
page 87

1 Sample answers: the White House, the Great Wall of China, the Taj Mahal

2 **a** RADAR, UNICEF, NATO
**b** OTT, FYI, BRB, BBC, ATM

3 **a** anger **b** excitement **c** indignation **d** excitement

4 **a** *The Wizard of Oz* **b** *The Comedy of Errors* **c** 'Livin' on a Prayer' **d** 'This Old Man'

5 Cape Canaveral, Shuttle Launch Experience, Butterbeer, NASA, Mission Control, the Richtesveld

PERSUASIVE TEXT
## Writing Work
page 88

1 Answers will vary. Sample answer: embedded video montage of some KSC highlights

2 **a** trustworthy, reliable, credible
**b** make the most of
**c** prejudiced and one-sided
**d** copied without acknowledging the source
**e** a regularly updated website or page with an informal style; literally 'web log' (diary)
**f** making inflammatory statements online (to create conflict, start arguments and cause division)
**g** protect
**h** collection

3 **a** True **b** True **c** False **d** False **e** True

4 Answers will vary. Sample answers:
**a** MEGA-HUGE rockets, ten storeys high, images on the page
**b** sounds … of a real launch, we are go, Flight!
**c** chewy hot dog, vacuum-sealed salad, BUTTERBEER
**d** strap themselves into a simulator, sweaty palms

5 Sample answers:
**a** so whatever
**b** It creates an informal and lighthearted tone that appeals to everyday tourists.
**c** Admission details are summarized.
**d** KSC highlights are in bullet points
**e** Go for it.
**f** It creates a friendly, familiar and persuasive tone.
**g** non-refundable!
**h** and, of course, BUTTERBEER!
**i** It conveys emotions including enthusiasm, annoyance and excitement.

6 Answers must come from the following list (six are needed): Kennedy Space Center, Shuttle Launch Experience, Mission Control, NASA, IMAX, Kennedy Space Visitor Complex, Cape Canaveral, International Space Station Center, Observation Gantry, Apollo/Saturn Visitors Center, Mt Fuji climbs, Australia Zoo, Orange River rafting

7 small chunks of text, bullet points, subheadings, key statistics and facts, relevant images, simple navigation menu, a maximum of three fonts, bold keywords

# ANSWERS

## UNIT 10: PERSUASIVE TEXT—PROTEST LETTER

### PERSUASIVE TEXT
### Comprehension Work page 93

1 **c** This is a **literal** question. In the annotations we read that the address on the top left belongs to the sender or writer so we know that Answer **c** is correct. Answer **a** is incorrect because it is the location of the proposed power plant. Answer **b** is incorrect because it is the address of State Parliament, where the letter is being sent.

2 '… we still rely on the burning of fossil fuels (in this day and age).'
This is a **literal** question. Locate the key phrase 'totally unacceptable' in the text *(line 32)* then quote or paraphrase the words that follow.

3 a signature
This is a **literal** question. Look at the elements at the end of the letter and name the element between the sign-off phrase and the writer's name as a signature. This is a stylised version of a person's name that is unique to them, personalises a document and certifies that they were the one to write it. It is meant to function like a written fingerprint.

4 **c** This is an **interpretive** question that calls on your vocabulary. You need to answer it by a process of elimination. Answer **a** is incorrect because 'reckoning' is making an educated guess, judgement or calculation. It can also mean punishment or justice. Neither meaning applies in this context. Answer **b** is close to a correct meaning but it is still incorrect because Answer **c** is the 'best meaning', as prescribed by the question.

5 **c** This is an **interpretive** question. Synthesise information from the annotation (on the letter's title) and your own understanding of the title as a summary. Also assume that the MP may not read the letter carefully—or at all. Answer **a** is incorrect because, as we read in the letter, the MP already knows about the proposed power plant. Answer **b** is incorrect because it is essentially a paraphrase of Answer **a**.

6 Alliteration, to emphasise both words and the idea that this development is 'dirty'. This kind of emphasis also brings other words to mind, like *disgusting* and *destructive*.
This is an **interpretive** question. There is no set answer to the second part of the question. It is up to you to draw a conclusion based on your reaction to the phrase as a reader. Your knowledge of common sound devices used in texts is called on here, along with your interpretation of the use of alliteration in the phrase 'dirty development'.

7 nearly 100 per cent environmentally friendly energy production and 250 000 new jobs.
This is an **interpretive** question that directly tests your synthesising skills. Locate the section in the text that discusses Germany's energy production *(lines 26–29)* and the key phrase 'everybody wins' *(line 30)*, then discern which facts in the section match this phrase.

8 **a** This is an **interpretive** question. It involves vocabulary, observational skills and elimination. Answering is easier if you already know the meaning of 'figuratively' but the parenthesis '(not literally)' in the question also tells you the meaning of this keyword. Checking the phrases in Answer **a** against this meaning is the main task. Eliminating Answers **b** and **c** are the remaining tasks. Answer **b** is incorrect because, while the last phrase in the set is not necessarily to be read literally, the other two are. Answer **c** is incorrect because, while all of these phrases verge on the figurative, they are far more literal than the phrases in Answer **a**.

9 'foreign'
This is an **interpretive** question. We read the answer in line 41. Locating it involves interpretation of the issue discussed in that section—overseas investors polluting Australia—which is fairly easy to identify by the words 'foreign' and 'corporate' (big business). The longer phrase, 'corporate fat cats', is a highly informal and derogatory term for wealthy business investors. All of these factors point to the fact that, as the question says, 'the power plant is not locally owned'.

10 the environment, public health and citizens' livelihoods (including jobs)
This is an **interpretive** question. The information in parentheses is an optional part of the answer. The hint indicates that 'the answers are made explicit in the last two paragraphs'. You are required to interpret three specific 'moral obligations'. Also, when re-reading the entire letter, we come across these obligations numerous times with different wording. This means that there is a back-up answering technique for this question.

11 **b** This is an **applied** question requiring careful reading of the question. The hint is vital in selecting the correct answer because it eliminates Answers **a** and **c**. Both of these answers name appropriate recipients of a copy of the letter but neither one names people that can be the recipients—that is, the addressees. A recipient of the letter needs to be someone who has the power to do something about the issue; someone in a position of authority

at government level. The State Minister for the Environment, like the State Minister for Energy and Resources, has this authority.

**12** **a** This is an **applied** question. You are required to apply the definition of 'backhanded compliment' to the phrase quoted in the question. Reading the hint helps considerably with this. Answer **b** is incorrect because the phrase 'the back hand' makes no sense. Also, this option includes two actual 'compliments', not insults disguised as compliments. Answer **c** is incorrect because no other MPs are mentioned and no generalisations are made about most MPs having a brain and/or a conscience.

## PERSUASIVE TEXT
## Spelling Work

page 94

**1** **a** proposal **b** thoroughly **c** foreign **d** current **e** wreak **f** greatly

**2** **b** able, renewable **c** cent, recent **d** reign, foreign **e** science, conscience **f** log, technologies **g** mate, climate

**3** **a** recent **b** centre

**4** **a** ear **b** file **c** start **d** adds **e** fits **f** fade **g** heat **h** feel **i** fuel

**5** Real words: **a** unrenewable **b** policies **c** atmospheres **d** foreigner

## PERSUASIVE TEXT
## Vocabulary Work

page 95

**1** **a** environmental **b** resent **c** degradation **d** conscious **e** police **f** climatic

**2** **a** scientific, neuroscience, discipline, unconscious, science fiction, subconscious
**b** policy, politician, politically, political, police force, metropolis

**3** **a** sincerity, insincere
**b** environmentalist, environs
**c** proposition, proposing

**4** **a** False **b** True **c** True **d** False **e** False **f** False

## PERSUASIVE TEXT
## Grammar Work

page 96

**1** **a** totally
**b** to give more force to the adjective 'unacceptable'

**2** **a** rarely **b** extremely **c** quite **d** strongly, urgently

**3** **a** carefully **b** cautiously **c** mindlessly **d** sloppily, really

**4** **a** Noun: protest. Verbs: admit, making. Adjectives: stressed, sleepless. Pronouns: I, me
**b** Nouns: MP, responsibility, conscience, people. Verbs: has, vote. Adjective: moral. Pronouns: his, her

## PERSUASIVE TEXT
## Punctuation Work

page 97

**1** **b**

**2** Sample answers:
**a** The numeral in this case is more eye-catching than the words.
**b** As in '100 per cent', the numeral stands out more effectively in this context.
**c** This figure is followed by 'tonnes'. Together, these three words seem larger than a single number ('8 000 000'), making the point about pollution stronger.

**3** Sample answers:
**a** The exclamation mark attracts attention, evokes scenes of protests or marches, and sets the tone of the letter.
**b** The all-capitals 'WHY' gives power and an outraged tone to the rest of the rhetorical question in which it appears.
**c** The exclamation mark conveys emotion (anger and indignation), leaves no room for debate or counterargument, and reinforces the adverb 'totally'.

**4** interrobang (?!), exclamation mark, selective italics

## PERSUASIVE TEXT
## Writing Work

page 98

**1** The issue is a proposed power plant that would create significant environmental damage if given the government go-ahead.

**2** There are many possible answers, including: petition, sit-in, media campaign, peaceful street march or rally, placards and banners, protest literature

**3** **a**

**4** **b**

**5** Answers will vary widely. In their answers, students need to ensure that, as the hint notes, the title is 'attention-grabbing, forceful and urgent'. Suggested titles do not need to contain two parts.

6 Mr Georgiadis is writing on behalf of all concerned local citizens.

7 A possible reason is to make the letter as fast and easy to read and digest as possible.

8 Answers will vary. Two possible answers are: repetition, particularly of key terms and phrases or of commands and demands; a quote from an authoritative source, such as a scientific research institute or governing body.

9 Sample answers:
**a** deeply concerned
**b** Stand up for the environment, for health, for jobs …
**c** strongly, urgently
**d** massive
**e** Has there been no thought given to the massive damage …?
**f** We urge you to do the right thing

10 Sample answers:
**a** The writer is trying to get the recipient to understand the projected impact of the proposed power plant on the local community and the fact that many citizens are concerned about the issue.
**b** The writer is trying to persuade the recipient to use their government power to prevent the plant from going ahead.

## UNIT 11: PERSUASIVE TEXT—FLYER

PERSUASIVE TEXT
### Comprehension Work
page 103

1 The *o* has been replaced by a diamond shape.
This is a **literal** question. Look at the restaurant's name at the top (banner) of both sides of the flyer and notice that a shape has been used in place of an *o*.

2 **a** This is a **literal** question. Locate the phrase 'again this year' *(line 5)* and look for the name of the award directly before it, leading you to Answer **a**. Notice that the collective name of the awards follows this phrase, making Answer **c** incorrect. Answer **b** is incorrect because the award is specifically for a seafood restaurant.

3 Australia, New Zealand and France
This is a **literal** question. We read the names of three countries *(line 10)*, directly next to where the restaurant's 'wine list' is mentioned.

4 **c** This is an **interpretive** question. We read that 'culinary veteran Jai Roney is at the helm' of the restaurant *(line 4)*. This idiom, which is also a boating term, means 'in charge'. Finding the correct answer is easier if you understand this expression. You will still arrive at the right answer if you notice that 'Jai Roney' is the only person named in the flyer, making him likely to be the person who runs the restaurant. Answer **a** is incorrect because there is no mention in the flyer of Newharbour marina precinct having a general manager or director. Answer **b** is incorrect because the manager is named in the flyer.

5 port-side and waterside
This is an **interpretive** question. Use the letter clues provided to find the answer. You also need to find two location terms in the flyer, and the common word fragment 'side' helps you with this. Finally, if you have the word 'port' in your vocabulary, you would know that it, along with 'marina', can mean 'body of water' in certain contexts. These clues lead you to the answer.

6 Sample answer: The word 'vista' means 'view', especially one that is pleasant to look at.
This is an **interpretive** question. We read about various visual features of the seascape near the restaurant—'sparkling waters; luxury yachts; the occasional dolphin' *(lines 13–14)*—all of which describe a pleasant view. These descriptions appear directly before the key phrase 'ever-changing vista' and the word 'picturesque', which points to the meaning of 'vista'. Also, the writer calls the area a 'stunning waterside location' *(line 2)*. The word 'view' alone is a correct answer but the second part of the definition makes the sample answer more correct.

7 none
This is an **interpretive** question. We read near the end of the flyer about 'a 20 per cent discount' but it's important to note the rest of the sentence: 'on a standard main meal (seafood platters excluded) when you mention this advertisement'. You need to deduce from this information that seafood platters are not included in the discount, as specified in the parentheses. An understanding of the word 'excluded' is necessary to answer this question correctly.

8 **c** This is an **interpretive** question. The keywords in the question are 'sound technique', 'subheading' and 'back'. Once you piece together the location and find the subheading 'Some morsels from our menu', you can eliminate Answer **a** rhyme and **b** onomatopoeia. This question requires a knowledge of the three sound techniques named.

9 **a** This is an **interpretive** question. The Hint should be particularly helpful in answering it. Looking at the other items in the menu that align with 'MP', we notice that they are all prices of dishes sold at the restaurant. This immediately indicates that 'MP' is also related to price. In most seafood restaurants,

fresh seafood that varies widely in price at market is sold at the day's market price, especially in the case of special 'fish of the day' dishes. Answer **b** is incorrect because it makes no sense as a term that would relate to the fish dish. Answer **c** is incorrect because the dish being described is not in the 'platter' category.

**10** **a** This is an **interpretive** question. To answer correctly, interpret the link between the phrase 'dipping sauce duo' on the menu *(line 35)*, the words in parentheses after it and the keywords in the question. Answer **b** is incorrect because neither of these items is a dipping sauce. Answer **c** is incorrect because one item is a fish and the other is a type of chilli. While the chilli is included in a dipping sauce, it is not a sauce on its own. In any case, the other item disqualifies this option.

**11** **c** This is an **applied** question. You do not need a knowledge of French terms to answer it. You need to apply the different possible meanings of the word 'fruits' to the question and then to eliminate two options. Answer **a** is incorrect because it does not have any clear link to the word 'fruits'. Answer **b** is incorrect because actual fruit pieces are not mentioned as being on the platter. You should also consider that if the question asks for the meaning of a French term, the word 'fruits' is unlikely to simply refer to fruits (bananas, apples, etc.). The term 'fruits de mer' literally means 'fruits of the sea' (that is, seafood), with the word 'fruits' denoting natural produce.

**12** house or in-house
This is an **applied** question. You only need to give one of the two possible answers. You are required to apply your knowledge of the word 'premises' from the question as you skim-read the flyer, looking for words with a similar meaning. Keep reading time short by going straight to the sections of the flyer that mention 'Some morsels from our menu' *(line 30)* as specified in the question. The two possible answers are located in the 'Entrée' section *(lines 34–35)* ('house aioli' is one of the dipping sauces) and next to the subheading 'Desserts' *(line 39)* (which are 'made in-house'). Further, it helps to understand the idiom 'house' as it is used in relation to businesses such as restaurants.

## PERSUASIVE TEXT
## Spelling Work page 104

**1** **a** ample **b** leisure **c** catering

**2** **a** décor **b** coordinate **c** precinct

**3** **a** sources **b** bait **c** dipping **d** star

**4** **a** ~~SO~~MORSELS/AMPLE/LEISURE~~ELS~~
**b** ~~MIN~~PRECINCT/RUSTIC/CATERING/~~STICT~~
**c** BOUTIQUE/DÉCOR/COORDINATE/~~ERION~~
**d** ~~PE~~PRESTIGIOUS/COMPLEMENTING/~~GRIGTIN~~

**5** **a** boutique, boutique **b** ample, luncheon
**c** marina, magnificent
**d** establishment, extremely

**6** Corrected passage: The appeal of a good seafood restaurant never goes out of date. Many patrons of a fine-dining business like Yellowfin will keep coming year after year because seafood is often hard to get or hard to prepare at home. People enjoy the convenience of a skilled chef doing the hard work for them.

## PERSUASIVE TEXT
## Vocabulary Work page 105

**1** Possible answers (there are many others): cosmopolitan, in-house, title, menu, boutique, zesty

**2** aioli, macerated, fondant, salsa verde, panna cotta

**3** **a** soft **b** stuffed **c** seafood

**4** **a** coordinate **b** morsels **c** ample
**d** rustic **e** culinary **f** complementing
**g** precinct **h** vineyards

**5** **a** décor **b** picturesque **c** marinara
**d** platter **e** intimidate **f** yachting
**g** cosmopolitan **h** alloy

## PERSUASIVE TEXT
## Grammar Work page 106

**1** A conjunction is a joining word in a sentence; for example, *and, because* or *but.* A conjunction can be used to connect two parts of a sentence. The word 'junction' means 'point where two or more things are joined'.

**2** A pronoun stands in place of a noun. It refers to a noun that has already been used or is about to be used. For example, *Josh did a big wash on Sunday. He wanted to have a week's worth of shirts ready.*

**3** In any order: verb, noun, adjective

**4** **a** noun **b** adjective **c** adjective
**d** verb **e** verb **f** noun or adjective
**g** noun **h** noun **i** adjective
**j** noun **k** adjective **l** noun
**m** verb (see note) **n** noun **o** noun.

Note: When 'coordinate' is pronounced 'co-ord-in-uht', it is a homograph for the original word in the

text (that is, it looks the same but sounds different); it is a noun meaning 'number or letter denoting a location'.

5 a decorate, decorated or decorating
b yachting c prestige d amply
e rustically f complementary

6 restaurant and catering

PERSUASIVE TEXT
**Punctuation Work** page 107

1 To 'read widely' is to read a range of different texts. 'Widely' refers to a wide variety.

2 Your writing will be clear because, as the first bullet point tells us, punctuation marks guide our understanding as readers. They are signposts and signals in sentences. When we use punctuation correctly, our meaning is clear.

3 a newharb.com.au/yellowfin
b décor
c some morsels from our menu …
d 6.5 (for baked ricotta)
e (seafood platters excluded)
f gluten-free
g Yell♢wfin
h take advantage of this special offer:

4 a Let's meet at the café for lunch.
b (but don't tell your Mum)
c French fries/straw chips are extremely fattening.
d You'll need these supplies:
e Take your car: we may want to leave the party early.

5 Corrected sentence: Our port-side setting presents diners with fabulous views of the Newharbour marina precinct: sparkling waters, luxury yachts, quirky tugs, rustic fishing boats; even the occasional dolphin.

PERSUASIVE TEXT
**Writing Work** page 108

1 Sample answers:
a A flyer may advertise a business such as a beauty salon or florist.
b A flyer may promote a community event such as Paramasala, an annual multicultural festival in Parramatta, NSW.
c A flyer may be aimed at raising awareness about skin cancers and how to avoid getting them.
d A flyer may be distributed around suburbs prior to an event such as a local or federal election to inform voters about their options.

2 At the top. Note: If the flyer is printed on two sides, the reverse may also have a banner.

3 Possible answers include any of the features listed in the bullet points above the question. Answers will only be correct, however, if specific reference is made to how or where they are seen in the flyer. For example: The restaurant flyer features a visual text variation on the reverse side, where a sample menu is printed. This section makes reading fast and easy, and is visually interesting.

4 Answers will vary, but students must name specific visual features and give corresponding information from the flyer to support their opinions. For example: The flyer would be more eye-catching with a bigger banner and a more exotic typeface for the name of the restaurant.

5 Sample answers: Ke$ha, P!nk

6 Suggested answer: A diamond suggests excellence, perfection, luxury and indulgence. Looking at it with another interpretation, the diamond shape can also be understood as stylised fish fins.

7 Sample answers: the perfect dining experience; intimate dinner; quirky tugs, rustic fishing boats; zesty salt tang; rainbow salad

8 Possible answers: the unfailing sea breeze; the warmth of gas heaters

9 Answers will vary but students must give reasons for their opinions and quote directly from the text. For example: The diction used to describe the dishes on the menu is effective because the writer has managed to appeal to the reader's sense of taste, touch and smell while keeping the expression economical and catchy; for example, 'dipping sauce duo'.

10 Answers will vary. You should mention how or why the image you have suggested is persuasive. For example: A couple enjoying a romantic meal by candlelight in the restaurant. This image would enhance the flyer's persuasive appeal by reinforcing and 'proving' the promises made in the text.

## UNIT 12: PERSUASIVE TEXT—ARTICLE

PERSUASIVE TEXT
**Comprehension Work** page 113

1 a This is a **literal** question. We read that 'More than 100 000 people are currently homeless in this country' *(line 5)*. Locate the keyword 'homeless' from the question in this context and link it with the statistic of '100 000'. Answer **b** is incorrect

because it is disconnected from the statistic. Answer **c** is incorrect for the same reason; also, the text says nothing about estimating Australia's entire population.

**2** **b** This is a **literal** question. We read that the 'Goodna Street Life Helping Hands Centre is in Goodna, Queensland' *(line 8)*. Goodna is named as a suburb in the state of Queensland. Answer **a** is incorrect because Queensland is a state not a suburb. Answer **c** is incorrect because 'a little corner' is a figurative expression used to introduce the centre affectionately.

**3** computer access
This is a **literal** question. We read that 'computer access' is available 'for people seeking employment' *(lines 13–14)*. To answer the question, locate the phrase 'people seeking employment' in the text and find the answer directly beside it.

**4** Sample answer: GSL's independence is positive because it allows for 'no-strings-attached charity to drive the operation' but negative because a lack of affiliation means a lack of 'sizeable' funding.
This is an **interpretive** question. Locate the word 'independence' *(line 15)* then identify the related positive point, which is directly beside it. You also need to interpret the mention of a 'downside' in the same paragraph as having the same meaning as 'negative' in the question in order to find the negative.

**5** Sample answer: It is important that GSL is shown to be a non-profit organisation early in the article because one of the key aims of the writer is to encourage people to provide GSL with financial support. They are only likely to do that if GSL is an entirely charitable organisation.
This is an **interpretive** question. You simply need to interpret the reason for identifying GSL in this way, based on the purpose of the article.

**6** Sample answer: The statistics in lines 25–28 mainly demonstrate that Helen's observation about homeless men is backed up by evidence.
This is an **interpretive** question. We read that the statistics 'reflect Helen's observation' *(line 25)*. Locating this phrase gives you the answer immediately.

**7** **a** This is an **interpretive** question. The clue to answering it is interpreting 'home' in the article's subheading 'Bringing the issue closer to home' *(line 29)* as Australia and synthesising the mention of the 'Aussie stars' with this reference and other references to Australia in the text. Answers **b** and **c** are incorrect because 'living in cars' and 'sleeping on couches' are not directly related to Australia.

**8** Sample answer: The implied meaning of 'mega-director' is that he (James Cameron) is exceptionally successful in the movie business—and therefore very wealthy. This sets up a massive contrast between his time as a homeless person and his life now, proving that anyone can be homeless if circumstances are against them.
This is an **interpretive** question that calls on your idiom vocabulary. 'Mega' is used colloquially to imply size, impressiveness and grandeur. You are not required to extend the implications of the term past its immediate context, as the sample answer does, but the best answers would include a comment like the sample answer's note about contrast.

**9** **c** This is an **interpretive** question. The separation and staggering (that is, structuring in layers or steps) of the final lines *(lines 50–52)* clearly draws attention to more than one element near the end of the article. You need to identify both Answers **a** and **b** as containing those elements and choose Answer **c** as a result. The elements named in both Answers **a** and **b** are correct in isolation, making Answer **c** the best answer.

**10** **c** This is an **interpretive** question. Your idiom vocabulary is again being tested in this question. You need to synthesise (link) the phrase 'did their time' with the idea of 'doing [serving] time' in prison. Answer **a** is incorrect because it is based on an incorrect definition of the idea of time in the phrase as it is used in context. Answer **b** is incorrect because we understand from reading the article that poverty and 'homelessness' are not what most people would call 'having a great time'.

**11** **a** This is an **applied** question. Choosing the correct answer relies upon your ability to apply the purpose and messages of the article to the three options and eliminate two of them. This is made easier by thinking about your own reaction as a reader to Helen's example. Answer **b** is incorrect because nowhere in the article does the writer state or suggest that Helen was once homeless. Answer **c** is incorrect because the writer implies throughout the article that Helen is not wealthy or famous; she is an ordinary, kind-hearted person.

**12** Sample answer: Jim Carrey might have developed his sense of humour through the experience of being homeless because he needed to find something positive in his life while he and his family struggled to have their everyday needs met. Humour can be a welcome distraction for people suffering in poverty.
This is an **applied** question that asks you to place yourself in Jim Carrey's position and think empathetically, then express those feelings and ideas in an answer.

# ANSWERS

## CHECK YOUR ANSWERS

### PERSUASIVE TEXT
### Spelling Work — page 114

**1** **a** independence **b** homelessness **c** crisis **d** sanctuary, temporary

**2** **a** tenacious **b** dignity **c** temporary **d** affiliated **e** opportunity **f** charity

**3** **a** accommodating
**b** accommodated or accommodating
**c** accommodatingly **d** facilitate
**e** size **f** sizeably
**g** independent **h** independently

**4** currently, maintain, facilities, various, including, onsite, intervention, lives, meal, dignity, struggling, poverty

**5** **a** 12 **b** 6

### PERSUASIVE TEXT
### Vocabulary Work — page 115

**1** **a** dignity **b** independence **c** facilities **d** eradicating

**2** intervention, couches, Australians, risk, particularly, single, raised, facilities, corporate

**3** **a** temporary shops, usually set up outdoors
**b** necessities for daily life
**c** native to a land
**d** associated with
**e** negative point or disadvantage

**4** **a** musician **b** rental **c** humour **d** volunteering **e** define **f** entirely **g** while **h** contributions

**5** **a** respect from everyday people
**b** a very challenging task
**c** once poor, now wealthy
**d** very generous
**e** served a sentence

### PERSUASIVE TEXT
### Grammar Work — page 116

**1** obviously

**2** tenacious, dollar, problem, dignity, admired, inspired

**3** Sample answers: repetition, unusual subject/verb/object order, impact punctuation (for example, exclamation mark, question mark, interrobang, ellipsis)

**4** **a** One of the strengths of GSL is its independence.
**b** Only a few are willing to do something about it.
**c** It's a big call but if anyone can make it happen, this tenacious, huge-hearted woman can.
**d** Of course the potential to become rich and famous does not make some people more deserving of charity than others!

**5** **a** volunteer or voluntary **b** risky **c** poor **d** entire **e** needy or needed **f** funded

### PERSUASIVE TEXT
### Punctuation Work — page 117

**1** Sample answers: A semicolon signals a connection between two ideas in a sentence.
A semicolon can be used to divide a sentence into two pieces but not to the extent that a full stop does.

**2** **a** ?! (interrobang)
**b** Sample answer: The interrobang is usually featured in highly colloquial or humorous texts, and the persuasive article 'Street cred' does not fit these descriptions.

**3** **a** ; **b** : **c** … **d** / **e** — **f** ’ **g** . **h** ( ) **i** ?! ,

**4** Answers will vary but students must name punctuation marks AND give their symbols.

**5** Answers will vary but the following elements should be mentioned: A semicolon divides the repetitive phrases including the keyword 'temporary' to draw attention to it; An ellipsis indicates a pause and suggests that a solution to the problem will follow; The italicised '*if*' emphasises that word in a challenging manner.

**6** Corrected sentence: These rags-to-riches cases might prove to you that homelessness does not define a person.

### PERSUASIVE TEXT
### Writing Work — page 118

**1** Possible answers include: colloquial language including idioms ('It's a big call'), indirect appeals ('Some of us'), earnest tone created by strong adjectives ('this excellent cause') and contact details (email address and Facebook group address)

**2** urging, influencing, convincing

**3** This pull-quote is effective because it explains the issue of homelessness in simple terms and points to one of the messages of the article, which is that everyone deserves dignity and kindness. It also shows the solution to the problem ('*if* somebody else will step in and help').

4 Answers will vary. Sample answer: 'Helen wants to make a lasting difference by eradicating homelessness in her community entirely.' This pull-quote sums up the mission of the main person featured in the article.

5 **a** True **b** True **c** False **d** True

6 They both involve the same technique: second person. The example given in the fourth point is not just a question but an example of second person address.

7 **a** present tense **b** quotes **c** homelessness **d** second person **e** verbs **f** question

## SAMPLE TEST PAPER 1

### SAMPLE TESTS
### Part A Reading and comprehension
page 126

1 its position on the windy North Sea

2 fuel made from waste products (namely, straw and household garbage)

3 pun

4 'My legs are gone.'

5 Two possible reasons (there are more): It suits the fact that the narrator is telling about a recurring nightmare. Repetition of this kind creates a sense of unease or panic.

6 'Relief breaks over me like a cool wave'

7 They indicate hyperlinks to other websites (specifically, these words and phrases are called anchor text).

8 She was writing in the Victorian era, when female writers were less likely to be published, so she took a male pen name.

9 A large, heavy object. This colloquial term is often applied to very thick books.

### SAMPLE TESTS
### Part B Language conventions
page 127

1 Sample answer: The effect is an emphasis on each word, which strengthens the idea of 'cleverness'. This is reinforced in other alliterative words that appear nearby, including 'customers … costs' (which are 'slashed') and (top of the) 'class'.

2 **a** 'a phantom itch', 'empty lower third of my bed and my body doesn't move'
**b** to create suspense (briefly) and build up to the narrator's revelation

3 The techniques listed (characterisation, description, conflict, motif, allusions) are summed up or defined as 'technical and stylistic features' (specifically, 'those technical and stylistic features of a literary gem'). The first part of the sentence is explained in the second part.

### SAMPLE TESTS
### Part C Comparing texts
page 127

1 Suggested answer: The purpose of Text 1, which celebrates the climate-saving achievements of the region of Thy, is to draw attention to the methods used and apply them elsewhere. Text 3, which celebrates the classic novel *Jane Eyre,* has the purpose of encouraging today's students to read it and appreciate its timeless qualities.

2 Suggested answer: Text 1 refers to fairytales primarily because they are associated with Denmark and make a good point of reference for readers. This reference is also used as a pun in the title. Text 2 uses the fairytale *Snow White* and the 'wicked stepmother' archetype (technically these are allusions) to explain aspects of the novel *Jane Eyre*.

3 **a** Text 1: news article format, beginning with the basic who, what, where of the story and elaborating on these details in short paragraphs

Text 2: told in flashback style, with a dream section followed by a reality section and a twist

Text 3: designed for a web page; features small chunks of text, bullet points and summarised publishing details

**b** Answers will vary but must refer to the purpose and audience of the chosen text.

### SAMPLE TESTS
### Part D Themes and meaning
page 128

1 Sample answer: Two themes explored in Text 3 are romance and timelessness. The novel being reviewed—*Jane Eyre*—falls into the genre of romance (along with others) so it is one of the key themes of the review. It is also named as one of the 'two good reasons why it's [the novel is] the goods'. The reviewer points out some of the romantic aspects of the story and goes to trouble to avoid 'spoilers' so that surprises in the story regarding the central romance will not be given away. Timelessness is a theme of the review only (not the novel): the reviewer explains why *Jane Eyre* is still appealing to readers today and why young readers in particular should persevere with reading it. Various features of Brontë's work are cited that make it a 'literary gem' and therefore one that is timeless (does not really date).

# ANSWERS

CHECK YOUR ANSWERS

## SAMPLE TEST PAPER 2

### SAMPLE TESTS
### Part A Reading and comprehension page 132

1. the biggest or most enormous turkey
2. chronological
3. This sentence is written in the second person.
4. the passing of time (we are not told how much)
5. sound / hearing / the auditory sense. This is because it is the only one available to her during the story.
6. Lizzie (main character and narrator), Marian (her mother), a nurse, a male nurse, a doctor and 'Nick' (a family member or boyfriend)
7. acknowledging and apologising for the gross misdeeds of the past
8. related to England or Britain, its people or its language (from the original name of the English: Angles)
9. It is asked rhetorically and to set up the article as an exploration of these issues, not as an answer to the problems. The question can also be seen as a challenge to everyone who reads the article to try to do something to aid reconciliation.

### SAMPLE TESTS
### Part B Language conventions page 133

Suggested answers:

1. **a** Idiom 1: an old gag. Meaning: an old joke or trick
   **b** Idiom 2: send ourselves broke. Meaning: used up all our money
2. the use of numbers, with a sense of counting up and down both slowly and quickly; the use of ellipses (…) to suggest that words are missing, show a trailing off and create suspense
3. The subheading sums up the current situation in Australia where true reconciliation is in doubt. In a similar way to the question that precedes the article, this question also poses a challenge to readers to help remedy the 'bleak' past and be a part of creating a 'brighter' future.

### SAMPLE TESTS
### Part C Comparing texts page 133

1. Two possible answers for each text (there are more):

   Text 1: to create humour; to invite personal reflection

   Text 2: to create empathy for those in a similar situation; to tell a story only by describing sounds
2. Two possible answers for each text (there are more):

   Text 2: situational conflict; inner conflict

   Text 3: community or societal conflict; racial conflict
3. Sample answers:
   **a** The type of person who seems to be targeted is someone who has had similar experiences to the writer. We know this because the writer is very specific about aspects of the family's Christmas ritual and seems to expect that the reader finds them familiar.
   **b** Text 3 has a wide target audience because this is every Australian's problem.

### SAMPLE TESTS
### Part D Themes and meaning page 134

1. Sample answer: Text 2 explores a very unusual problem from the perspective of the person going through it. She (Lizzie) is in a coma. Specific ways in which this problem are explored include dialogue, suspense and action. In the dialogue, the problem is implied and explored, as are associated problems (such as the need for constant physiotherapy). Suspense that revolves around the problem is created by the narrator's rising and abating panic. Actions of minor characters are related by the narrator. These revolve around the central problem of the coma. The narrator's own action is conveyed in a very restricted manner because of the situation (such as moving one finger) but it is powerful enough to serve as the climax of the piece.